# Like An Illusion

# Like An Illusion

## Lives of the Shangpa
## Kagyu Masters

### Nicole Riggs

Dharma Cloud

Eugene · Oregon

Published by Dharma Cloud Press, an imprint of
Red Eye Books
Eugene, Oregon 97408
Printed in the United States of America

*Cataloging-in-Publication Data*

Riggs, Nicole.
  Like an illusion : lives of the Shangpa Kagyu mas-
ters / Nicole Riggs. -- 1st ed.
  p. cm.
  Includes bibliographical references and index.
  LCCN: 00-136086
  ISBN: 0-9705639-0-6

  1. Yogis--China--Tibet--Biography.   2. Lamas--
China--Tibet--Biography 3. Yoga (Tantric Buddhism)
I. Title.

BQ7930.R54 2001              294.3'923'092'2
                             QBI00-857

Cover and interior design by Colman Fockens

This book is printed on acid-free paper

# Contents

# Foreword by Bokar Tulku Rinpoche

KEENLY INTERESTED IN Tibetan Buddhism, Nicole Riggs is particularly devoted to the masters and teachings of the glorious Shangpa Kagyu tradition, which is one of the Eight Great Chariots of the Practice Lineage. I am pleased that she has translated the *Lives of the Shangpa Kagyu Masters*.

The essential meaning of the life stories is that these masters, from Vajradhara, Niguma, and the scholar-adept Khyungpo Naljor on down through the succession of lineage holders, have all been widely learned in all fields of knowledge as well as exceptional in their scholarship, discipline, and benevolence. They turned away from the eight worldly concerns. They perceived samsara and nirvana to be like an illusion and they realized the natural state which is like space. Their love and compassion was impartial and pervasive. They saw the faces of innumerable *yidam* deities. Dharma protectors and guardians were at their service. Their activities for the benefit of others arose naturally and were spontaneously accomplished.

Simply hearing the life stories of such genuine beings blesses our mindstream. Guided by faith and devotion, our renunciation, compassion, wisdom and so on, grow and flourish. We can actually realize the natural state of Mahamudra and become guides for other beings. It is my prayer that this will occur for whoever comes across, sees, or hears these life stories.

Bokar Tulku
April 15, 1998

# Translator's Note

THESE LIFE STORIES point to a profound truth. At the same time, they share with Milarepa's finest tales the fresh and immediate sense of 'living dharma,' with humorous anecdotes and touching portraits. I have sought the spirit of the original and have at times disregarded a dictionary equivalent in search of a more fundamental accuracy. The Tibetan term *'dod chags*, for example, is generally translated as 'attachment and aversion,' but in Niguma's famous verse to Khyungpo Naljor I have translated it 'love and hate' because the whole stanza in the original is pithy and dramatic. My aim has been to bring to life the feeling-tone of the original.

For the same reason, I translated as many of the technical terms as possible and kept capitalization and italics to a minimum. For example, I have translated the term *'od gsal* (literally 'clear light' or 'luminosity') as 'clear-light nature of mind' to convey Kyabje Kalu Rinpoche's definition, "The open and luminous nature of mind is what we call the 'clear light.'"[1] Nevertheless, I retained original technical terms where no satisfactory equivalents exist, such as dakini, *siddhi*, or yidam.

Challenges abounded in translating *Like an Illusion*. The stories were written in the colloquial dialect of a thousand years ago in West-Central Tibet, and many words and expressions of that time are no longer used. Because of the complexity of Tibetan Buddhist terminology, it was necessary to provide endnotes, often giving the Tibetan and Sanskrit equivalents of an expression. These I have sought to keep as brief and unobtrusive as possible.

In the text, Tibetan names are given an approximate phonetic translation. To acknowledge the Indian source of this lineage—the dakini Niguma and many other teachers of Khyungpo Naljor were Indian—

the names of all Buddhas, deities, and Indian teachers are given in Sanskrit.

To make the text accessible, an abridged translation is presented here. To the best of my knowledge, this is the first translation of the Shangpa Lives in any major foreign language, and should open the door to other translations in the future. In abridging the stories, I mostly excluded long lists of teachers and teachings, condensed the first chapter into one introductory verse, and combined into one two stories of Shangtönpa, which were in many parts identical. However, I chose to present a full, unabridged translation of the Life of Khyungpo Naljor, the principal yogi of the lineage.

The original Tibetan print was carved on blocks at Jamgon Kongtrul's retreat in Palpung through the efforts of Kyabje Kalu Rinpoche.

I take full responsibility for any mistakes in the text. I sincerely thank the Lamas, teachers, scholars, and hidden yogis who generously helped me on the way, particularly Lama Wangchen, Lama Chödrak, Trinley Döndrup, Keith Dowman, Jeremy Morrelli, and Ngödrup Burkhar. I am very thankful for the years of teachings I received from Lama Tashi Namgyal. Jeff, I couldn't have done it without you! I am grateful to Bokar Tulku for singing Niguma and Sukhasiddhi's songs. May all beings experience the clear-light nature of reality!

# Introduction

*Meaning of Like an Illusion*

READERS INSPIRED TO Buddhism because of its refined philosophical understanding of the nature of reality may well be baffled by the tales contained in *Like An Illusion*. Here is a master subduing a local demon, here is a mendicant crossing a river, here are thieves setting upon villagers, here is a leper asking for a cure, and here is a master drinking beer. Readers might not expect such behaviors of Buddhists. How is it, they may wonder, that practitioners who spend much of their lives in meditation retreats seem to end up in adventures rivaling those of *Indiana Jones*?

It would be a mistake to dismiss the tales of *Like an Illusion* as adventure stories. Buddhism is a philosophy of liberation, so it is natural that the central focus of this text is not story-telling, but liberation from cyclic existence. Many dreams and miracles occur in *Like an Illusion*, but to interpret them as purely 'fantastic' is to ignore their soteriological aspect and function. Consider the excerpt below. Khyungpo has been searching for the teacher Niguma, and here he has just met her for the first time:

> The yogi Khyungpo rose in the sky to a height of about fifteen thousand feet. He found himself on top of a golden mountain. Above his head, Niguma's retinue was performing the mystical dance of the tantric feast, and from the four sides of the mountain flowed four rivers of gold. The yogi looked

down at the streams of gold and asked, "Does such a golden mountain really exist in India, or did the dakini[2] make it appear?"

Niguma sang:

Whirling in the ocean of samsara
Are the myriad thoughts of love and hate.
Once you know they have no nature,
Then everywhere is the land of gold, my child.

If on all things, like an illusion,
One meditates, like an illusion,
True Buddhahood, like an illusion,
Will come to pass, due to devotion.

But what does it mean to say that phenomena are like an illusion?

The Tibetan expression for 'like an illusion' (*sgyu ma lta bu*) occurs frequently in Buddhist writings. It has become the norm to translate the word *sgyu ma* as 'illusion' as I have done here for poetic feeling, although that is perhaps not a completely accurate translation. 'Illusion' in English suggests a fancy, something imagined, nothingness. In the Tibetan, however, *sgyu ma* is closer in meaning to 'magical scene.' A magician, given his skill, the right tools, and a certain environment, will create a 'magical scene.' This magical scene is like an illusion in the sense that it has no inherent nature and simply arises in dependence upon causes and conditions.

When the practitioner takes the content of the miracles he witnesses to be inherently real (which means when he believes the mountain "really exists"), he 'falls,' so to speak, for an appearance in which he plays a part. The appearance arises in dependence upon his mental preconceptions and other causes and conditions. However, his 'fall' is not to be judged too harshly because his tendency to grasp at appearances has developed into a habit over many lifetimes. He fails to see the lack of inherent existence in appearances and thus believes in their reality.

In the remarkable stories presented in *Like an Illusion*, it is the limits of belief or conceptual thought[3] which are being tested—not the limits of reality. The Shangpa lineage promotes the middle way philosophy of Tibetan Buddhism, steering clear of the conceptual extremes of existence and non-existence. Lamas, dakinis, and protectors provide the antidotes to extreme positions. The dakini Niguma does not say either that the mountain "really exists" or that she "made it appear." She does not say that things are completely real, or that they are purely illusory: she says they are *like* an illusion. She immediately makes the same point about the one who seeks liberation and the goal of that effort: they, too, are like an illusion.

Khyungpo is on top of a mountain witnessing an amazing display of gold streaming down. In the face of this appearance, Niguma is counseling him to take the whole thing with a grain of salt. She is the facilitator of the truth, which must take place *in* Khyungpo's mind. Her miracles are techniques intended to overcome Khyungpo's instinctive urge to look upon the world as if it either "really exists" or has been "made to appear." Since phenomena arise interdependently but have no inherent existence, Niguma's aim is to induce in the yogi who has been fooled by appearances a not-finding of the object imputed.

Meditating on the not-finding of the imputed object leads to an understanding that things have no inherent nature. "Once you know they [thoughts of love and hate] have no nature, then everywhere is the land of gold, my child," says Niguma. Equanimity, then, is the key. And equanimity arises out of meditation experience. When a practitioner gains the direct, intuitive experience of reality (the nature of which is no different than the nature of mind) he no longer functions from the dualistic base of self and other, external and internal. Therefore he sees the absence of any true nature in thoughts of love and hate. He perceives them as being of the same taste. While the mountain is understood to have no true nature, it nevertheless appears, and the appearance itself is perfect and blissful: the mountain appears like an illusion, and the appearance is golden.

At this point, the experience of reality is liberated, and it is called 'sameness' (*mnyam nyid*). Few of us have such an experience, of course! It is my hope that these precious Shangpa stories will lead readers to a golden mountain of realizations.

### Historical Background

*Like An Illusion* PRESENTS THE LIFE stories of masters of the Shangpa Kagyu lineage,[4] marked, as are all phenomena, by impermanence. Originating in teachings that the Kashmiri women Niguma and Sukhasiddhi received directly from Vajradhara, the lineage was established by Khyungpo Naljor (990-1139). The Shangpa lineage takes its name from the valley of Shang, west of Lhasa, where Khyungpo established his monastic seat after seven journeys to India and Nepal in search of authoritative teachings. At the core of the teachings and practices are the Six Yogas of Niguma and the Mahamudra Reliquary.[5]

Toward the end of his life, graced with visions of deities and of his Lamas, Khyungpo sang this song:

> Alas! All composites are transitory:
> Just like clouds in the sky,
> They gather
> And then disperse.

Khyungpo is credited with building one hundred and eight monasteries (although that number is auspicious in Tibetan conventions and may not be the actual number of monasteries built). The 11th century was a time of Buddhist expansion throughout Tibet, with the erection of many famous monasteries, such as Reting, Drikung, Sakya, and Tsurpu.

Over the next three centuries, the lineage was transmitted from teacher to disciple and Shangpa masters became respected for their realizations. Hundreds of disciples gathered around Mokchokpa's cave, and Sangye Tönpa's fame extended across the Indian subcontinent. The masters shied away from institutions and focused on practice first and foremost.

But the lineage, like clouds, passed from gathering to dispersing. Shortly before passing away, Khyungpo told his disciples, "After my death, don't cremate my body. Place it in a bronze and copper casket filled with gold, silver, and jewels, and present offerings to it. If you do so, this area of Shang will become like a second Bodhgaya and my lineage will flow like a river."

After he died in 1139 A.D., disciples placed Khyungpo's body in a casket filled with gold and silver, but monks from Eastern Tibet demanded the body. In the mounting tension, the decision was made to simply cremate the body, in defiance of Khyungpo's words.

The later obscurity and near-extinction of the Shangpa tradition suggest the haunting truth of Khyungpo's prophecy. Indeed, although the Shangpa tradition retreated from society and politics, it was still influenced by them. This is illustrated in occasional comments, such as Zhönnu Drup's mention of advancing Mongol armies, and of Drikung and Sakya monks forming themselves into battalions (the Tibetan term *ser dmag* specifically means monks-turned-soldiers).

The life stories in *Like an Illusion* end with an account of Taranatha's childhood. Taranatha (1575-1634)[6] was to become a controversial figure in an increasingly unstable period. In the last decade of his life, the 1630s, Tibet was plunged into a civil war, which was eventually won by the Gelukpas, with the support of Mongol armies.

The shift of authority to the Gelukpas imposed limitations—sometimes crippling ones—on other schools of Tibetan Buddhism, including the Shangpa Kagyu. The dispute with the Gelukpas had its philosophical manifestations as well. Taranatha became a target because of the position he held on the ultimate nature, declaring it to be 'Empty-of-Other' (*gzhan stong*).[7] The Empty-of-Other view approaches the ultimate in positive terms, in contradistinction to the Middle Way philosophy, which expresses the ultimate by negation.[8] The monastery of Jonang was the seat for holders of the Empty-of-Other view. It had been rebuilt and expanded by Taranatha, but with the advent of the fifth Dalai Lama, it was closed down. A ban was placed on the publication of the Jonang texts. Since Taranatha held the transmission for both the Shangpa and the Jonang traditions, his repression drove the Shangpa lineage underground.

For two hundred years, the Shangpa tradition endured in relative secrecy, a fact that is in keeping with the emphasis on concealment and discretion we find throughout the life stories. Many of the teachings were absorbed into other lineages, such as the Sakya and Geluk traditions. For example, the cycle of teachings on Six-Armed Mahakala, now widespread throughout Tibet and of great importance to the Geluk tradition, originated with the Shangpa lineage.

It was only in the mid-19th century that the eclectic master Jamgon Kongtrul Lodrö Taye revitalized the lineage as an independent tradition. He compiled the Shangpa teachings to which he devoted an entire volume in his Treasury of Oral Instructions (*gdams ngag mdzod*). His work was continued by Kyabje Kalu Rinpoche, who made the Shangpa practices part of the three-year retreats carried out in Tibet and in the west. Kyabje Kalu Rinpoche also imparted the instructions to teachers of other traditions such as the Dalai Lama, the Sixteenth Karmapa, Shamar Rinpoche, Tai Situ Rinpoche, Jamgon Kongtrul the Third, Gyaltsap Rinpoche, Dezhung Rinpoche, and Tenga Rinpoche.

Kyabje Kalu Rinpoche passed away in 1989. His reincarnation, Yangsi Kalu Rinpoche, was born in September, 1990. The transmission is now held by Bokar Tulku Rinpoche under whose guidance Yangsi Kalu Rinpoche is studying.

## *Why does a master write about his life?*

WE FIND SEVERAL reasons why a master might choose to record his life story: to inspire disciples; to demonstrate the truth of causality through short anecdotes; to clarify doctrinal differences; and to develop and safeguard the lineage. This soundness of the lineage can only be guaranteed if disciples are provided with clear internal evidence that the line of transmission is unbroken. The stories have a *foundational* purpose by impressing upon us the aptitudes of the individual masters of the lineage.

And how do we, as readers and disciples, discover the master? First, as a precocious child with an early renunciation for the snares of samsara. Next, as a student encountering Lamas and teachers. We are shown the teachings and empowerments the master receives.[9] We follow him into retreat where his meditative challenges and triumphs are revealed. We are impressed with his ability to visualize deities. We see disciples gather around him. We find him in a monastery or, as in the tradition of independent yogis, in the wilderness.

The pattern bears a decided resemblance to the phases found in the hagiographies of the Buddha, and this can be illustrated in the parallel between Buddha Shakyamuni and Khyungpo Naljor: the tantric view of enlightenment asserts that Buddha Shakyamuni was already a fully enlightened being who simply *manifested* as a human and displayed the phases of his life for the benefit of others. So, too, for Khyungpo Naljor: at his birth, his family was visited by the Indian adept Amogha, who prophesized, "This emanation will travel all over India." The connotation of the word "emanation" is that Khyungpo Naljor himself is a fully enlightened being who manifests as Khyungpo the yogi in *this* life. Correlations between the Buddha's life and the master's life, between the Buddha's realization and the master's realization, provide the master with a powerful seal of validity. If the Buddha's teachings are considered authentic, so must the master's.

Seeing the Lama as the actual Buddha (*sang rgyas dngos*) is, then, of fundamental importance in the development of the lineage: it is the crux of the *Lives of the Shangpa Kagyu Masters*. The Tibetan expression for 'lives' (*rnam thar*) literally means 'complete liberation.' The protagonists of the Shangpa Lives are presumed to have reached full liberation. To emphasize that the stories are not merely chronological accounts, I have most of the time translated the term as 'lives' rather than 'life-stories' or 'biographies.' These stories are at heart the unfolding of the masters' awakened experience. They are also the dakinis' teaching on the nature of reality, replete with supernatural elements, ironic anecdotes, humor, and compassion; they are songs and poetry celebrating the elements of nature; advice on particular practices; and help on overcoming specific obstacles. In short, the lives presented in *Like an Illusion: Lives of the Shangpa Kagyu Masters* offer a glimpse of enlightenment, a suggestion of liberation, and praise to a genuine tradition.

The question arises whether writing an autobiography creates potential conflict with central tenets of Buddhist philosophy. Is not an autobiography both an egocentric task (focusing on oneself), and a reification (delineating oneself from others)? It is important to understand that the Tibetan autobiographical mould demands humility of the author. Modesty—self-mockery, even—is expected of the master who writes his autobiography. Rigongpa, for example, called himself an alms-seeker (*ldom bu pa*). Sangye Tönpa said at the end of his life, "I may have brought just a very little bit of benefit to beings." [10]

The restraint of the autobiographies is in sharp contrast to the tone of the biographies written by others. Whereas the autobiographer begins his story with a straightforward 'I come from such-and-such place; my family is such-and-such,' the biographer opens with reverent displays of admiration. The Life of Shangtönpa, for example, begins with elaborate praise and goes on to describe its subject as "the unrivalled lord across the three pure states, the torch of Dharma which dispels the darkness of ignorance, the wish-fulfilling gem that grants all needs and desires, the great vessel carrying those who wish it across the ocean of samsaric attachment, the teacher who sets us on the path and guides those seeking liberation."

The combination of humility in the autobiographies and praise in the biographies places the stories squarely within an accepted writing mould. The master does have realizations, but does not personally boast of them. He is an acceptable exemplar, and his lineage is validated.

The stories in *Like an Illusion* strengthen the lineage by revealing relationships between its practitioners. Throughout the text, masters refer to one another in direct, sometimes prophetic terms. The dakini Sukhasiddhi makes appearances throughout the Shangpa Lives: for example, she transmitted her teachings to Khyungpo and vowed to "bless all holders of the lineage," and her presence is indeed felt in every life story. She also sang to inspire Mokchokpa burdened with hardships in his cave. She appeared to Kyergangpa, Rigongpa, and later Sangye Tönpa. She sang this pithy verse:

> The sky is empty and non-conceptual.
> Cut the root of this conceptual mind.
> Cut the root and relax! [11]

These references serve to insure the direct line of transmission. Legitimacy is further enhanced by the exchange of teachings between the Shangpa and other Buddhist schools. Khyungpo Naljor studied with a hundred and fifty Lamas, beginning in the Bön tradition and moving on to the Nyingma school before turning to the Kagyupas. When Mokchokpa received the Six Yogas of Naropa as well as Mahamudra[12] teachings from Gampopa, a bond was established with the Karma Kagyu tradition. References to the Karmapas (holders of the Karma Kagyu transmission) are frequent. The Shangpa master Khyungpo Tsultrim Gön expressed strong faith in Rangjung Dorje, the Third Karmapa. The next Shangpa lineage holder, Ridrö Rechen Sangye Senge, spent time at the Karmapas' monastic seat in Tsurpu where he received teachings from the Fourth Karmapa Rolpe Dorje (1340-1383).

Many of the Shangpa masters were active Sakya practitioners as well. Sangye Tönpa and Zhönnu Drup both practiced the Sakya Path and Fruition teachings (*lam 'bras*). Tangtong Gyalpo (1361-1464) is another example of a master holding the Sakya and the Shangpa traditions: he received transmissions from the Lama Müchen Gyaltsen and through a direct vision of the dakini Niguma.

A relationship also developed with the Great Pacifier tradition (*zhi byed*) through the master Kyergangpa whose family was connected to the Great Pacifier teachings of Padampa Sangye.[13] Kyergangpa received the instruction in real life as well as from Padampa Sangye in a dream. The Gelukpas too had links with the lineage: the Shangpa master Jakchen Jampa Pal (1310-1391) was one of the Lamas of the great Tsongkhapa and through him the Shangpa teachings entered the Geluk school.

Finally, the lineage is solidified by the realizations of the masters succeeding one another in the Shangpa Lives. Khyungpo Naljor said to his disciple Mokchokpa, "What you have realized, I have not, so you are greater than me." Mokchokpa in turn told his own successor, "Kyergangpa, I am like a cow and you are like the *dzo* born of the cow." A *dzo* is a female yak, much larger and more powerful than the milk cow, and we are to understand that the disciple's realizations are also vaster in scope and more powerful than those of his teacher.

All these foundational activities provide the roots for the tree of the lineage; now disciples can savor its blossom. Within the scope of establishing a tradition, the blossom is the dakini Sukhasiddhi's pledge that she will always bless and protect the lineage; it is the comfort that faithful practitioners of the lineage, past, present, and future, shall enjoy rebirth in a pure realm, a theme reiterated in every story; it is the assurance that all the teachings have been transmitted; it is the expectation for the practitioner of finding refuge in the masters' compassion; it is, finally, the promise that the practices disclosed in this tradition have brought past masters to awakening and provide a proper, valid path to enlightenment.

### *Woman or Dakini?*

TWO WOMEN GAVE birth to the Shangpa lineage, the dakinis Niguma and Sukhasiddhi. Their stories start the string of biographies in *Like an Illusion*. Other women appear in the stories, in roles ranging from patron to mother, student, and teacher. The feminine dakini also appears frequently, symbolizing ultimate realization.

Niguma received a transmission of the four complete empowerments of tantra directly from Vajradhara. Her instructions form the corpus of the Shangpa meditation practices, and today, three-year retreats offered at Kalu Rinpoche centers around the world include the Six Yogas of Niguma. Sukhasiddhi, the other dakini in the lineage, is always presented as peaceful, beautiful, and ripe with blessings that she continually bestows on the lineage. Khyungpo Naljor names both women as two of his four root Lamas.

Examining *Like an Illusion* shows that references to women are somewhat sparse, given their pivotal role in the tradition. The lives of Niguma and Sukhasiddhi account for twenty out of the seven hundred and fifty folios of *Like an Illusion*. These two women are pillars of the tradition, and yet less than five percent of the text is dedicated to them! Their accounts are not only quantitatively minimal, they also exhibit very little qualitative detail. The account of Niguma in particular consists mostly of praise in verse. Some might claim that the brevity of Niguma's story is merely proof of her unencumbered progress on the path, but this interpretation risks beatification of a certain type of perfect woman, leading to a conceptual pitfall that places women at one extreme or the other—the 'perfect woman' is denied any complexity.

Of Niguma and Sukhasiddhi's vicissitudes along the path, very little is shared with us. They did exist as historical beings: Niguma was related to Naropa,[14] and Sukhasiddhi was a beer merchant. But once they receive teachings, they immediately transform into awakened dakinis. No individual details are given. The same observation can be made about other women who appear in the text:[15] readers receive no information on their reality as human practitioners faced with challenges and finding the inner resources to overcome difficulties.

Is the dearth of details on women in *Like an Illusion* really indicative of a fundamental bias? Sangye Tönpa said, "Mental imputations do not need to be cleared from the outside; rather, the qualities will arise from within" (*sgro 'dog phyi nas gcod mi dgos par yon tan nang nas shar yong ba*). Defining women as an entity is a conventional designa-tion, and on this, Mokchokpa said, "Cut through your doubts on the conventional level / You have no need of conventional reality." The conventional focuses on the *contents* of existence, such as women and men, but Buddhism looks at the *nature* of existence, which is the same for women and men. Experience is a moment-by-moment dance between senses, sense objects, and sense consciousnesses. In a prison or in a palace, during a rape or a tantric feast, what matters is to vividly recognize the inherent clear-light emptiness of the experi-ence.

In the tantric context of the Shangpa lineage, the focus for practice shifts from extinguishing or transforming emotions and sensations (such as one's concepts about women) to recognizing their nature as intrinsically pure and empty of inherent existence. In *Like an Illusion*, the tantric view of reality is presented through association with the dakini, who is female and playful, although sometimes wrathful. The yogi Khyungpo Naljor meets with Lion-Faced Singhamukha and she tells him, "The supreme instruction is / To recognize the dakini as your own mind."

The dakini is placed at the objective end of desire, but she looks right back at the subject and points to his externally-directed hunger as the pivotal axis for the shift in perception. The dakini mischievously and blissfully displays what is being projected, reflecting her intrepid wisdom. Free of delusions herself, she is able to give back to the prac-titioner exactly what he is producing, as if on a stainless mirror. As a result, there is equivalence between physical beauty and mental real-izations. For instance, Sukhasiddhi was sixty-one when she attained enlightenment and yet, the text says, she became a dakini with the appearance of "a beautiful sixteen-year old girl, white in color, her hair flowing down her back. She was so beautiful that one never tired of looking at her." It seems that Sukhasiddhi's heightened awareness corresponds to man's heightened fantasy! She is, however, reflecting back to the practitioner his own enlightened nature, which is displayed as physical beauty.

The dakini is dynamic because she does not merely take in, she also reflects and seeks to foster enlightened realizations in the practitioner. When a vision overwhelms Kyergangpa, a goddess appears and tells him:

> My child, look into your own mind.
> . . . . . . . . . . . . . . . . . . . . . . .
> It is all illusory, appearance-emptiness,
> Like the reflection of an image.

The dakini reminds the disciple to examine his own conceptions and mental creations. She often couches her advice in affectionate terms ("my child") as if to ease the harsh reality of facing one's illusions for what they are. When Sangye Tönpa puffed up with pride at his accomplishments, a dakini appeared and made him climb a sand hill, but he slipped back with every step. The dakini mocked him, "What's the problem with a sand hill? I thought you said you were so extraordinary!" In this way, Sangye Tönpa had to face his own delusions.

The conclusion drawn from the text is that readers uncomfortable about the absence of details on women in *Like an Illusion* are challenged to set aside dualistic preoccupations and concentrate on achieving an internal blossom of experience, which is what the dakini is all about.

## Secrecy

FROM THE OUTSET, the Shangpa masters have revealed a penchant for secrecy. As Niguma ordained, the lineage was kept secret in a one-to-one guru-to-disciple transmission for seven generations. Only after two centuries, with Sangye Tönpa, was it taught more widely. The word 'secret' (*gsang*) appears throughout the text in five main contexts:

1. It offers protection for the neophyte who is introduced to esoteric practices;
2. It exemplifies restraint by the master who keeps his qualities secret;
3. It is a prohibition in this degenerate age keeping out those who lack comprehension;
4. It enables retention of sexual fluids in a tantric context;
5. It represents concealment of extraordinary abilities.

In the case of secrecy as protection, the injunctions to secrecy imply esoteric tantric practices with exclusive initiations. The Lama guides his disciple, granting him an initiation or empowerment (*dbang*), which enables him to proceed with a particular practice. Next he will likely give the disciple a reading transmission (*lung*) and offer clarifications and specific explanations. In this process, the Lama must decide what is appropriate for the disciple and protect him by revealing only the practice and level of interpretation for which he is suited.

The Life of Zhönnu Drup offers the example of Sangye Tönpa agreeing to pass his transmission to Zhönnu Drup, "[You Zhönnu Drup] are the right person. To you, I shall reveal [it] all without exception, I won't keep any secret." The implication here is that the master may break the seal of secrecy around the transmission only for a mature and compassionate disciple. Conversely, the neophyte is protected from exposure to practices or understandings for which he is not prepared.

The master's humility means that he is not interested in vainly displaying his talents, so here too, secrecy is called for. We know for example that Zhönnu Drup "always kept concealed his experiences and realizations, and carried on his life with modesty, never making any claims."

In the title of Kyergangpa's Secret Lives, secrecy has the meaning of prohibition. Here, what is secret is what only few can perceive, namely a past life. Kyergangpa agreed to reveal his past lives only "at the insistent request" of a small group of disciples, and the account ends with a warning of severe harm to anyone who lacks faith or devotion for the story. When Kyergangpa opens the secret of his past, it is with the understanding that his listeners have absolute faith that he, Kyergangpa, is the same character who lived in previous lives under a different name, in different circumstances.

It is easier to understand secrecy as prohibition if one remembers that, according to many Buddhists, we live in a degenerate age (*kaliyuga* in Sanskrit). In such an age, people are apt to misunderstand extraordinary abilities. They may become envious, resentful, or skeptical, with the result that these emotions fatally thwart spiritual progress. Rigongpa gave the sober advice, "In these degenerate times, many beings, upon hearing the Dharma, do not understand it—so it's best to stay quiet." Secrecy here is the seal of prohibition keeping out those lacking comprehension.

Secrecy also has the meaning of retention in *Like an Illusion*. In a tantric context, secrecy is retention of the sexual fluids, or bodhichitta. Bodhichitta is generally understood as the dynamic wish to attain enlightenment in order to liberate all beings.[16] However, in relation to this discussion of secrecy as retention, bodhichitta refers to the male and female sexual fluids. The male sperm is called white bodhichitta, and the female fluid, red bodhichitta. They are also called seed essence (*thig le*, Skt. *bindu*). Esoteric sexual tantric practices call for mastery of the movement of this seed essence within the body, and if undertaken by practitioners with the correct understanding, these can lead to an intimate experience of primordial awareness (*ye shes*, Skt. *jnana*).

Khyungpo Naljor received a teaching on the four ways of mastering the seed essence—descending, retaining, reversing, and spreading—from the female teachers Sumatimaha, Gangadhara, and Samantabhadri. In these practices, when one's bodhichitta is retained, it remains potent; when disseminated, it wanes. In this context, the injunction to keep within one's attainments takes on the tantric meaning of retaining one's sexual fluid and sending up and spreading the

resultant energy, so that it becomes the experience of bliss-emptiness.

Retention of the sexual fluids gives the master powers (*siddhis*) such
as flying in the sky, bringing down a rain of flowers, transforming his
appearance, and so on. These extraordinary abilities are to be concealed, however, and concealment is the fifth meaning of secrecy in
*Like an Illusion*, as exemplified in Rahula's verse:

> Lest anger and jealousy increase,
> Whatever talents you may have,
> Like a candle inside a flask:
> Always keep them secret.

As seen above, in this degenerate age, secrecy can be a prohibition
keeping out those who are jealous or lack the proper understanding
and that is the implication of the metaphor, "Like a candle inside a
flask." For the most part, the master conceals his extraordinary abilities, but at times, exhibiting such powers can be a didactic tool. If
displays of supernatural powers inspire disciples to practice, the master will perform them.

Beginning with Niguma's seal on the lineage for seven generations,
secrecy marks every phase of the Shangpa master's progress on the
path: he is given secret practices, holds himself in humble restraint,
prohibits those who lack understanding, retains bodhichitta in his
advanced practices, and conceals from many his subsequent attainments.

## Compassion: Human, All Too Human

AVALOKITESHVARA, THE DEITY of compassion, told Khyungpo:

> Whatever you do, whether you walk, stand, sleep or sit,
> Always remember your kind mothers who still experience suf-
> fering.

> Arouse immeasurable compassion
> And anchor it with the iron hook of mindfulness.
>
> From the snowy mountains of love and affection
> Flow the cooling rivers of great compassion,
> Extinguishing the flames of afflictive emotions.[17]

Compassion is the wish to free all beings—friends and enemies alike—from suffering. It is a central feature of *Like an Illusion*. Both in their actions and in their teachings, the Shangpa masters display compassion. They are moved by the suffering of others, and their response typifies what we call 'compassion with reference to beings' (*sems can la dmigs pa'i snying rje*). They are not perfect gods; they are human beings who have dedicated all their time, energy, and abilities to attaining enlightenment for the sake of others. We benefit from their example because we gain inspiration and a sense of self-confidence in our practice.

Kyergangpa's story, for example, is particularly touching. It enables the modern reader (doubtless plagued by obstacles and moments of despair) to see that his samsaric predicament itself has a long tradition. Kyergangpa was recognized as an emanation of Avalokiteshvara, the deity embodying compassion. He meditated for years with, as he said, "no signs [of accomplishment] whatsoever" (*rtags ci yang ma byung*). When at long last he gained a vision of Avalokiteshvara the Lord of Great Compassion, he burst out an ironic greeting, "O Lord of Little Compassion!" Compassion does not come easily, as this anecdote illustrates.

There's also compassion in Kyergangpa's candor. He is aware of his failings, he is 'human, all too human' to use Nietzsche's phrase. His frankness reminds us that hardships are common to all and that obstacles *can* be overcome.

When he met Lama Tsari Gompa, Kyergangpa lied to him about his lack of funds. However, he soon acknowledged his lie, and not only to the Lama—who saw through it—but, by setting the episode down on paper, to his readers and disciples as well. In another instance, he faced fickle patrons and jealous teachers: these, he explained, were the result of his own karmic ripening. If a Lama as great as Kyergangpa had obstacles to surmount, and was able to overcome them, then we can too.

Overcoming hardships and wishing others to be free of suffering are themes in the story of Sukhasiddhi, an old woman banished from her home by her own family due to her compassion for an individual even less fortunate than herself. She was forced to sell beer to earn a living. In another example, Rigongpa spent much of his time subduing havoc-wreaking protectors, activities that reveal his compassion for the targets of the protector's wrath. Similarly, Zhönnu Drup watched with compassion as strife destroyed the Sakya school.

But the Shangpa masters' compassion extends beyond commiserating with the beings of samsara, to the analytical stance which questions the experiential nature of compassion itself. Shangtönpa's compassion for sentient beings was so intense that he often couldn't stop crying over their travails. But he made his own compassion an object of meditation and asked himself: who is it that experiences compassion? Toward whom is it directed? And what is the nature of the compassion itself? Shangtönpa's reflections led to an understanding of egolessness and thus freedom from suffering because, as Rahula said to Khyungpo Naljor, "The root of suffering is clinging to ego."

Reflecting on egolessness, the masters begin to understand the illusory nature of reality. At this point, their compassion deepens into what is called 'compassion with reference to reality' (chos la dmigs pa'i snying rje). Suffering arises not simply from the particular samsaric circumstances of individual beings, but from a fundamental ignorance on their part. The masters find that ignorance confuses beings who end up producing conditions for their own misery. All beings mistakenly posit inherent existence to the ego, objects, and experiences, when there is in fact no inherent existence to anyone, or anything. This basic misconception is the root cause of suffering for sentient beings and understanding it is compassion. Niguma's morning practice puts it succinctly, "Sentient beings fill all that space fills. Every one, without a single exception, has been my parent. Each and every one has helped me in countless lives. All of them, though wishing happiness, accomplish suffering. Oh pitiable ones, wandering endlessly in samsara..."[18]

Compassion with reference to reality requires an understanding of the ultimate nature of reality. It motivates the practitioner to help *others* perceive the nature of reality. It is no surprise, then, that the masters' acts of compassion—at least in the Christian sense of altruism—do not predominate in the text. The starkest example is the protector Mahakala, whose story closes *Like an Illusion*. Mahakala always appears as a wrathful deity holding a knife, a skull-cup of blood, a lasso etc., but he is in essence Avalokiteshvara, the deity of compassion, and he accomplishes the benefit of beings.

In fact, in exposing delusions, the Shangpa masters seem at times anything but meek or kind! They do not hesitate to challenge the boundaries of the acceptable, shocking their disciples out of conventional concepts about reality in order to perceive the innate purity in all phenomena. In the Life of Rigongpa, Kyergangpa told Rigongpa to drink beer, eat in the evening, associate with all sorts of people, wear old rags, and not bother with either aspiration or dedication prayers during teachings. Rigongpa's unorthodox behavior forces a reassessment of what it means to be enlightened, and what it means to be compassionate.

Compassion, therefore, gives form to, or *informs,* the master, who takes the shape best suited to benefit others. At this highest level of realization, compassion is expressed through the enlightened emanation-body (*sprul pa'i sku,* Skt. *nirmanakaya*). In a statement that is as much aspiration as it is prophecy, Kyergangpa announced he would display millions of bodies in order to lead beings to maturation. In another example, the Buddha "displayed various manifestations; these aspects constitute the enlightened emanation-body. The body connected with the various means of benefiting others until samsara has come to an end—that body is the enlightened emanation-body."

The ultimate compassion, as *Like an Illusion* reveals, is to realize emptiness, directly and correctly. Dualistic notions of self and other disappear, and compassion manifests spontaneously, naturally, without conceptualization. This last phase of compassion is called 'non-referential compassion' (*dmigs pa med pa'i snying rje*).

The phases of compassion illustrate a progression of awareness from a motivation to obtain enlightenment for the sake of others, to an understanding that others are suffering due to their misconception of reality and, lastly, to the ultimate compassion of realized emptiness. This last phase is the goal of the Shangpa masters and is synonymous with enlightenment.

## Renunciation and Commitment

RENUNCIATION AND COMMITMENT are essential in Buddhist practice. In *Like an Illusion*, the master renounces the world and develops a bond with an authentic teacher. When the term renunciation (*nges 'byung*) appears in the text, it implies renunciation of samsara, the relentless cycle of existence.

The three approaches or vehicles[19] of the Buddha's teachings provide three different perspectives on renunciation. In *Luminous Mind*, Kalu Rinpoche put it this way, "The hinayana path teaches renunciation of impurities ... The mahayana approach proposes to change those 'contaminated' qualities into their opposites," whereas "the vajrayana [tantra] involves transcending perceptions of pure and impure."[20] We find examples of all three in *Like an Illusion*.

To ground her practice of tantra, the Shangpa master uses the hinayana revulsion toward worldly affairs as her starting point. For example, the Shangpa master, Sangye Tönpa, perceived "this samsaric bondage as a prison, an inferno. I realized all things of this world, family, home, country, and the like, to be ephemeral and impermanent, actually deceitful. A falsehood."

Furthermore, as a tantric practitioner rooted in a mahayana understanding of emptiness and driven by the compassionate aspiration to benefit all beings, the Shangpa master learns to recognize mental grasping as something to be renounced. Although one conceives of, and grasps onto the phenomena of existence as intrinsically real, existence is actually a state of flux. Khyungpo Naljor spoke beautifully of this ephemerality, likening it to "the gathering and dispersing of clouds in the sky." With the cessation of conceptual labeling, the world is seen in its emptiness. "If conceptual thoughts of samsara and nirvana are abandoned, then the two become one reality."[21]

In tantra, lust and disgust for the world are embraced in a dynamic dance. Using powerful techniques to remove the subtle stains obscuring her consciousness, the master habituates herself to experiencing worldly objects as the mandala, and herself as great bliss. It is in this context that Tara told Kyergangpa, "See your afflictive emotions / As self-arising, self-liberated."

The tantric path of recognizing the innate purity in all phenomena is said to be faster but also more dangerous. The tantric practitioner develops the habit of perceiving herself and all other beings as deities and the environment as a pure realm. But in practice, she is still subject to the law of cause and effect; her actions bring specific results. She trains in perceiving everything as pure, but she must not delude herself that a pure outlook overrules the law of cause and effect. A grave error is made if she uses the fire of tantric techniques to assert, however unconsciously, the validity of the ego. This is precisely the point made by a young dakini to Sangye Tönpa when she told him that he was still under the delusion of dualistic perception: "Perceiver and perceived: gold perhaps, but still golden shackles!" Only genuine compassion and commitment to the Lama's precepts will keep one from falling into extremes.

Even when the practitioner does not fall into the dangerous pit of ego / no-ego, the path may simply become so daunting that it is abandoned. Either way, the *samaya* vow keeps her safely on the tantric path. The quintessential tantric yogi, Rahula, told Khyungpo, "Meditate in accordance with karmic cause and effect. And above all, keep *samaya*."

The term *samaya* is often translated as 'tantric commitment' and plays a crucial role in *Like an Illusion*. The Tibetan equivalent for the Sanskrit term *samaya* is *damtsik* (*dam tshig*) and stands for '[giving one's] word to a genuine being' (*dam pa'i skye bo tshig*). The key here is 'genuine being.' A genuine being (*dam pa*) refers to an individual who has realized the ultimate truth (*don dam*), the nature of reality. When practicing tantra, the Shangpa master relies on a Lama to initiate her and give her teachings and explanations, and she has the conviction that the Lama is a genuine being who has realized the nature of reality.

Outer tantric commitments consist of keeping harmony with one's Lama (contradicting one's Lama is the first and most serious downfall) and fellow practitioners. Inner tantric commitments demand consistency in tantric practice. Since a tantric commitment is a powerful vow and breaking it is said to have dire consequences, it becomes, coupled with a renunciation of the mental trappings of dualistic fixation, an incredibly powerful force driving the Shangpa master's engagement on the tantric path.

### Solitude: Like a Wounded Antelope

TO REALIZED MASTERS, the transmission is the clear-light nature of mind, and contaminations are deluded perceptions. The Shangpa masters repeatedly tell their disciples that practicing in solitude is the best road to realization. In one of the most beautiful songs in the text, Rahula advised Khyungpo Naljor:

> Until you achieve stability,
> You are harmed by the distractions of the world.
> Therefore, like a wounded antelope,
> Stay alone, and practice.

Worldly entanglements pull a practitioner back into conceptual reality, and solitude is a way to avoid these traps. Mokchokpa admonished Gyatön Namkha, "A practitioner returning to lay life / Is the bedrock of samsara!"

It is in a retreat setting that the master can refine his tantric experience, which aims not to extinguish the world, nor to transform it, but rather to directly intuit it, in order to benefit others. A period of solitary retreat for intense and undistracted practice is *de rigueur* for a genuine practitioner. The typical life story includes a period of meditation practice, much of it in solitude, and often culminates with a return to the world to engage in activities such as establishing monasteries and otherwise propagating the Buddhist teachings. When the master knows how to sustain the experience he has developed in retreat, he re-enters the world and becomes active. At that point, whether he lives in the midst of worldly activity or in solitary mountain peaks, his awareness does not dim, as Niguma made clear to Khyungpo:

> Whirling in the ocean of samsara
> Are the myriad thoughts of love and hate.
> Once you know they have no nature,
> Then everywhere is the land of gold, my child.

The master often assumes responsibilities within the social structure. He gathers disciples about him and, perhaps, builds a monastery to ensure the success of his lineage and of the Buddhist teachings in general.

But not the Shangpa lineage. This tradition is marked by its lack of institutionalization. Although Khyungpo Naljor settled into a normal religious life after seven journeys to India and Nepal, building monasteries and establishing a tradition, the holders of his lineage, starting with his principal disciple Mokchokpa, largely avoided monasticism. Mokchokpa started a religious community after his retreat site proved too small to accommodate his growing retinue of disciples, but even then he expressed a wistful longing for "meditating

alone in solitude." With the exception of Khyungpo Naljor, the masters of this lineage follow a non-traditional path and make it clear
that they prefer being alone, even in their dying days.

Iconoclasm is, of course, not unknown in Buddhist hagiography.
Many of the *mahasiddhas*, or great adepts, of India and Tibet—such
as Sukhasiddhi's Lama, Virupa, who paid for his drink at the tavern
by holding the sun up on his dagger—expressed individualistic pro-
clivities. In Tibet, the great poet-yogi Milarepa (a contemporary of
Khyungpo Naljor) was particularly critical of "artificial scholar-
priests."[22] By the time *Like an Illusion* was written, this individualistic
behavior with its emphasis on solitude had itself become a tradition,
albeit an unorthodox one, developing parallel to the more conventional path.

Given the Shangpa emphasis on solo praxis, it is no surprise that
the masters' anti-traditionalist feelings extend to their attitude toward
relics. Long-life rituals and relic-veneration (the sight of relics was
said to inspire disciples) were well established by the time of the
Shangpa lineage, but the text reveals the masters' ambivalence about
the worship of them. In response to their disciples' requests, most of
the Shangpa masters leave relics that will provide inspiration, but at
the same time, they shun posthumous glory. When students sought
to perform long-life rituals for a dying Sangye Tönpa, he replied, "It's
all the same to me [whether you do the long-life rituals or not], all I
need is meditative absorption in the clear-light. Nothing else is of
any benefit." His successor, Zhönnu Drup, asked that after his death,
his bones be scattered in the river, and expressively forbade the building of big relics-shrines. Khyungpo Tsultrim Gön requested that after his death, his body be cremated or given to the birds.

The appeal of solitude and the resultant anti-traditionalist senti-
ment are often supported by textual anecdotes that offer evidence of
institutional backbiting. One example will suffice here. Khyungpo
Naljor gained respect in the community, and many young monks were
attracted to his teachings. As his success increased, the elders of the
nearby study center grew jealous. They huddled together, "If all our
monks turn to Khyungpo for teachings, it will be the end of our

school." The example makes the point that institutions can be a powerful agency of the mind's conventional structuring. In contrast to this reifying tendency, Shangtönpa said he abstained from "the obsession with leading a monastery."

Just as teachers want to preserve their schools, others also seek to advance themselves. The text offers many ironic vignettes about the pitfalls of conceit, and draws a distinct contrast between boastful beings engaged in furthering their own interest, and the genuine masters who practice alone. Taranatha's father described a particular Lama as "one of those opportunists who goes around saying the *mani* mantra[23] to fill his purse and his belly."

A startling contrast is presented in the tale of Lama Burgom Nakpo which appears in the Life of Mokchokpa: Mokchokpa saw a small hut hidden between the trees and learnt that Lama Burgom Nakpo lived there. The sight inspired him and he set out for the hut. There, he saw a man, wearing a yogi's cotton robe, who invited him inside. Mokchokpa asked where Burgom Nakpo was and the man in the cotton robe replied, "That's me. I have no attendants." Burgom Nakpo is the exemplar for the practitioner in solitude: modest yet realized.

The Shangpa masters express uneasiness with scholars (*dge bshes*) as well. These provide an ideal target not so much because of their self-absorption, but because they represent beings "with only intellectual, not actual understanding." Even if one accepts that an intellectual understanding of the ultimate is a pre-requisite for a direct perception of reality, there is a point at which the intellectual approach must be set aside. Sangye Tönpa said, "In this short life, endless intellectual pursuits are like a deer chasing a mirage, his thirst unquenched—so drink of the pure nectar." As this advice illustrates, the Shangpa lineage emphasizes solitary practice over scholarly study. Sukhasiddhi in particular is associated with direct experience, not intellectual analysis.[24] As a result, her instructions were always pithy and straightforward:

> The sky is empty and non-conceptual.
> Cut the root of this conceptual mind.
> Cut the root and relax.

This is the experiential immediacy of the Shangpa Lives: direct genuine experience born of solitary practice, free of mental fabrications.

## Dreams and Visions

THE PRACTITIONER GAPA Chögyal obtained teachings but he was unclear about their source, so he asked his Lama, Khyungpo, whether he had actually received instructions—or whether they had occurred in the realm of dreams. In response, Khyungpo Naljor sang:

> The Buddha's body, the Buddha's pure land,
> The Buddha's entourage, the Buddha's teaching,
> Are all like an illusion.
> Reality or dream, where is the difference?

Dreams, visions, and displays of magic are central to *Like an Illusion*.[25] The stories answer Gapa Chögyal's question about dream and reality. They are, in fact, a series of teachings on Dream Yoga. Khyungpo Naljor used lucid dream techniques to help a confused disciple. Mokchokpa had prophetic dreams. In dreams, Kyergangpa had visions of deities and Padmasambhava,[26] and Rigongpa subdued spirits. Shangtönpa first saw his yidam deity[27] in a dream—and later in real life.[28]

Dreams provide an ideal analogy for reality, the nature of which is described variously as a dream, a mirage, a rainbow, or a magical apparition. The phenomena that arise in a dream *seem* real to the nonlucid dreamer, yet they have no substantial reality. Dream appearances are a series of moments of experience that lack inherent truth. The dreamer's misconception of reality lends the dream its 'true' quality. The similes of reality and dream highlight the illusory nature of phenomena. They arise yet have no true nature. They have no true nature, yet they arise.

A parallel can be drawn between non-lucid dreaming and samsara on the one hand, and lucid dreaming and nirvana on the other. The Shangpa tradition is tantric in nature, so the likening of dream and reality goes beyond the mere absence of inherent existence to an assertion of the clear-light nature of mind. A distinction is made between the relative mind, which is mistaken perception, and the ultimate clear-light nature of mind, which is unmistaken. Mokchokpa taught:

> Mind's true nature has no arising.
> The clear-light nature is the realization of this non-arising.

With lucid dreaming, it's possible to continue the dream even when we become aware that we are dreaming. This is the point at which we can interact dynamically with our dream apparitions. Sangye Tönpa said, "At night, the clear light of non-conceptual luminous bliss arises spontaneously." Just as dreams do not cease because we recognize them for what they are, the appearances of the external world do not cease for the mind aware of its own clear-light nature.

The predominance of dream-accounts in *Like an Illusion* reflects Dream Yoga, the third of the Six Yogas of Niguma.[29] The Shangpa masters, and in particular those known as the Seven Shangpa Jewels, exhibit extraordinary mastery in their practice of Dream Yoga. Their lives can be seen as a series of teachings on Dream Yoga. Kyergangpa used his Dream Yoga practice to travel to Mount Potala and receive pithy verse instructions from Tara. Sangye Tönpa, in his autobiography, described the Dream Yoga activities of training, multiplication, emanation, and transformation. When Mokchokpa had difficulty in visualizing and therefore emanating *garudas*[30] in his dreams, the yogi Chöyung pragmatically suggested that he go to the nearby monastery and study drawings of the *garudas* on its walls.

In *Like an Illusion*, dreams are a means of receiving teachings, prophecies and instructions. They function as an aspect of meditation practice, and they are also a metaphor for reality, teaching the practitioner the illusory nature of existence.

### Miracles and the Two Truths

AS THE SPRING flowers blossomed, Khyungpo spent time with
his monks in Pangkar. One day, he performed a miracle: he
manifested before each one a beautiful goddess of the Heaven
of Thirty-Three,[31] so beautiful the monks couldn't stop staring at them. Every one of the goddesses was smiling, graceful and lovely. This sight aroused great pleasure in the monks.
The next day, they were summoned to another gathering and
all went eagerly.

But this time, Khyungpo emanated the wrathful god Yama,
Lord of Death,[32] eating human flesh. The Lord of Death
looked terrible, with red eyes, mouth gaping, fangs bared,
laughing loudly and shouting "DEATH AND DESTRUC-
TION!" In his hands, he held sharp weapons. His retinue surrounded him, reciting mantras. The monks were struck with
fear and many fainted. When they regained consciousness,
they asked Khyungpo if he had emanated the goddesses and
Yama. In response, Khyungpo sang this song:

All objects of pleasure and horror
Arise from one's own mind.
. . . . . . . . . . . . . . . . . . . . . . . . . .
Understand that they are self-arising illusion,
And they no longer have any power to bind you.

Miracles and the supernatural appear at every turn in *Like an Illusion*
and other similar texts. They play an important part in Tibetan Buddhism, which was made possible in part by its assimilation of local
customs. When Indian Buddhists such as Atisha carried teachings back
from India to Tibet in the 11th century, they incorporated aspects of

the existing Bön religion of Tibet. The Bön viewpoint was 'shamanis-
tic' insofar as it dealt in communications with the supernatural world.
In fact, Tibetan popular culture saw social and natural relations in
terms of non-human beings (gods and spirits) harmful or beneficial
to humans. Such a cultural conception required rites and magic to
appease, subdue, or eradicate the spirits, and Buddhism assimilated
this impulse. Khyungpo Naljor performed an exorcism to stop thieves
from chasing him, and Sangye Tönpa became "a *garuda* in order to
tame the local demon."

Miraculous displays are also an essential component of the tantric
movement of Buddhism, which took hold in Tibet from the 11th century onwards. One only needs to read the life stories of the great
adepts[33] to appreciate the recurrence of miracles as powers (*siddhis*).[34]
The ability to pass through matter, fly, manipulate the elements, play
with lucid dreams, and so on, are all enumerated as part of the *siddhis*
of realized adepts.

When a master realizes Mahamudra, *siddhis* arise spontaneously.
Realizing Mahamudra means understanding (not intellectually, but
directly) the emptiness of inherent existence in self and phenomena.
Since emptiness pervades all phenomena, the master who realizes
this is freed from the limitations of self and other, internal and external. His perceptions are unhindered and his actions can defy conventional logic—he can perform miracles.

Following an experiential realization of the nature of phenomena,
which appear and yet are unborn, Rigongpa caught a lightning bolt
in his hands and played with it by rolling it back and forth on the
folds of his robe. An "excellent experience of Illusory Body" enabled
Mokchokpa to "levitate in the vajra posture[35] above [his] cave."
Khyungpo Tsultrim Gön stayed in a cave, but through his clairvoyance, saw what happened in the valley down below. These miraculous feats illustrate the masters' realization of illusory reality.

Tantra works on a psychophysical level, so that when the practitioner masters a specific tantric deity, he is able to manifest that deity in
a physical sense. Khyungpo Naljor, for example, mastered the wisdom gained through the practice of the Five Tantric Deities. He was

able to display for a disciple "the Five Tantric Deities present in [the] five chakras[36] [of his body]," saying, "from now on, never see me as ordinary, not even for a moment." This miraculous display was a physical sign of realization. So, too, Mokchokpa displayed the forms of Vajrayogini and Tara, Kyergangpa manifested as Avalokiteshvara, and Rigongpa as Vajrapani, and so on. After Zhönnu Drup "abandoned ego-clinging, [he] meditated until his body was the body of the deity, and his mind was the body of reality."[37] Since tantric deities offer a means for a direct, unmistaken understanding of the nature of reality, the ability to appear as a tantric deity is synonymous with a realization of the nature of reality.

This, then, is the background against which miracles come to life in *Like an Illusion*. They vividly illustrate the two truths of emptiness and dependent arising.[38] Ultimately, the nature of reality is empty of inherent existence and the nature of mind is empty of inherent existence, so there is no difference between them.

Buddhism teaches that the two truths are inseparable: if phenomena do not have an independent, inherent existence, it follows that they exist *in dependence* upon causes and conditions. Thus emptiness (ultimate truth) is inseparable from dependent arising (conventional truth). As an example, the first teaching that Kyergangpa, in a past incarnation as a monkey, gave the king and the king's retinue was to understand that "cause and effect arise interdependently."

Miracles are a rich medium for this intricate dialogue of reciprocal cause and effect. Two relevant excerpts from the Life of Rigongpa emphasize respectively the ultimate and the conventional. In the first example, Rigongpa pointed to emptiness as the basis for his equanimity. "I stayed in the midst of chaos and slept in frightening places, between warring armies. When people told me that I shouldn't stay unprotected in hostile places without a single assistant, I simply thought to myself, 'There is no truly existent nature to self and other, enemy and friend, fights and struggle. They are but self-arising illusions.' My realization that appearances do not inherently exist made me fearless. In short, I saw that all phenomena, sights, and sounds, do not truly exist." By turning this around, we see that whenever, in any of the stories, a practitioner gets scared at the sight of various bizarre manifestations, the fear is due to the attribution of inherent existence. This is the point made by Gyaltsen Bum as he tells his disciples of miraculous experiences: "It should be understood that all miracles, great or small, are one's own mind. Neither gods nor demons have any real impact."

The other example from the Life of Rigongpa aims more at the conventional truth of dependent arising, with anecdotes involving Dharma protectors so real that they actually killed humans who disrespected Rigongpa! In one such instance, Rigongpa was meditating in a hut when a shepherd approached and insulted him. Two days later, the protector Drakshema tore out the shepherd's heart, saying, "A couple of days ago, this man insulted you, teacher!" The protectors continued their rampage despite Rigongpa's pleas not to harm any beings. Given the interdependence of phenomena and the play of cause and effect, it seems that a shepherd was killed as a result of showing disrespect for a Lama, and also that someone, a protector, did the killing as a result of hearing the shepherd show disrespect.

These examples illustrate that while appearances do not truly exist, they nevertheless do appear and do have a conventional, imputed existence. The master inculcates the ultimate understanding that the imputed nature of phenomena does not inherently exist. Khyungpo Naljor offers a clear example. After "[flying] through the mountain, levitating in space in the vajra posture, and displaying one and many forms," he sang this verse:

> Phenomena appear and yet have no true nature.
> Immature beings take them to be real
> And are confused.
> Appearances do not truly exist!

"Phenomena appear." Here is an acknowledgement of dependent arising, or the conventional truth. But lest that leads to the extreme of eternalism, or reifying phenomena as inherently 'there,' Khyungpo continued with a nod to emptiness, ultimate truth: "… yet have no true nature." The "yet" establishes the proper dialectical balance. It is, however, the next two lines that are particularly relevant. The term "immature beings" (*byis pa*) specifically refers to beings who lack insight into reality and as a result impute a fixed nature upon phenomena. Immature beings "are confused" by this process—the determinate phrasing suggests that the imputations placed on phenomena do gain a sort of autonomy, so that beings become confused. Not only do they become confused and thus create imputations, but having created these imputed concepts, beings are confused *by them*. The imputation itself becomes a basis of imputation. Later, Khyungpo reiterated the point. He displayed many bodies in the sky and sang a song including this verse:

> Although illusory phenomena
> Have no true nature,
> We cling to them as real
> And are deceived.

The use of "deceived" (*bslus*) suggests, even more than "confused" (*'khrul*), the impact of mistaken imputations. Miracles, by playing upon imputations, are fully involved in the cause-and-effect dialogue that is taking place all the time, both as results of our concepts and as causes for them. Only when the realization of the ultimate nature of reality dawns within, is Niguma's "golden mountain" indeed attained.

# I

# Vajradhara

WHY THE NAME Vajradhara? In Sanskrit, *vajra*, meaning 'diamond,' implies solidity, an essence, not a hollowness within. It cannot be taken away. It cannot be cut. It cannot be dismantled. *Dhara* means 'to hold.' Whoever holds diamond-like reality is rightly called Vajradhara.

> If you possess the wisdom of all the Buddhas
> And if you're endowed with bodhichitta,
> You are the victor Vajradhara.

This brief account of Vajradhara was set down by the mendicant yogi Mokchokpa, so that all those in the Shangpa lineage may gain realizations.

# 2

# Life of Niguma

HOMAGE TO ALL the holy Lamas! From the sky-like body of reality, the sun-and-moon rays of your form bodies dispel the darkness of mind of all disciples. I bow down at your feet, holy Lama.

I will now give a brief account of the wisdom dakini Niguma. It starts with Niguma's birthplace, the magical city of Peme in Kashmir. In the time of the Buddha Kashyapa, much before Shakyamuni,[39] there was a saint[40] called Midday Sun. In those days, an ocean covered the site of the future city, Peme. The saint, Midday Sun, went to the area and decided that a temple should be erected. In order to develop the site, he asked for the *nagas'*[41] assistance, saying, "I need you *nagas* to give me some of this land."

But the king of *nagas* replied, "Well, I'll give you as much space as you take when you sit in the vajra posture!" So the saint made himself very big. As he sat in the vajra posture, he covered the whole of Kashmir. True to their word, the *nagas* changed the ocean into solid ground, and the saint built a temple named Intimate Nectar.

When this was done, to charm and amaze the people, Midday Sun invited a great magician to build a city around the temple. The magician created the city in the likeness of Tanaduk.[42] Its unique beauty gave the name Peme—the Incomparable—to the city. Before the magician had time to disassemble the magical city he had created, the people killed him. To this day, Peme the Incomparable remains. The glorious city of Peme had no rival in all of Jambudiva.[43] There were thousands of women beer merchants, and both Ratnavajra and the sage[44] Naropa lived there.

And now, let us turn to the wisdom dakini. Niguma was the daughter of the Brahmin Shantasamnaha and the sister of the sage Naropa. In her past lives, she practiced the path for three immeasurable eons. In this life, she came to reality itself just by meeting a realized Lama and receiving a few teachings.

Her impure illusory body arose as perfect body. She dwelt in the three pure states[45] and saw the face of Vajradhara himself. She received the four complete empowerments[46] from the emanated mandala of tantric mahayana.[47] She developed omniscient wisdom in the sutras, tantras, oral instructions, and teachings. She saw all phenomena as they are and as they appear.[48] She herself attained Cloud of Dharma, the tenth level of a bodhisattva.[49]

Niguma released even the subtlest veil to the knowable[50] and became in essence the three bodies of enlightenment,[51] indistinguishable from the Buddha. For her own benefit, she brought to completion abandonment and cultivation.[52] For the benefit of others, she manifested the two form bodies. This she will do until samsara is completely empty. In particular, through her activity and blessings, she gazes with impartial compassion on all the holders of the [Shangpa] lineage.

Niguma granted the four complete empowerments to the adept Khyungpo Naljor in the emanated mandala. To him, she transmitted the most profound tantras, intimate advice, and oral and written teachings. She also gave him the essential pith instructions that enable worthy disciples to attain enlightenment in one body and one life.

She commanded that, for seven generations, these ear-whispered instructions should not be propagated outside the one-to-one guru-to-disciple transmission. She promised that all disciples and lineage holders would go to the Pure Land of the Dakini, because this lineage was special above all others.

*Eulogy to the Dakini Niguma*

HOMAGE TO YOU, wisdom dakini!
You have overcome fixation on mere illusion
And have cleared the subtlest veil to the knowable.
You remain in the diamond-like *samadhi*[53] of clear light.
You are truly the great conqueror!

Three-fold purity[54] is the perfection of generosity.[55]
You realize the meaning of the all-pervasive realm of reality,[56]
And have powers such as seeing, blessings, and meditation.
To you, I bow down!

The subsiding of desires is the perfection of ethics.
You realize the supreme meaning of the natural realm of reality,
You understand that the realm of reality is perfect and self-arising.
To you, I bow down!

To be impervious to anger is the perfection of patience.
You realize the correspondence of cause and effect within the realm of reality,
You, dakini, have attained meditative powers.
To you I bow down!

Energy in one's practice of virtue is the perfection of perseverance.
You realize that the realm of reality is utterly free of grasping,
You master a hundred thousand *samadhis* benefiting self and other.
To you I bow down!

Unwavering wisdom is the perfection of meditative concentration.
You realize that the realm of reality is not different from all other things,
Dakini of powers,
To you I bow down!

Knowing all phenomena to be unborn is the perfection of knowledge.
You realize that purified afflictive emotions are one with the realm of reality,
Dakini of powers,
To you I bow down!

The accomplishment of wisdom is the perfection of skillful means.
You realize that the realm of reality and essential characteristics cannot be differentiated,
Dakini of powers,
To you I bow down!

Focusing on the highest good is the perfection of aspiration.
You realize that the pure realm of reality neither increases nor diminishes,
Dakini of powers as numerous as the atoms in the trichiliocosm,
To you I bow down!

Vanquishing the armies of Mara is the perfection of power.
You realize [the realm of reality] to be incomparable courage and strong wisdom,
Dakini of powers as numerous as the atoms in a thousand Buddha realms,
To you I bow down!

Perceiving things as they are is the perfection of primordial
    awareness.
You realize that the realm of reality is free of mental
    obscurations in meditation and post-meditation,
And know that whatever is empty neither increases nor de-
    creases.
To you, dakini who has realized this pure state, I bow down!

You are truly a daughter of the Buddha, a mighty tenth-level
    bodhisattva.
Seated on a lion throne in the sky in this trichiliocosm,
You grant the Great Light Rays Empowerment.[57]
To you who removes veils to the knowable, I bow down!

In the mansion of the Queen of Akanistha,
You grant the empowerments of undefiled great bliss.
In a flash, you illuminate the Dharma.
To you of perfect and impartial knowledge, I bow down!

The uncompounded realm of reality
Is inseparable from wisdom and love.
Foundation, accumulation, and all-pervasive [activity] are self-
    accomplished.
To you who actualizes the body of reality, I bow down!

Without deviating from the body of reality,
You spontaneously manifest the two form bodies
Through merit engendered in times past.
To you who acts until samsara is empty, I bow down!

### Supplication to the Dakini Niguma

THE BLISS BODY is emptiness-compassion inseparable. Glorious
    guide, mighty tenth-level bodhisattva who wears bone orna-
    ments, I supplicate you.

Dakini, I supplicate you, from your non-referential compassion, please guide all sentient beings, my mothers, from this vast ocean of samsara to the realm of unfolding pure bliss.

Dakini, I supplicate you, please pacify obstacles and adverse conditions for all mother and father beings fortunate enough to enter the path of Dharma. Grant your blessings that our experiences and realizations may increase forever more, and that we may traverse the five paths[58] and the ten levels.

Dakini, I supplicate you, from the time of Ananda's enlightenment,[59] and for as long as there are sentient beings within samsara, please act for the benefit of others through non-referential, non-conceptual compassion.


THIS WAS A short account of the complete liberation of the wisdom dakini Niguma, set down for the understanding of all her disciples by the tantric alms-seeker Mokchokpa, whose full name is Rinchen Tsöndrü, in the monastery of Gyere. By this virtue, may all the sons and daughters of the lineage live up to this life story. By the pure virtue of this text, may I and all disciples of the lineage and all sentient beings quickly attain unsurpassable enlightenment.

# 3

# Life of Sukhasiddhi

TO THE GLORIOUS wisdom dakini Sukhasiddhi, known as Dewe Ngödrup in Tibetan, I pay homage!

In a town in Western Kashmir lived a family of eight: two elderly parents with three sons and three daughters. The family was terribly poor and hungry. They had run out of food and had nothing to eat except for a pot of rice. So one day, the three sons headed south to look for food. The three daughters went north and the father went west. Meanwhile, a man even more destitute than the family came to the door and asked the woman for some food. The old lady opened up the pot of rice, cooked it, and offered him some.

The father had found no food and was weak with hunger. He thought, "Why search for more food? We still have that pot of rice at home." So he returned home. The three sons turned back without finding anything, and likewise the three daughters. They all arrived at once and had hardly stepped back in when they barked, "Mother, open up that pot of rice and give us some! We're hungry and tired."

"You all went looking for food! I thought you'd come back with something!" the mother replied. "While you were gone, a very poor person came to the door, and I gave him the rice to eat . . . It's all gone." This angered the husband and children. They cried out in one voice, "You have done this before! Instead of going out and looking for food as we do, you just give away the little we have left! Now, because of you, we have nothing to eat. We're sick and tired of it! You continually make us miserable! Go away, we don't want you around here anymore!" Then they threw her out of the house.

The old lady left Kashmir and headed west for Uddiyana,[60] where, it was said, all the men were dakas[61] and all the women, dakinis, and one's mind became naturally clear upon arriving there. Because it was harvest time, she obtained a bag of rice and decided to make beer from it and become a beer merchant.

At that time, the great teacher Virupa[62] lived in the forest of Uddiyana. A yogini known as Avadhutima was staying with him, and together they practiced the yoga of sexual union. This yogini often came to Uddiyana to buy beer. Because the old lady's beer was the tastiest, Avadhutima only bought it from her. One day, the old lady asked her, "Yogini, who are you taking this beer to?"

The yogini answered, "To a great yogi who lives up in the forest."

"Well then," said the old lady, "let me give you my very best beer, and please, I don't want any payment for this."

Later, as Virupa was drinking what his consort had brought him, he asked, "Yogini, how come this beer is free?"

The yogini explained, "This is a gift from the beer merchant, a woman of unusual faith. I told her there was a Lama in the forest and I needed beer for him. She felt great devotion and offered her best beer."

"Yogini," answered Virupa, "I should liberate this woman from the three realms of samsara. You must tell her to come."

The yogini fetched the old lady, who, filled with faith and devotion, went to meet the yogi with a jug of beer and some pork meat. Virupa immediately gave her the four complete empowerments for the yogic practices as well as the secret practices of the generation and completion stages.[63] Right when he bestowed the empowerments, the old lady became a wisdom dakini.

When her husband and children threw her out of the house, Sukhasiddhi was fifty-nine years old. When she reached Uddiyana and became a beer merchant, she was sixty. By the time she met Virupa and received the empowerments, she was sixty-one. You could say that she was physically old. But through the power of her realizations, her body was thoroughly purified and transformed into a rainbow body. She now appeared as a beautiful sixteen-year old girl, white in color, her hair flowing down her back. She was so beautiful that one never tired of looking at her. She dwelt in the sky and became known as Sukhasiddhi, dakini of magical illusions.

This dakini, now Virupa's secret consort, was the extraordinary victor Nairatmya.[64] Even now she roams the six times and looks with eyes of divine wisdom upon the innumerable beings of the three realms. To those with sacred outlook[65] she teaches the Dharma. To those who perform secret practices as well as those who pray devotedly to her, she grants blessings and bestows both extraordinary and common *siddhis*. Merely hearing her name, let alone her life story, brings great faith.

*The following is what the great disciples of the Shangpa lineage have said of Sukhasiddhi*

THE LORD KHYUNGPO Naljor, the one with the seed of faith deep within his being, said, "I went searching for her all over India. One day, in a sandalwood forest, she appeared in the sky at the height of about seven palm trees in the midst of rainbow brilliance and surrounded by countless dakinis. After making an offering of five hundred measures of gold, I begged for pure instructions. Sukhasiddhi granted me the four complete empowerments for the uncommon secret practices. She also gave me the Six Yogas' secret practices, and the threefold oral instructions. Then, she gave me all the mother tantra instructions, which make enlightenment possible in a matter of mere years or months.

"For me, Khyungpo Naljor, of my four root Lamas—Niguma, Rahula, Maitripa and Sukhasiddhi—Sukhasiddhi has been the kindest. In the beginning she was kind by making prophecies [concerning my practice and attainments]. In the middle she was kind by acting as my tantric partner and bestowing all empowerments without exception. And in the end, she was kind by giving me the oral instructions for putting these into practice. Her kindness is such that she has never left me: I can always see her, whether I am in India or Tibet. Disciples in the future should practice this secret *sadhana*."[66]

Lama Mokchokpa in Tibet had this to say about Sukhasiddhi: "While practicing in Dingma, Sukhasiddhi appeared and gave me many prophecies. Remembering these, I am inseparably united with her."

Lama Kyergangpa said, "When I went to the Jokhang temple in Lhasa,[67] Sukhasiddhi taught me the yogic practices of the completion stage and then gave me the four complete empowerments. Since then, I've experienced continuous union with her."

The great teacher Rigongpa Sangye Nyentön stated, "The instant I went into Kyergang Cave, I saw the face of Sukhasiddhi. Three times, she said to me, 'Rest in non-referential awareness.' Since then, I see her face always. I received instructions on the four complete empowerments. Then, she made prophecies such as, 'You will be a powerful yogi and will master the three doors of emancipation'[68] and so forth."

All you disciples who would also like to be enlightened in a year or a month, this is the teaching: remain in solitude and practice this secret *sadhana*!

MAY VIRTUE INCREASE!

# 4

# Life of Khyungpo Naljor

I, KHYUNGPO NALJOR, reverently bow down at the feet of Chakrasamvara, Mahamaya, Hevajra, Guhyasamaja, Vajravarahi, and Mahakala. I bow down at the feet of all the Lamas, yidam deities, dakinis, and Dharma protectors. This account of my life is written for the benefit of all future disciples of the lineage. Listen to it with sincere devotion.

I, the insignificant monk Khyungpo Naljor, was born in Nyemo Ramang in the Gangkarda area, to nobility, the Khyung family. My father was Khyung Gyaltak and my mother, Goza Trashi. As I entered my mother's womb, my parents and all the people of the area became prosperous and happy. When I was born, in the tiger year, the Indian adept Amogha made the following prophecy:

> This emanation will travel to India.
> He will gather the heart essence of all sages and adepts.
> He will lead numerous beings to maturation and liberation.
>
> He will train disciples by displaying various emanations
> And proclaim the essence of mahayana beyond extremes.
> Throughout the ten directions, he will resound the lion's roar
> Of the ultimate tantra—bliss-emptiness inseparable.

His body is in nature Chakrasamvara,
His speech Mahamaya
And his mind, glorious Hevajra.

His navel chakra—the emanation center—is Guhyasamaja
His secret chakra, the bliss-holding center,[69]
Yamantaka.

All these mandalas adorn his body,
But he also manifests them
For the sake of his disciples.

Moreover, by taking on the form of various yidam deities,
He trains
Even those students hard to discipline.

He will reach a hundred and fifty years of age,
And his teaching life will come to an end
Amidst several omens and miracles.

Then, Khyungpo Naljor will travel
To the Blissful Pure Land,
Revered by all the Buddhas.

There, he will attain enlightenment
And turn the wheel of mahayana Dharma.

All the faithful descendants of his lineage
Will definitely be reborn in the pure realm.

Amogha returned to India, flying through the sky like a bird.

When I was five, my parents revealed this prophecy to me. By the time I was ten, I excelled in reading, writing, arithmetic, and both Chinese and Indian astrology. At twelve, in accordance with the tradition on my father's side of the family, I studied the Bön teachings. Later on, I practiced Dzogchen, and finally, Mahamudra. Then, taking jewels and gold dust to present as offerings, I left for India and Nepal, unconcerned about comforts for myself and endured much hardship.

Over the course of seven journeys, I studied with a hundred and fifty sages and fifty great adepts. I adopted four as my glorious root Lamas. Of these, the two wisdom dakinis [Niguma and Sukhasiddhi] had direct transmissions from Vajradhara—the enlightened enjoyment-body, the sixth Buddha.[70] They took delight in me and granted me the ultimate oral instructions. I cut off all distractions and practiced single-pointedly. All doubts were allayed and I obtained both extraordinary and common *siddhis*. This has been a brief summary of my life. Reflect on it with great faith.

My family was inclined toward the Bön religion, which had been practiced by ancestors on my father's side. Because of this, when I turned thirteen, I studied under the Bön teacher Yungdrung Gyal. Soon, I had mastered all inner and outer Bön teachings. I blessed more than seven hundred practitioners with sacred water. I also wrote several treatise books and difficult commentaries. Through my work, I helped spread the Bön teachings to the provinces of Central, Eastern, and Western Tibet. In brief, I became a skilled Bön adept, and many great teachers and disciples came to see me. In particular, the scholar Gyal from Rong came to the area with three thousand offerings—horses, silver, and so on—and asked if I would give a teaching on the profound meaning that would resonate with all people, regardless of their abilities. I sang the Song of Seven Instructions for students of superior, average, and mediocre intellect. Throughout the song, Gyal and fifty students under my guidance penetrated the meaning of view and meditation. Many more had actual visions.

But I started to have some doubts as a Bön practitioner. I thought to myself, "There is no one contesting my abilities, no one debating me. No Indian adepts or translators ever translate these Bön texts. So, when I ask for a debate, people refuse, telling me I'm not a Dharma practitioner, I'm a Bön practitioner!"

I now recalled the prophecy made by Amogha that I would go to India. I gathered several measures of gold and went to my parents, explaining my plans for travel. But they would have none of it, saying, "Son, we are getting old. Please don't go to India until we die." Deferring to my parents, I decided to at least entrust my youngest Bön disciples to a scholar, telling them to listen, learn, and practice. I then went to the Dzogchen Lama Jungne Senge, to whom I presented a liberal gift of gold, silk, and horses and from whom I requested teachings on the three Dzogchen collections—the Space collection, the Mind collection, and the Pith Instruction collection—which I then preached. Soon, I became renowned for having taught the eighteen sections of the Mind collection [of the Dzogchen tradition] to more than three hundred monks. In this way, I gathered disciples from all directions.

I now reflected, "As for Dzogchen, the view is the highest and the activity is the most powerful. But I need a skillful practice to bring together view, meditation, and action." With these thoughts, I left all my disciples and went to Lhasa. I studied the entire cycle of Nirupa's doctrines and other teachings at Shomara in Töling. Nirupa gave me the Perfect Non-Abiding Mahamudra Root Tantra, the Inconceivable Explanation Tantra, the Secret Non-Duality, the Unsullied One, the Manjushri Uttering the Names, and all the *doha* songs of enlightenment. Furthermore, Nirupa gave me the Yamantaka Black Wrathful Tantra and *sadhana*, the Vajrabhairava Tantra and *sadhana*, and all of his own—Nirupa's—teachings. My devotions, my diligence, and my good practice all pleased Nirupa who said several times, "Khyungpo, now you are like me, we're equal in realizations. You know all that I know. You're outstanding."

This raised doubts in my mind. "Well," I thought, "I have been taught the entire doctrine and have spontaneous devotion for the Dharma. I have studied all the teachings. Yet, in truth, I don't have the slightest sign of extraordinary or even common *siddhis*! Now, my Lama Nirupa is the greatest adept in Tibet, so if he says that he and I are equal, it must mean that he hasn't attained any realizations either! I think I really need to go to India."

With my mind made up, I left for India. On the way, I stopped at my aunt and uncle's. They were childless and very wealthy. But when I asked to borrow some gold and turquoises, my uncle refused, saying, "You're no good! First you were a Bön practitioner, then a Dzogchen disciple, and now you are leaving both of these behind! Look at you: you have neither entourage nor money, and you want me to lend you gold and turquoises? Forget it!" My aunt heard this. Now she took me aside and said, "Khyungpo, your uncle doesn't want to lend you what you asked for. But here are turquoises and eleven measures of gold. Now, go and practice Dharma for the benefit of your unfortunate aunt and uncle." With these words, my aunt walked me out.

I then sold the fields I owned for gold, to which I added the gold collected from my students in the past. Then I exchanged my uncle's turquoises for gold. Now loaded with gold, I headed toward Nepal. On my way, I met the learned Vasumati and gave him three measures of gold as an offering for which I was given the teachings of Virupa, the secret general tantra empowerments, and among the Krya Tantras: the Excellent Courage Tantra, the Supreme Awareness Tantra, the Perfect Accomplishment Tantra, and the Meaningful Lasso Tantra, as well as fifty Krya tantric cycles with corresponding *sadhanas*.

After my encounter with the learned Vasumati, I walked on and met the learned Atulyavajra who told me, "You can stay here in Nepal with me for the next three years. I'll teach you the Dharma. Or, if you prefer, I'll lead you to Bodhgaya to see Lama Dorjedenpa who's been recognized as the second Buddha." I went to India and met Lama Dorjedenpa:

I, Khyungpo the yogi,
Cannot bear the pain of samsara.
Fear arises deep within me
As I see no end to this cyclic existence:
The suffering of birth,

The suffering of death,
The suffering of the lower realms.

I am not afraid of death:
Rebirth is what I fear.
Based on actions, we get a certain rebirth,
And in this samsara, we wander powerless.

All that you and I can do
Is to know death comes for us too.
Since I could die at any time,
To the Dharma I give this life of mine.

I have not stayed in Nepal.
India is now my goal.
With no concern for life or limb,
I've left for Bodhgaya
The place where a thousand Buddhas will appear.

To Bodhgaya the Vajra Seat,[71]
I come with pure attitude.
I see the face of Dorjedenpa
Prophesized as the second Buddha
By the victor Shakyamuni.

I give him five hundred measures of gold from Gulang—
It is just like seeing the Buddha himself.
My hair stands on end, I weep profusely.
Genuine faith arises within me.
In a fit of utter devotion,
I join my hands and ask him this:

Be a fountain of teachings, my monastic preceptor,
Please give me the *vinaya* code of discipline.[72]

Once I have aroused the great bodhichitta mind of compassion,
Please teach me the mahayana doctrine.

Once I have received the maturing tantric empowerments,
Please grant me the liberating teachings of the generation and
completion stages!

Such is my request to Dorjedenpa.

The glorious Lama Dorjedenpa smiled with pleasure. This is what he
said in reply:

In the borderland of the red-faced demons,[73]
People are filled with wrong views—their mindstreams are
flawed.
People in Tibet don't know how to practice Dharma correctly:
They all want the teachings but don't have what it takes to prac-
tice.
They want to act for the sake of others but have no maturity
themselves.
They're so jealous and petty.
Yet from that land of non-practitioners
Who think they know everything about the Dharma,
One such as you has appeared, Khyungpo,
One with great faith and determination, fearful of the death-
rebirth cycle.
For the sake of the Dharma, you have traveled all over, with no
concern for your own life
And now you are in India!
You have auspicious karma indeed!

In a past life in Tibet, land of snow,
You were a great *shravaka* of unlimited powers, known as Great
Magician.

At that time, there were many non-Buddhists, gods and *nagas*,
    harm-doers,
Elementals, and human beings, yet you subdued them all.
You had an entourage of *shravaka* practitioners.
You crossed rivers and mountains and flew like an eagle through
    the sky.

You are a great saint, capable of taking all sorts of emanations,
Neither I nor any other Indian scholar can adequately act as
    your preceptor.
In the snowy land of Tibet,
Go see Langri Tankpa, the Golden-Hued One,
An emanation of Amitabha.
And let him be your preceptor for full ordination.[74]

For now, here in Bodhgaya and other holy places,
I will teach you everything—*vinaya* code of discipline,
    Prajnaparamita and tantra—
Just as you requested.

When Lama Dorjedenpa gave me the new Dharma name of Tsultrim
Gön, his nose started to bleed, which showed I was so mighty that
even the name Khyungpo Naljor should not be changed. The Lama
said, "Yogi Khyungpo, this is the great result! Now, let's start: first,
you need to be taught the *vinaya* code of discipline, root sutras, and
*shastras*."

Next, I went to Shri Bhadrasajnana who was staying up on a moun-
tain. There, I was granted the generation of bodhichitta, the Five
Treatises of Maitreya, the Five Divisions of the Yogacharyabhumi of
Asanga, as well as the Seven Treatises on Valid Cognition. After that,
I went south to the Bhiksha charnel ground in Kaushambhi, where I
met Vairochana Rakshita[75] who was staying in a small hut teaching
the Dharma to thirteen sages. Vairochana gave me the Thirty-Two-
Deity Mandala of Guhyasamaja, the Thirteen-Deity Mandala of
Hevajra, the Thirteen-Deity Mandala of Chakrasamvara, the Five-

Deity Mandala of Mahamaya, the Thirteen-Deity Mandala of
Vajrabhairava and the empowerments of the Five Tantric Deities.[76]
During his stay in Shravasti, Vairochana Rakshita gave me the Buddha Skull Tantra, and the Equalizing Enlightenment Tantra, *sadhana,*
and empowerment.

Finally, I returned to my Lama Dorjedenpa in Bodhgaya and received empowerments in the single great mandala of the Five Tantric
Deities based on the Ocean of Gems Explanation Root Tantra. Here
is my song on this:

> Empowerments, transmissions, and *sadhanas*
> Of the Five Great Tantras
> Are particular in this:
> From the Liberation Tantra of Supreme Bliss
> Come teachings on cause, path and fruition.
> If great bliss is accomplished,
> Diamond-like bodhichitta[77] itself becomes the practice of great
>     bliss—
> Glorious Guhyasamaja,
> Essential Mahamaya,
> Quintessential Hevajra,
> Grand Chakrasamvara (magical emanation, partaker of plea-
>     sure),
> And wrathful Vajrabhairava.
>
> These five ultimate teachers
> Join together the tantras of both skillful means and wisdom.
> The maturing empowerment consists of outer, inner, and se-
>     cret levels.
>
> As for the two stages on the [tantric] path,
> They are the generation stage and the completion stage.
> Appearance is generation, emptiness is completion,
> And these two are inseparable, just like the reflection of the
>     moon in water.

The completion stage is itself subdivided in two—
With one's own body, or with another's body[78]—
Inseparable from the union of bliss and emptiness.


Fruition blooms as extraordinary and common *siddhis*.
The common *siddhis* are the eight great accomplishments.[79]
The extraordinary *siddhis* consist of the manifestation of the
    four bodies,
Naturally arising, spontaneous, naturally subjugating.


If you have pure karma, if you exert yourself one-pointedly
If you're able to maintain your *samaya*,[80]
You'll definitely reap the fruit.
Use the skillfulness of your own body—the path of means,
Or the karma mudra of another's body.[81]
This then, is the supreme precept: elevate to the tantric path
    the qualities of sensory objects.[82]
We have this instruction from the following preeminent lin-
    eage:


Nagarjuna the great teacher prophesied by the Buddha him-
    self;
Kapala who became a great adept through the Yoga of Clear
    Light;
Kukkuripa[83] manifesting dogs for his practice of karma mudra;
Luipa the Fish Eater, the famed adept;
Shridhara Harikela the blessed.


From them all comes the lineage gathered through:
Dombi Heruka;[84]
Kushulupa;
Mahavajra;
Yeshe Nge the Glorious;
Vairochana Rakshita
Sumati the yogi;

Tathagata Rakshita;
Amoghavajra;
Dorjedenpa my Lama;
Who passed it on to me.

Then Lama Dorjedenpa gave me the Yamantaka Black Wrath-
ful Tantra.
It is descended through:
Lalitavajra;
Padmapada;
Indrabhuti the Young;[85]
Shridhara Amoghavajra;
And Vairochana Rakshita.

I also received the Seven-Fold Vajrabhairava Realization, the practice
of Adamantine Light, the Three-Fold Realization, and the oral instructions of the six parameters [in tantric scriptures].

Dorjedenpa further taught me the Akshobhya Tantras and *sadhanas*,
the Tara Tantra instructions, the Manjushri Uttering the Names
Tantra, *sadhana*, and empowerment, the Mantrayana Admiration, the
gradual path of practice and the gradual path of debate; the Krya
Tantras and *sadhanas*, the Charya Tantras, the Yoga Tantras and the
Anutarayoga Tantras. A stay in a monastery in Kashmir and later in
Bodhgaya gave me opportunities to receive from my Lama the Vajra
Under Earth (Krya) Tantra, Taming the Elements (Krya) Tantra, the
Supreme Dancer, the Spirits-Tree Tantra and the tantras of the peace-
ful and wrathful deities. I presented my Lama, now staying on the
summit of Mount Malaya, with an offering of thirteen measures of
gold. At dawn on the tenth day of the month, we performed a tantric
feast. Here is my song:

A rain of flowers came down,
The sky filled with dakas and dakinis.
Music, light and rainbows stirred the space.

As offerings were dedicated to the deities,
Dorjedenpa spoke thus to me:

O noble son, go back to Tibet,
Liberate many beings in that land of snow.
In the future, your teachings will spread
Thanks to a yogi, holder of your lineage.
He will have all the teachings,
And will show the bodhisattva path without error, no matter
    what.
He'll attain the highest level of non-abiding.
His own disciples will gain realizations on the path.

Between the causal vehicle of signs, with its four philosophical
    tenets,[86]
And the resultant vehicle [of tantra],
There is a difference:
The first employs the causes (of enlightenment) as the path;
While the second focuses on the result (i.e. enlightenment) as
    the path.

In the stages of [first] direct perception and [then] inference,
Use the four axioms
To establish the three characteristics.[87]
That is the gradual path of debate [for the causal vehicle of
    signs].

The tantric and the mahayana paths
Are differentiated by
The thirty-seven limbs of enlightenment[88] and the five paths.

The gradual path of practice
Which leads to concise pointing-out
Is the second gradual path. [The first was the gradual path of
    debate.]

These two gradual paths actualize the path of seeing [the third
    path].
Untainted by wrong views,
It is the path of actualizing wisdom.
Those who integrate the actual meaning,
Free of extreme views [such as eternalism and nihilism],[89]
Engage in the great Middle Way.
And with repeated practice of calm abiding, insight,[90] and
    samadhi
On the paths
Comes the supreme path of mind.

You'll gain realizations equal to mine,
And I was prophesized by the Buddha.
You will attain enlightenment.
You will go to the Blissful Pure Land.

As for those quarrelsome beings who are hard to teach,
Do not be upset by them but keep meditating on bodhichitta.
You will have tens of thousands of students
In the vicinity of a self-arising Chakrasamvara mandala.

This is the prophecy I have received.

Now, three students of Maitripa were staying by the shore of the
Ganges, practicing Vajrabhairava. These three were known as the
three Vajra brothers because of their names—Kshetavajra,
Atulyavajra, and Ratnavajra.[91] I saw them practice Yamantaka so I
presented each of them with a measure of gold and requested the
Vajrabhairava empowerment, the Red and Black Yamantaka Tantra
and sadhana, and the Exorcism of Yamantaka. I practiced each for
seven months. Soon, I had a vision of Red Yamantaka, followed by
one of Black Yamantaka with entourage. From the dakini Kanakashri
of Devikoti, I received the Samphuta Exposition Tantra, the Comple-

tion Stage Thatness Compendium, the Ocean of Wisdom, the Wisdom Deliverance, and the Array of Vows Tantra.

After he gave me Vajrabhairava teachings, the Brahmin Ratnapala said, "You have an aunt who once gave you some turquoises. You should now give her a talisman to ensure male progeny." Following this prescription, I decided to head straight to her place. On the way, I saw an army of bandits approaching me in the great plains of Palmo Tang, so I performed an exorcism: I took blood from a goat and smeared it on one of the bandits, reciting incantations. The man instantly died. In no time, the other robbers were writhing in the throes of a painful death. I pointed my fingers menacingly at the remaining bandits. This incident gave me fame as a blood-exorcist yogi!

After this, I continued on and reached my aunt's place. At dawn, a white goddess appeared and said, "Three boys will soon be born thanks to the talisman you brought [for your aunt], Khyungpo. The eldest will be a lord-protector of the Shangpa lineage; the second son will spread the Shangpa teachings; and the youngest will truly understand the Shangpa teachings. When you, Khyungpo, become known as the Lama from Shang, these three will be great Dharma patrons and every year they will lay out liberal offerings of gold and silk and horses." The goddess wrote down names for the three boys on the reverse side of the talisman and disappeared. And indeed, over three years, three boys were born, who grew up to become important Dharma patrons for me.

I traded for gold all the offerings that my students had presented in the past. Furthermore, on my way, I discovered a gold mine in Gulang and picked up thousands more measures of gold. Finally, my disciples in a village of Mangyul repeatedly requested empowerments, and each request was buttressed by offerings of gold.

In Nepal, I received the Four Pith Instructions of the Anutarayoga Mother Tantra and the Chakrasamvara Root Tantra from the great Pamtingpa. And I left again for India. Back there, I returned to Lama Dorjedenpa and devotedly presented a hundred measures of gold. My Lama announced, "I received a prophecy that you should request the Dharma from Danashila, a disciple of Naropa." So I headed for

Nalanda and Danashila gave me the following: the Completion Stage Thatness Compendium, the Vajra Peak Tantra, Practicing the Lower Realms Tantra, the Guhyasamaja Tantra, and the teachings on Hevajra, as well as many oral instructions.

From the great yogini Sumatikirti, I received many Chakrasamvara teachings as well as the Six Teachings of Krsnapada and the Chakrasamvara Root Tantra. From the glorious Ramapala in the Kusha Grass East Garden I requested secret Mahamudra practices. From the noble Nateghandapa who was dwelling in the Jewel West Garden, I was given the Wisdom Accomplished, the Precious Wheel Empowerment, the Body Speech and Mind Tantras, the Wisdom Intention, and other Anutarayoga Tantras, topped with many transmissions and instructions.

From the Jetsunma Ratnadevi who was staying in the village of Kamkata, I was granted the Mahamudra essential practices. In a charnel ground in Jalandhara, a student of Kukkuripa known as the adept Suryagarbha gave me the Seven Teachings of Kukkuripa and several *sadhanas* on Vajrayogini.

Lama Maitripa, staying south in the Bamboo Grove, transmitted the Perfect Non-Abiding Mahamudra Root Tantra, the Five Tantric Deities, songs of enlightenment, Mahamudra Pure Wisdom, and a plethora of instructions on taking the three bodies of enlightenment as the path, as well as Manjushri Uttering the Names Tantra and the Hevajra Tantra and *sadhana*.

Maitripa settled for a time in the great Bhiksha charnel ground of Kaushambhi, and I offered him seven measures of gold, saying, "Lama, since there is little wealth in Tibet, please give me a practice for the quick accumulation of wealth."

Maitripa replied, "For this sort of thing, you need the wish-fulfilling protector [Mahakala]. He is also called the nullifier of the karmic board, the sandalwood tree lord-protector, the dark lord of compassion. He is the Six-Armed Wisdom Protector. He protects beings fearful of the bardo and has gods, demons, and humans under his control. He has mastered the three gatherings—beings, wealth, and good conditions. He destroys all enemies and is invulnerable. In little time, he brings about all extraordinary and common *siddhis*. By attaining the extraordinary *siddhis*, common *siddhis* appear naturally; and by attaining common *siddhis*, extraordinary *siddhis* also appear naturally."

Hearing this, I asked, "Who is this being to whom I should make my requests?"

And Maitripa told this story:

"In the past, Avalokiteshvara engendered the bodhichitta mind of great compassion in the presence of the Buddha Amitabha. He decided that he would not become a Buddha until the ocean of samsaric suffering was completely empty. So he made the following prayer, 'If my aspiration ever becomes corrupted, may my head be shattered into a thousand pieces!' That's how strong his vow was.

"Avalokiteshvara spent his time on Mount Potala, meditating during the six times of day and night[92] with compassion toward all sentient beings. He labored for the benefit of whomever was to be trained. Then, after he had liberated countless sentient beings by his thoughts and deeds over many eons, he looked once again at samsara from Mount Potala. He saw that the world of confused beings had neither increased nor diminished. If anything, samsara seemed to have degenerated; afflictive emotions had become more pronounced. Seeing this, Avalokiteshvara felt daunted and thought, 'I have been unable to liberate even a single sentient being!' But with that thought, he abandoned his bodhisattva aspiration, and his head burst into a thousand pieces.

"Buddha Amitabha appeared and said, 'O noble son, you have deviated from your vow, that is not good. In order to acknowledge your mistake, you must renew your vow, this time even more strongly.' After he had finished speaking, Amitabha took the thousand pieces of Avalokiteshvara's head and fashioned eleven faces, which he blessed.

"Avalokiteshvara thought, 'I can't possible renew my vow in stronger terms than before.' So, for the next seven days, he remained in a daze, unconscious. When he awoke, he saw that because of obstacles, the lifespan of sentient beings was much shorter and full of hindrances. Beings were powerless and completely at the mercy of causes

and conditions. They were poor, miserable, and they had few opportunities to practice Dharma. Not keeping their *samaya*, they committed much evil.

"Seeing that even those practicing Dharma couldn't overcome their
fear of the bardo, Avalokiteshvara decided, 'May I be the deity that
beings can see through prayer, even if they don't practice much. May
I be the one who subdues at once all demonic obstructions and enemies. May I perfect the three gatherings—beings, wealth, and good
conditions. May I be the powerful lord through whom beings can
rapidly attain extraordinary and common *siddhis*.' And the essence
of this vow became the blue-black syllable HUNG in the heart center
of Avalokiteshvara, from which sprung the Six-Armed Wisdom Protector [Mahakala]. Like a wish-fulfilling gem, the protector was to
answer the needs of beings according to their individual wishes. And
the earth shook in six ways in respect for Avalokiteshvara's aspiration.[93]

"Seeing this, Amitabha Buddha and his entourage appeared with
countless Buddhas. They all joyfully exclaimed to Avalokiteshvara,
'O noble son! You are acting to benefit beings according to their individual wishes. We rejoice!' From the heart centers of all the Buddhas
came the blessings of Yamantaka's enlightened activity. Then, the
great esoteric dakinis bestowed their blessings and the dakas gave the
wisdom protector the powers of pacifying and enriching.

"As a result of all these blessings, harm-doers, demons, devils, and
even Mara perform actions associated with the empowerment of the
Buddhas' enlightened activities. Consequently, whoever practices,
gives generously, or even just thinks about Mahakala will be bestowed
all realizations. Even those who do not practice will receive blessings
and see the face of the deity."

Lama Maitripa looked at me and continued:

"Now for Shavaripa. In an earlier life, he was a great Brahmin. At
the time, he was known for his musical skill and delighted the Buddha with his singing in the area of Dhanyakata,[94] which counted thirty-
three cities. In his life as Shavaripa, he practiced in a thatched hut in
the charnel ground Shady Cool Grove. Shavaripa first heard the loud

sound of a *damaru* drum[95] and bells. Then he saw the renowned wisdom protector Mahakala who told him, 'O noble son, you are now the holder of my practice.' So Shavaripa set the practice in writing. Jetsunma Vajrayogini, Avalokiteshvara, and Tara appeared and gave him their own *sadhanas* as well.

"Well, so much for that story. Now, when I received the Mahamudra Tantras and pith instructions on Mount Glory to the South, I had a vision of the protector for twenty-one days. And as for you, Khyungpo Naljor, you must offer tormas[96] of black barley and bundles of incense. Do not throw rocks at black dogs. If you never waver in your faith and devotion, you will see Mahakala as inseparable from your Lama.

"Practice as I say, in the mountains and in other solitary places. With such practice, a good disciple will actually see the face of the deity and receive all *siddhis* in as little as thirteen days." Thus he prophesied. And Maitripa repeated this exhortation three times.

Then, with five hundred measures of gold on me, I traveled throughout the four corners of India, meeting Lamas and asking who had actually seen the Buddha. All sages and adepts said the same thing: Naropa's sister Niguma, who dwelt in the three pure states, was able to receive the Dharma directly from Vajradhara. They all also said that no matter where you are, with sacred outlook you will see Niguma's face. But if your outlook is impure, she won't be found, no matter how hard you look. Niguma truly dwelt in a pure state and possessed the rainbow body. Still, I was told, she could be frequently seen in the great charnel ground of Sosa Ling celebrating tantric feasts with her entourage.

Just hearing the name of the dakini made me weep. My hair stood on end. I felt overwhelmed with devotion and immediately left for the charnel ground of Sosa Ling, repeating the mantra *Namo Buddha* on the way. Suddenly, the dakini appeared in the sky in front of me, at the height of about seven palm trees, her body dark brown in color. She was wearing bone ornaments. In her hands, she held a skull-cup and hooked knife. She was dancing and displaying one and many forms. As soon as I saw her, I thought, "This is the dakini Niguma." I

prostrated and made several circumambulations. Then I knelt down
and asked for the pure oral instructions. But Niguma shouted, "Hey
you, watch out! I am the cannibal flesh-eating dakini. HA! Flee now!
As soon as my retinue comes, we will devour you!" In response, I
simply made more prostrations and circumambulations and once
again knelt down, requesting the secret oral instructions. Niguma
now said, "So you really want the mahayana oral instructions? Well,
you'll need some gold for that. Have you got any?" At this, I presented
my five hundred measures of gold. But the dakini grabbed the gold
and hurled it in the air, scattering it all over the forest. Seeing this, I
thought, "Oh, she really must be a cannibal flesh-eating dakini. She
doesn't even care for my gold!" The dakini's eyes darted about left
and right, and her immeasurable retinue of dakas and dakinis appeared
from the sky. Some in a flash created three-tiered heavenly mansions,
some built mandalas of colored sand, and others gathered the implements for a tantric feast.

On the evening of the full moon, the dakini Niguma bestowed upon
me the empowerments of Dream Yoga and Illusory Body Yoga. Next,
she said, "Hey, little monk from Tibet, come on up here!" By means
of the dakini's magical ability, I rose in the sky to a height of about
fifteen thousand feet. I found myself on top of a golden mountain.
Above my head, the dakini's retinue was performing the mystical
dance of the tantric feast, and from the four sides of the mountain
flowed four rivers of gold. I looked down at the streams of gold and
asked, "Does such a golden mountain really exist in India, or did the
dakini make it appear?"

The dakini sang:

> Whirling in the ocean of samsara
> Are the myriad thoughts of love and hate.
> Once you know they have no nature,
> Then everywhere is the land of gold, my child.
>
> If on all things, like an illusion,
> One meditates, like an illusion,

True Buddhahood, like an illusion,
Will come to pass, due to devotion.


"Now, a dream will come to you through my blessings," she said.

Indeed, I had the following lucid dream: I went to the realm of
gods and demi-gods. I was being eaten alive by large demi-gods when
the dakini appeared in the sky saying, "O son, do not wake up." At
that very instant, I received the instructions on the Six Yogas. After I
woke up, the dakini appeared and said, "No one else in India has ever
received the Six Yogas in one session."

She gave me the following teachings: three complete transmissions
of the Six Yogas, the Vajra Verses on the Three Ways of Integrating
the Path, the Stages of the Illusory Path, *sadhanas* and empowerments
of the Five Tantric Deities, the Nine-Deity Emanated Mandala of
Hevajra, the Thirteen-Deity Mandala of the Weaponed One, the
Hevajra Tantra and songs, the Samphuta Exposition Tantra and
*sadhana*, the Gradual, Complete, and Condensed Generation Stages
for the Weaponed One, the Oral Instructions on the Completion Stage
Thatness Compendium, empowerments, tantras and *sadhanas* for the
Sixty-two-Deity mandala of Chakrasamvara, the Thirteen-Deity
mandala of Chakrasamvara and the Five-Deity Mandala of
Chakrasamvara, pith instructions on the Kalachakra and the Weap-
oned-One, teachings on the Red and White Forms of the Dakini,
methods for removing veils, the Five Tantric Deities, the
Chakrasamvara Completion Stage in Five Steps, all the seed essence
completion stages, and all the points of the Vajrayogini transmission.

Next she said, "Except for Jetsun Lavapa and me, no one in India
knows the instructions and empowerments of these Six Yogas. Do
not allow these special teachings to spread. Maintain a one-to-one
guru-to-disciple transmission for the next seven generations. Only
then should these teachings be more widely revealed."

After this prophecy, I made an offering of a hundred measures of
gold to Maitripa and requested the Five-Deity Mandala of
Chakrasamvara teachings on the Five Paths in a Single Session, the

Red and White Forms of the Dakini, and the Six Practices of the Kalachakra.

Thus, carrying five hundred measures of gold with me, I went to northern India. Once there, I asked around, "What Lama has actually met the Buddha?" Thirteen adepts, who included the sage Lalitavajra, Aryadeva and the dakini Sumati, replied, "We can give you instructions and empowerments, and then we will make you a prophecy." Hearing this, I offered my five hundred measures of gold and was granted many instructions and empowerments. Then the adepts said, "We thirteen realized beings have a Lama, the wisdom dakini Sukhasiddhi. She has passed down the inner instructions of Nairatmya to Aryadeva who attained the eighth level of a bodhisattva within seven months. As for our prophecy: you, Khyungpo, will be blessed and taught by Sukhasiddhi, the dakini who receives teachings directly from Vajradhara and Nairatmya."

Aryadeva then gave me the inner instructions. I asked, "Where is the dakini staying? What is her lineage?" Aryadeva wrote down where she was staying at that time. Then he said:

"O noble son, listen carefully to what I have to say, and bear it all in mind. In Kashmir lived an old woman and her family. At that time, there was a great famine, and her family had nothing left to eat except for a pot of rice with less than a week's supply in it. So one day, her children said, 'Old woman, you look after this pot of rice, keep it for "Uncle Endless Season!"[97] We're going to look for food.' Her sons and daughters headed out to look for food. Meanwhile, a monk came to her door and said, 'Old woman, I am Uncle Endless Season! Please give me something from your pantry!' The woman gave the monk rice from the pot, and she ate a little of it herself.

"Later, her husband and her sons came home empty-handed. No sooner had they returned than they said, 'Hey, old woman. Open up this pot of rice and give us something to eat!' But the mother replied, 'While you were gone, a monk came to the door. The sight of his robes and alms-bowl and staff filled me with devotion. I gave him the rice.'

"This angered the children. 'The old hag has brought us to nothing,' they spat out. 'This won't do! The little we had, she gave away. Oh no, this won't do! Let's throw her out.' So her family chased her out of the house.

"The old lady wandered around and asked for advice about where to go. Everybody told her that the western land of Uddiyana was peopled by dakas and dakinis. There, finding nourishment came easy. As soon as she heard this, the old lady decided she should go to Uddiyana. Since she had no more food, she begged for some rice. Soon, she had more than twenty pounds. Carrying it all, she continued on her way. Before long, she reached the town of Bhita, where she decided to make liquor out of the rice she had gotten from begging.

"At that time, the Jetsun Virupa was staying in the forest near Uddiyana, practicing tantric union with his consort. His consort-yogini often went to town to buy beer and meat for tantric rituals. Soon she began to purchase her beer from the old woman. One day the old lady asked her, 'Yogini, who is the beer for?'

"The yogini answered, 'I buy it for a great Lama who is staying in the nearby forest.'

"'Look,' the old woman said, 'because I haven't accumulated virtue, I am poor and destitute. I got old and my husband and children threw me out of my home. I don't care for possessions, so please take this beer. I don't want any money for it.'

"From then on, the old woman carefully picked out her finest beer of the day and offered it to the yogini. One time, the Lama was enjoying the liquor his consort had brought him, and asked her, 'Yogini, how is it that this beer costs us nothing?' The yogini replied, 'There's an unusual lady in town who is very devoted to the Dharma. Since I explained to her that I needed the beer for a great Lama, she has refused payment and she insists on giving us her finest beer.'

"When he heard this, the Lama said, 'Yogini, I must guide this old lady out of the three realms of samsaric suffering. Bring her here!' The yogini went back to town and gave the old woman the Lama's message. The old lady was delighted. She took two jugs of her best beer and some pork meat to present as gifts to Lama Virupa. That night, Virupa granted her the four complete empowerments of Vajrayogini's secret practices and at that very instant she became a wisdom dakini.

"The old woman was fifty-nine when her own family evicted her. She was a beer merchant at the age of sixty and met Virupa at sixty-one. So she was in her early sixties when she received the empowerments, and yet she suddenly looked like a beautiful girl of sixteen. She appeared in the sky like a magical illusion, her body white in color. From then on, she became known as Sukhasiddhi, the wisdom dakini inseparable from Nairatmya, and able to receive the Dharma directly from Vajradhara.

"Well, that is the story of this dakini Sukhasiddhi. People with sacred outlook will see the dakini everywhere. But if they do not perceive appearances as pure, no matter where they look they will never find her. Sukhasiddhi often stays in a place known as Sandalwood Medicine Park. On the tenth day of each phase of the moon, she's there, teaching the Dharma to an assembly of dakinis. She displays the Dharma through words. Go there and pray to her. After you receive the four complete empowerments and oral instructions, all the teachings will be revealed to you. This is my prophecy." Aryadeva had finished speaking.

I loaded my five hundred measures of gold and walked toward Sandalwood Medicine Park, repeating the mantra Namo Buddha. In the sky above the park, I saw the dakini surrounded by her retinue, her body white in color and her hair flowing down her back. Her two hands were placed in the mudra of birthlessness and rainbow luster surrounded her. At this sight, I felt goose bumps all over my body and my eyes filled with tears. Overwhelmed with the same joy that arises on the first level, I experienced undefiled bliss. I made an offering of flowers, water lilies, lotuses, moon-lilies, and other presents. I prostrated and made a hundred thousand circumambulations. I knelt down and asked for the pith instructions. The dakini sang:

Virupa, Nairatmya
From them and from Vajradhara

I received the manifest path of tantra:
The four complete empowerments that lead to maturation,
The generation and completion [stage] teachings that lead to
   liberation.
You have offered gold, rare gems,
You prostrate yourself fully, my lowly foot on your head—
What you're receiving today is the very best.
Now I will liberate you.

Three times she said, "O, noble son, you're wonderful. O, noble son, you're wonderful. O, noble son, you're wonderful." I offered five hundred measures of gold and the dakini said, "I will directly bless all your female and male disciples, all holders of the lineage. They will go to the Pure Land of the Dakini."

She granted me the four complete empowerments in the emanated mandala, introduced me to practices of the navel [emanation center] and secret chakras, and transmitted practices for the generation and completion stages—all pith instructions without exception. The first great kindness of the wisdom dakini Sukhasiddhi was to give me the four complete empowerments in the emanated mandala. Her next great kindness was to appear as a goddess and be my tantric partner. The final great kindness of the dakini was to give me all secret pith instructions.

She prophesied that I would attain the fourteenth level of a bodhisattva[98] and inhabit the Blissful Pure Land. She further said that she would always hold all my students, my students' disciples, and holders of the lineage in great compassion and establish them in the Pure Land of Bliss-Emptiness. Consequently, my lineage holders will be distinctly more advanced and will gather superior merit and wisdom.

Following this special encounter, I made liberal gifts of gold to the dakinis Sumatimaha, Gangadhara, and Samantabhadri. Pleased with my faith, they gave me instructions on the mother tantras completion stage, the four ways of mastering the seed essence—descending, retaining, reversing, and spreading—as well as many guiding instructions on wisdom.

Next, I went to Bamboo Grove. From the sage Sukhavajra I received the Yamantaka Black Wrathful Tantra, the Seven-Fold Vajrabhairava Realization, the Three-Fold Vajrabhairava Realization, the All-Victorious Wrathful Tantra, the Lhamo Namzhal, the Biped Raven Teachings, methods for reading skulls, and the Akshobhya Tantras and *sadhanas*.

I also went to the sage Lalitavajra and offered a hundred measures of gold. There, I was granted the eighteen *sadhanas* of the goddess Remate and the protector Mahakala, exorcisms for both Buddhists and non-Buddhists, treatises on making medicine, the Nyitrö Tantra, teachings on protection from lightning and hail, seven medicinal sets, and many oral instructions.

After that I went to Maitripa who transmitted empowerments in the emanated mandala of Vajravidhu: he gave me the tantra and the *sadhana* for the Eleven, the Five, and the Solitary Deity. During the empowerment, his vase, vajra,[99] and bell stayed suspended in space. Maitripa also gave me cups made from the skull of a Brahmin and said, "You, Khyungpo, will one day be able to grant empowerment in the emanated mandala of Vajravidhu."

This concluded my search for oral and written instructions. I returned to Tibet and felt I ought to give gold for the teachings I had received, so I began to retrace my steps to Bodhgaya. There, I performed a tantric feast. At dawn, Lama Maitripa, dakini Sukhasiddhi, and noble Tara approached and foretold that I would guide disciples in the very place where Chakrasamvara and Kasarpani appeared.

Shortly thereafter, I reached Nepal where monks, local kings, and others asked for empowerments and transmissions. Soon I reached the upper part of the Nepal-Tibet canyon, at the invitation of old students. Much merit was created.

Continuing on my way, I discovered thirteen gold mines, including Dzambu and Gulang. In each place, I gave bodhisattva vows and granted empowerments. And every time, there was another thousand measures of gold on the ground. After that, I accepted invitations to southern Latö, Tsongdü, and Nyemo in Western Tibet. My hosts presented me with golden books, horses, turquoises, silk, satin and other beautiful things. I thought, "Well, now that I have a lot of wealth for offerings, I can go back to India."

I hoisted five hundred thousand measures of gold, hired five hundred servants, and returned to Bodhgaya. Once there, I performed an offering at the request of the local king. For ten days, I made a daily offering of eighty measures of gold in Bodhgaya. A rain of flowers fell from the sky, sounds and lights stirred the air, and dakinis danced. Miracles took place—offerings by gods and men alike. The king, many sages, my Lama Dorjedenpa, and householders all saw me and expressed their delight, "What a great Tibetan yogi!"

I presented vast offerings of gold for Lama Dorjedenpa, the wisdom dakinis Niguma and Sukhasiddhi, the hundred and fifty Lamas, the three Vajra brothers, and others. After I performed a tantric feast, the Lamas gave me oral instructions and made several prophecies. Since Maitripa wasn't there, I laid out another large gift of gold for the wisdom dakini Gangadhara and was granted many more teachings.

One more liberal offering in Bodhgaya, and I left for another trip to Tibet. There, I went to the [Red] Temple in Töling[100] accompanied by the scholar-translators Dharma Lodrö and Gayadhara.[101] I told them, "My books are worn out and moldy. I will have to go back to India yet again!" As it happened, the sage Atisha[102] was there at that time, and when he heard me, he replied, "I have the same Indian texts here and I've asked Rinchen Zangpo[103] to translate them." So I was able to restore my texts by comparing them with the manuscripts in Atisha's possession. Rinchen Zangpo and Dharma Lodrö translated them from Sanskrit into Tibetan. The sage Atisha also gave me bodhichitta generation, Guhyasamaja empowerments, the teachings on Guhyasamaja, Yamantaka, and Vajrabhairava, Maitreya's Ornament of Clear Realization, Ornament of Sutras, and Sublime Continuum, as well as numerous other teachings.

As I was returning to my homeland, I met up with two other great practitioners, Jotsun Khyung of Gomo and Ngultsun Trangpo, who were also on their way back after receiving spiritual teachings. They suggested, "Let's go to Lhasa." We all went, carrying a golden umbrella. On the evening of the thirteenth day, they offered me the golden umbrella. They presented ritual alms and lit butter lamps, and said many prayers. Then, as a jest they said, "Let's see what kind of dreams we'll have now!"

The next morning, we all discussed our dreams. I said, "In my dream, the Shakyamuni statue in Lhasa spoke these words to me: 'In a past life, you were a great *shravaka*. Now, you come from the north, and your previous karma has awakened. You endured hardships, went to India, and realized reality itself.[104] You brought many disciples to maturation in the snowy land of Tibet. Both you and they will go to the Blissful Pure Land.'"

In turn, the other two were asked about their dreams. Jotsun Khyungpo explained, "In my dream, a drum was resounding from the top of a hill. Then, a heap of bows and arrows fell at my feet." This turned out to be true.[105] Next, Ngultsun said, "Well, as for me, I was sitting on top of a pile of barley, and many people kept on bringing me more!" Ngultsun later became very wealthy!

At this point, I took full monastic ordination from Langri Tankpa and went to Penyul, but I found myself running out of food. I remembered Lama Maitripa saying that throughout my practice, the protectors would always provide for food. Yet no protectors seemed to help and I was out of supplies for my torma offerings. One night, I went to the entrance of my cave and shouted, "Kshetrapala! Dzinamitra! Takiradza! Drakshema! I am running out of food, I can't continue doing torma offerings!" The following day, people came up the mountain with gifts of silver, horses, food, tea, and the finest nourishment, such as meat, butter, and milk. For the next few weeks, I gave bodhisattva vows and performed empowerments. Soon, I had gathered two thousand disciples—so many in fact, that they couldn't all fit in the cave! So the monastery of Cheka was erected in the Jokpo Valley of Penyul.

During that period, I arranged to be in retreat and practice during the waning moon. During the waxing moon, I elucidated the texts and gave oral instructions. At one time when I was meditating in Lenpa Chilbu, a vast assembly of dakinis gathered and said, "You have disciples in your monastery in Shang. Go and take care of them."

One morning, it started to snow heavily. I had just settled myself when an Indian yogi approached and said, "I was told I should meet you."

I waved him off, "I'm in retreat now, and receive no visitors."

"But I have come a long way from India to see you," the Indian yogi protested, "and I am ill." So I examined the Indian yogi and explained, "You have a circulation problem." I proceeded to bleed the yogi, saying that this would cure him. But he replied, "Bleeding is no good for a yogi!" So saying, he levitated in the sky, his body in the vajra posture and blood poured from his body. Returning to the ground the yogi now declared, "Ouch! Now it looks like I have a problem with the energy flow in my body." So I began to massage him with a red ointment, saying that this was the cure he needed. Again, the Indian yogi replied, "That massage is no good for a yogi!" Then, levitating in space as before, semen shot out from the pores of his body with a brisk sound and was then withdrawn back in.

Many dancing dakinis appeared in the sky, and at that moment, I thought, "This yogi is really an adept." I performed prostrations and circumambulations and offered him a gold mandala. The Indian yogi requested me to hold all beings in my compassion, adding, "Gunakara, Ratnakara, Abhiyukta, and Jnakara all told me that it would be of great benefit if I went to Tibet. I went and now I have met you. I have come from India this very morning and I have only just now crossed this Tibetan ravine."

I asked, "Where does your Lama reside? What is your lineage and what is your name?"

The man replied, "To the south is the city of Bhirajo. That area is sacred to Vajrayogini. I am of royal caste: my father is Unaladhava and my mother is known as Puchanimi."

This yogi, Rahula, stayed in my Cheka monastery for eleven months and gave me many helpful explanations on difficult commentaries. He granted me the empowerments of the Five Tantric Deities, followed by their respective four complete empowerments, as well as *samadhi* empowerments, and *sadhanas* for each of the deities. He further transmitted the Hevajra Tantra, the Samphuta Exposition Tantra, the Chakrasamvara Root Tantra, the Rali *sadhana*, the Hevajra *sadhana*, the Saroruhavajra, the Four-Fold Thatness, the Four Seals of Mahamudra, the Completion Stage in Five Steps, Luipa's Chakrasamvara, the Solitary Daka, the Three Transmissions of Vajrayogini, Mahamaya, the Seven Teachings of Kukkuripa, the Great School of Commentary on Thatness, Shantipa's Five-Fold Thatness, the Seven-Fold Vajrabhairava Realization, the Yamantaka Black Wrathful Tantra, and so forth.

As for the completion stage, I got the Completion Stage of the Five Chakras, the Big-Vase Breathing Technique, the Liberation of Constrictions in the Chakras, the Wisdom Skylight Transference of Consciousness Practice, the Three-Fold Completion Stage Thatness, the Chakrasamvara Completion Stage in Four and Five Steps, the Guhyasamaja Five Paths in a Single Session, Mind-Energy Inseparable, songs of Mahamudra, and pointing-out instructions such as Mahamudra Pure Wisdom. Rahula further taught me the Two Truths of the Madhyamika Middle Way, Practicing the Lower Realms Tantra, the Vajrapani Tantra for Subduing the Elementals, the Three Dzalima *sadhanas*, the Akshobhya Tantra, the Vajravidhu, the Four Blessings Deities,[106] *sadhanas* for the four retinues of Six-Armed Mahakala, the Nyitrö tantra, the One-Hundred-Eight Hail Balls, as well as advice on guarding the teachings.

One day, he said, "You and I, master and disciple, must build a stupa[107] and consecrate it." Rahula then emanated many forms and, assisted by dakinis, consecrated the stupa. He held up his vajra and bell and they remained hovering in space. Rahula now said, "I will be going to Nepal, but until I do, you be the teacher and I, the student!"

So in Rong, I gave the empowerments of the Five Tantric Deities. To fifty disciples in Dam, I gave empowerments in the emanated mandala. Then, in Shang, Jang, and Tanak, and in the northern and southern districts of Latö, as well as in Mangyul, I granted the empowerments of Guhyasamaja and Vajrabhairava and gave

empowerments to thirteen disciples in the emanated mandala of
Vajravidhu.

On the fifteenth day of the month, I performed a hundred tantric
feasts. That day, Rahula said, "There's just no basic stability in this
land of Tibet. How can any illusions be performed here? I've accomplished immortality [as everlasting] as the sun and moon [and can
perform miracles. Khyungpo,] come ride my magical horse, let's go
to India. I've still got a bit of advice to pass on."

My thought? "Well," I said to myself, "what more can there possibly be? No matter what teachings I bring back from India, they'll be
of no use to thick-headed Tibetans!"

[But reading my thought], Rahula declared, "I must go to Bodhgaya
tonight for a tantric feast. You and your poor attitude, don't bother
coming to India with me." With these words, Rahula took off in the
sky like a bird. I prayed and cried to Rahula, and he returned, and
sang these six verses of nectar:

> The root of suffering
> Is clinging to ego.
> Therefore, without bias, attachment or aversion,
> Rest in the meaning of equanimity.
>
> This present life is impermanent
> And the next life is uncertain.
> Therefore meditate in accordance with karma and result,
> And above all, keep *samaya*.
>
> Until you achieve stability,
> You are harmed by the distractions of the world.
> Therefore, like a wounded antelope,
> Stay alone, and practice.
>
> Lest anger and jealousy increase,
> Whatever talents you may have,
> Like a candle inside a flask:
> Always keep them secret.

The abiding nature is transcendent union
Therefore meditate on whatever arises as illusion.
Appearances have no inherent existence.
So think this way of your body.

Fulfilling all your needs for this life
And guiding you on the path in future lives
Is the Lama, like a Buddha.
Think of him always.

Rahula then left for India.

In Nyemo, after I manifested an army to repel enemies, all the local people became deeply devoted and entered the path of Dharma. In my Cheka monastery, I gave the teachings of Rahula to a great many students. I stayed there three years expounding on the Dharma, during which time many dakinis appeared, including Singhamukha.

Afterwards, I was invited to Shang, where I also had a monastery. I went there with three thousand servants. I spent three years in the Shang region, erected a total of a hundred and eight monasteries and appointed abbots for each of them, instructing them, "Concentrate mostly on practicing my teachings and especially on meditation."

I gathered three thousand disciples from Central, Eastern, and Western Tibet, but then I fell ill. For eleven days, thirteen principal teachers and disciples presented great torma offerings to the protector. When the torma offerings were being carried, the protector could actually be seen, his body white in color. I soon recovered. From then on, the entourage of the protector as well as Hayagriva and his eight deities behaved like my servants and performed enlightened activity on my behalf.

At dawn on the eighth day of the last month of summer, I saw nine Hevajra emanation deities and thirteen Hevajra deities carrying weapons. They gave me the Four-Fold Thatness teachings. Then, on the fifteenth day of the same month, Manjushri appeared. He opened a small treasure chest, and taught me the Treasure Box of Visualization. That pith experience was deeper than the teachings I had previously received in India. As a result, all diseases and obstructions were cleared. On the third day of fall, I saw thirteen Tara and Vajravidhu deities surrounded by ten Herukas. When I was granting the empowerments, my vase, vajra, and bell hovered in space.

Three times, the man Treo Jangchub Gyal presented offerings, and three times he asked me to bestow empowerments. However, I forgot all about the request and left for Kyosang. Treo Jangchub caught up with me and supplicated yet again, "Please give me an empowerment today—any empowerment."

"I'll do just that!" I replied. There and then in the meadows, I granted him empowerments in the emanated mandala. Right away, the illness and demons plaguing Treo Jangchub cleared off.

Another time, I had assembled a thousand monks to practice, but all were distracted by thoughts of food. They were slacking in both their study and their meditation. I became dejected at the poor practice of my Tibetan students and thought of going back to India. But Tara appeared and advised, "Do not deviate to the hinayana: put on the armor of a bodhisattva." I settled inside a small vase and for the next seven days I savored the food of *samadhi* meditation. During that time, a young monk underwent a profound experience of great compassion just by sitting on my bed.

As the spring flowers blossomed, I spent time with my monks in Pangkar. I manifested before each monk a beautiful goddess of the Heaven of Thirty-Three. Each goddess was so beautiful one couldn't stop staring at them. Every one of them was smiling, graceful, and lovely. This sight aroused great pleasure in the monks. The next day, they were summoned to another gathering and all went eagerly. But this time, I emanated the wrathful god Yama, Lord of Death, eating human flesh. The Lord of Death looked terrible, with red eyes, mouth gaping, fangs bared, laughing loudly and shouting, "DEATH AND DESTRUCTION!" In his hands, he held sharp weapons. His retinue surrounded him, reciting mantras. The monks were struck with fear. Many fainted. When they regained consciousness, they all thought, "This must be wrathful Yama pointing out our karma . . . and we

must be in the bardo!" They asked me whether I had emanated the
goddesses and Yama. In response, I sang this song:

> All objects of pleasure and horror
> Arise from one's own mind.
> To the yogi, this appearance
> Of the flesh-eating form of Yama, Lord of Death, brandishing
>     weapons,
> Taking our life even now
> Is seen as illusion.
> And that is liberation.

> Beautiful goddesses adorned with gems,
> Sweet sounds and music,
> The entourage of sensory delights:
> Understand that they are self-arising illusion,
> And they no longer have any power to bind you.

I taught about the bardo and many other topics. All became diligent
in their practice and meditation.

One day, the scholar Gyal from Rong approached me when I was
meditating in a cave, and donated a hundred horses, a bag of silver,
and rolls of satin. Then he asked, "Khyungpo, you've gone three times
to India. You've sought a hundred and fifty Lamas, and you have four
root Lamas. You have become an accomplished master, and you understand that appearances have no inherent existence. Won't you show
me some of your miraculous powers? Can you fly back and forth
through this rock? Can you sit in space in the vajra posture?" So I
flew through the mountain, levitated in space in the vajra posture,
and displayed one and many emanations, witnessed by the people in
the area. Seeing this, Gyal and the monks were overcome with faith.
"What meditation and oral instructions bring about these abilities?"
they asked.

I sang this song in response:

If on all things, like an illusion,
One meditates, like an illusion,
True Buddhahood, like an illusion,
Will come to pass.

Phenomena appear and yet have no true nature.
Immature beings take them to be real
And are confused.
Appearances do not truly exist!
E MA HO!

Then I gave many more teachings. Könchok Gyal from Rong felt such great faith that within eleven months, he had a vision of his yidam and realized that appearances have no inherent existence.

One morning in early spring, many dakinis appeared to me and spoke these words: "On the day of the waxing moon, and again on the day of the waning moon, be sure to perform a hundred and eight tantric feasts. Your body, speech, mind, navel and secret chakras will become inseparable from the Five Tantric Deities. All will perceive this. The deities will be inseparable from yourself."

On the seventh day of the last month of spring, after the hottest time of day, I was falling asleep when the wisdom dakini Samantabhadri appeared and said, "You will gather a hundred and eighty thousand beings. You will fulfill the requirement for five heart son-or-daughter-disciples and one later one. Your life itself will reach its fulfillment at a hundred and fifty years of age. You will then attain the ultimate Blissful Pure Land." These words woke me up. I considered gathering people to give them these details. I would also explain that I knew the thought and latent potential of every sentient being. But the dakini Sukhasiddhi appeared and said:

Impure beings hold wrong views
And cannot be tamed even by the Buddha.

They cling to harmful influences even in the presence of omni-
    scient ones,
So conceal your qualities, O yogi.


This she repeated three times. Therefore, in the tradition of this
[Shangpa] lineage, I kept my qualities concealed until I achieved complete mastery.

Many families from Eastern Tibet had assembled; when it came
time to give me offerings, fights broke out. At that very moment, I
emanated a hundred and eight thrones and appeared on each one. As
a result, every person was able to present offerings in front of one of
the hundred and eight thrones.

During that same time, I perceived that my young room attendant,
Rinchen Dorje, was holding wrong views and seeing me, the Lama,
as ordinary. I told Rinchen to recite the hundred-syllable mantra, to
do the practice of Empty Enclosure Resounding with A[108] and to
meditate for seven days. When the seven days had elapsed, I called
Rinchen into my room. "How do you see me?" I asked.

Rinchen replied sincerely, "I see you as a Lama wearing a fur-
trimmed coat."

[So I made him practice some more,] then asked again, "And now
what do you see me as?" This time, the young attendant prostrated
and said, "Now, I see you as the mandala of the thirteen Hevajra deities wielding weapons."

"You should also see the Five Tantric Deities present in my five
chakras. Go back out and practice!" Rinchen left to practice more.
When he finally returned, he saw me as Hevajra and I said, "From
now on, never see me as ordinary, not even for a moment." And
Rinchen sang this praise:

As for the deities of your enlightened emanation-body,
I see the Five Tantric Deities in your five chakras.

As for the hundred and eight thrones,
I can never look enough at your emanations,

Each one proclaiming the mahayana Dharma free of extremes—
Your manifold manifestations teach throughout the ten directions.

I praise you, Buddha-Lama, heart-emanation of the ocean of
   the victors.
Please keep all of us sentient beings on the pure path,
Confused as we are by ignorance.

From then on, not even for an instant did the slightest wrong view
arise in Rinchen. He became a great attendant and minded my every
word.

   I taught the Five Treatises of Maitreya and the general and secret
tantras. But the monks of Central, Eastern, and Western Tibet often
argued with one another about who was to serve me food. They were
about to break their *samaya*, so the four guardian kings[109] appeared in
front of the quarrelsome monks at a height of seven palm trees in
the sky, with a gathering of deities. They gave the following warning:

Birth in a place from which there is no liberation
Or losing your tenuous connection with a place of liberation,
These come from quarrels and disagreements.
Let's not even get into the importance of keeping your *samaya*!

For those who can surmount the difficulty of living in harmony,
Attaining enlightenment in one life is not so difficult.
[Lama Khyungpo], let us, the deities gathered here,
Serve you during the teachings.

Come sit at a height of seven palm trees in the sky—
Bring down a rainfall of Dharma!
Sound the conch shell of Dharma!
Raise the banner of Dharma!

So I committed to a seven-month vow of abstaining from food prepared by humans. During these seven months, I appeared in the sky
at tree-height, teaching the Five Treatises of Maitreya, and all the
general and secret tantras, instilling in many an understanding of the
Middle Way view. At that point, the deities appeared and said these
words in unison:

> You fulfill the intention of your teacher, Lama Dorjedenpa.
> You delight all the deities.
> You liberate all beings.
> You perform great activity for the Buddha's teachings.
> Well done!

This they repeated three times, upon which they brought down a
heavy rain of flowers, and disappeared. At dawn on the thirteenth
day of spring, Buddha Amitabha appeared and displayed the Blissful
Pure Land, and revealed several prophecies to me, including the following:

> This is your last rebirth.
> In the Blissful Pure Land,
> You will subdue all sorts of demons,
> Gain genuine enlightenment,
> And set in motion the cycle of teachings.

> Whoever is taught by you
> Or even just hears the name Amitabha
> Will enjoy a miraculous birth
> In the Blissful Pure Land.

> You will have three main lineage holders[110]
> Who will go to the Pure Land of Joy,
> To the Blissful Pure Land, and to other pure realms
> To attain perfect enlightenment.

Shortly after this revelation, a hundred and eighty thousand people assembled to listen to me, and my popularity aroused jealousy in the monks of the local monastic school. The envious monks huddled together to hatch a plot, "We can either submit to Khyungpo, or we can try to corner him when there aren't too many monks around, and finish him off for good!" Now while this was going on, several of the younger monks of this same school had come over to me to study the Dharma. This further infuriated the three elders of the school who discussed the situation thus, "If all our monks turn to Khyungpo for the Dharma, it will be the end of our school. We simply have to form an army and fight back."

As soon as this news reached my attendant Rinchen, he ran to me and exclaimed, "The monks from the school are forming an army! Either we fight and one of the monasteries gets destroyed, or we run away right now!" But I refused to consider either possibility. "In my Dharma," I said, "there can be no harm done to other beings. I will certainly not start to form battalions! As for running away, that would mean leaving this monastery and starting from scratch somewhere else, and I won't do that either!"

The army of the monastic school, five thousand soldiers strong, set upon my monastery at the crack of dawn one fall day, when there were few monks near me. Rinchen ran to me and cried, "I told you that an army would come against us, but you didn't listen! Now we're surrounded by soldiers. What are we going to do?" By means of my *samadhi*, I manifested an emanation army, which emerged victorious from battle without wounding or killing any man. This display convinced the monk-soldiers from the school to take me as their root Lama, offering me everything they had.

Around that time, famine gripped the land. I made prayers to noble Tara and was blessed with some prophecies. One morning, I went to a large valley and planted barley seeds. By that same evening, an enormous harvest-field had appeared. In that way, I brought an end to the famine.

On the eighth day of fall in the tiger year, I granted empowerments in the emanated mandala of the Four Blessings Deities to fifteen disciples who, from then on, experienced many visions of the deities.

Not long after that, the scholar Gapa Chögyal presented me with large offerings and received the Five Treatises of Maitreya, and teachings on the Eight Thousand Verse Prajnaparamita as well as the Prajnaparamita condensed into a singular syllable. He studied and meditated on this for a year but still had doubts about the view of Prajnaparamita, so he came to me and explained, "Well, there's not much point in my requesting teachings from all the Tibetan Lamas. If you, Lama Khyungpo, were to use dreams to request the pure view from the Great Mother Prajnaparamita, perhaps she might reveal it to me. While we're at it, since many in my family have had a short life, perhaps you could make a request to Amitayus for a long-life practice. And for that matter, since I have such a hard time arousing compassion, Avalokiteshvara might be entreated to bring about effortless compassion in my being!"

But no matter how many requests, no matter how much Geshe Chögyal practiced, he still did not gain any realizations. He prayed to Vajrapani for tantras and instructions and he practiced Tara for three years. He even had an enlightened activity empowerment, yet showed not the slightest attainment! So he begged me to ask the Jetsunma in the pure realm of Uddiyana for even just one pith instruction on appearance and existence, and I used dream yoga in the following way:

First I went to Akanistha. There, an immeasurable entourage of Buddhas of the ten directions with their sons and daughters surrounded the Great Mother Prajnaparamita. They were all seated on tiger skins, their hands in the mudra of teaching. I presented thousands of offerings and requested the Dharma from them. They gave me the Three-Fold Instructions on the Ultimate Unborn Nature.

Then I went to the Blissful Pure Land. On top of the bodhi tree was the protector Amitabha, surrounded by Avalokiteshvara, Hayagriva, Vajrapani, and countless other bodhisattvas. Amitabha taught me the Dharma through signs and I brought down a shower of flowers. I emanated from my body many young men and women consorting together. After presenting an offering, they requested, "Amitabha, please protect sentient beings from a short life in the realm of Jambudiva." In response, both Amitabha and the deities of the bodhi tree proclaimed the Dharma and performed the Long-Life Practice of the Nectar Vase.

Next, I went to Mount Potala. I found Avalokiteshvara teaching the Treatises of Maitreya to some harm-doers. A brilliant radiance issued out of him and his two retinues,[111] and entered my three chakras[112] of body, speech and mind. From these pure centers of light came these pure Dharma verses:

> If free-flowing compassion has not arisen
> From the birthless nature of all phenomena,
> The mother-beings of the six realms[113]
> Cannot be brought to maturation and liberation.

> Whatever you do, whether you walk, stand, sleep, or sit,
> Always remember your kind mothers who still experience suffering.
> Arouse immeasurable compassion
> And anchor it with the iron hook of mindfulness.

> From the snowy mountains of love and affection
> Flow the cooling rivers of great compassion,
> Extinguishing the flames of afflictive emotions.

> Thus I am the embodiment of great compassion.

Through this and other means, Avalokiteshvara taught the *samadhi* of all-pervasive compassion.

Continuing with my dream, I went next to Alakavati.[114] The Lord Vaisravana was teaching the Demon Vehicle Tantra, the Heart of Demon Life and the Wish-Fulfilling Demon Tantras. Since it was evening on the tenth day of the month, I laid out a proper offering and the following morning at dawn, I went to Uddiyana to receive the empowerment of the mandala of the Five Tantric Deities from Singhamukha, the lion-faced dakini, surrounded by the four classes of dakinis. Singhamukha spoke these words:

Vajra Dakini protects from obstacles.
Ratna Dakini obtains people and wealth.
Pedma Dakini attracts all consorts.
Karma Dakini accomplishes all activity.
If you're gripped by passions,
Then you're in essence at the mercy of the dakinis.
So remember—whatever comes up in the external world,
Recognize the dakinis as your own mind.

Recognition of the essence of mind and of mind itself as a non-
    conceptual diamond:
That is Vajra Dakini the Diamond, protecting from obstacles.

Contentment without needs is a precious treasure:
That is Ratna Dakini the Gem, fulfilling all human wishes and
    desires.

Non-conceptual lotus, free of attachment:
That is Pedma Dakini the Lotus, attracting all consorts.

Action free of arising, free of cessation:
That is Karma Dakini the Action, performing activity.

Yogis who do not recognize this,
Though they may practice for eons,
Will never develop realizations.
Therefore, the supreme instruction is
To recognize the dakini as your own mind.


And then Singhamukha and the dakinis gave many other teachings
such as the Three Arisings and the Three Gatherings.

So this was the dream I seized for the purpose of benefiting the
scholar Gapa Chögyal's practice. I gave instructions to Gapa Chögyal
who then presented a hundred and eight tantric feasts, practiced the

instructions, and realized the meaning of the unborn ultimate nature. He had visions of Buddha Amitabha. Non-referential compassion arose spontaneously. He became like a servant to the sons and daughters of the Buddhas and performed enlightened activity just like Karma Dakini. At that point, he asked me, "Precious Lama, in the dream, instructions were requested from the Buddhas. Did this request actually happen or not?"

In reply, I sang this song:

> The Buddha's body, the Buddha's pure land,
> The Buddha's entourage, the Buddha's teaching,
> Are all like an illusion.
> Reality or dream, where is the difference?

These words inspired great faith in the scholar Gapa Chögyal.

Here is another story: some people once requested that I use the practice of Dream Yoga to protect them and their cattle from harm by the three demons, Baranakpo (of the Shap region), Nyentang Lha, and Jowo Benchen. So I manifested as Vajrabhairava. In the daytime, I brought down thirteen strikes of lightning. At night, in the state of awareness during sleep, I rode a buffalo and shouted, "PEM! PEM!" and destroyed everything. Soon, the demon Baranakpo said, "Please, great Lama, I can't bear this any more. All my relatives are going to be struck by lightning and the buffalo will destroy all our dwellings. Now, I am vomiting blood, and soon I'll be dead! Here are a hundred horses, please, just take them!"

I replied, "This half-heartedness won't do! You must pledge your heart and soul to me. Make a commitment to stop harming people and to act as a spiritual friend. If you don't do it, I'll truly destroy you!" Hearing this threat, Baranakpo pledged his life to me and acted as a spiritual friend. From then on, he's been performing the enlightened activity of protecting horses and cattle.

Then, I brought down a hundred lightning bolts all at once on the rooftop of Nyentang Lha, the second of the three demons. The whole house shook and crumbled and I manifested as Zurpu Ngapa, King of the scent-eaters of the bardo,[115] and was let in by Nyentang Lha. I granted the empowerments of the mandalas of the Five Tantric Deities in exchange for his life. I also went to Lake Manasarovar and granted the empowerment of the mandala of Vajravidhu in exchange for the lives of the demons and their promise to become deities assuring wealth and prosperity.

Finally, having emanated as the mandala of Wrathful Yama, I subdued Jowo Benchen, *nagas* and spirits, and commanded them to cause no harm to beings, except for those who break their vow and take an evil path. I also taught them methods for presenting offerings. In dreams, I appeared as Vajrabhairava and subdued gods and demons, and my powers increased. This was my subjugation of the demons Baranakpo, Nyentang Lha, and Jowo Benchen.

On the seventh day of the second month of fall, with flowers still in blossom, when my following was great and included my finest students, at the culmination of my life, all of my Lamas from southern India appeared and granted the four complete empowerments for seven days. These wisdom beings[116] dissolved into me, saying, "There is no greater human disciple than you, Khyungpo Naljor. You are the best."

Then, on the thirteenth day of the same month, my Lamas from western India appeared together with the protector Amitayus and granted empowerments for seven days at which time these wisdom beings dissolved into me, saying, "There is no greater human disciple than you. If you wish to go now, you can reach the Blissful Pure Land and attain the rainbow body without abandoning this physical form." But I declined the offer, feeling that I had not yet completed my task of teaching the Dharma. I thought, "I've now gathered a great many disciples. I should pass on these teachings." In response, Amitabha and the Lamas asserted that I would attain enlightenment without abandoning this physical form, and that after leaving this fully ripened body, I would go to the Blissful Pure Land and become a Buddha there. Finally they repeated three times the following prophecy, "Khyungpo, if your body is not cremated after your death, this area of Shang will become a second Bodhgaya and this Dharma lineage of yours will flow continuously, like a river." In the late summer, my disciples gathered together and I turned the wheel of Dharma three times for both old and new students, and completed all my teachings.

I, Khyungpo, have gone to India seven times. I have met a hundred and fifty Lamas and pleased them with my offerings of gold, my faith and devotion. From these Lamas, I requested empowerments, blessings, tantras, *sadhanas*, teachings and specific oral instructions. Of these, I adopted thirteen as my principal Lamas and four as my root Lamas. The two unrivaled wisdom dakinis [Niguma and Sukhasiddhi] graced me with empowerments, blessings, tantras, *sadhanas*, and instructions on how to put these into practice, pith oral transmissions and so forth.

Through these transmissions, I have been able to satisfy you, my students. In general, the oral instructions I have transmitted are vastly superior to others. Given at the beginning, it helps beginners. Given in the middle, it helps those in the middle. Given at the end, it helps those at the end. Thus I have given you everything, I have left nothing out.

Have no doubts or hesitation, practice with perseverance and it will be impossible for you not to attain enlightenment—superior students in this fully ripened body, average students in the habitual body, or inferior students in the mental body of the bardo.[117] Surely, there have been no other teachings and oral instructions like the ones I have given in India and Tibet.

As for this monastery here in Shang: it was prophesied by Lamas and yidam deities. Now it's a base for disciples from Central, Eastern, and Western Tibet. From this ground grows the trunk of flawless awareness, my disciple, Meu Tönpa, who has gained mastery of Vajrabhairava and Manjushri.[118] The branch of altruistic aspiration is embodied in the bodhisattva Yorpo Gyamoche, who has received teachings from Manjushri. The branch of immeasurable compassion is Ngultön Riwang, inseparable from Avalokiteshvara. Arousing love in an unbiased way, the disciple Könchok Kar from Latö is the very essence of Chakrasamvara and the protector [Mahakala]. The realized Zhangom Chöseng manifests the inseparability of clear light and deity body, and attracts consorts.

The fruit [of this tree] is my one later disciple, Rinchen Tsöndrü Mokchokpa, who brings to fruition the practices of Dream Yoga and Illusory Body Yoga. These are my six disciples, who have been foretold. They have received teachings from yidam deities and the nature of reality has penetrated their minds. So all you students must abandon doubts and jealousy, and see them as inseparable from myself.

I've fulfilled the ultimate three: the ultimate gathering of disciples totals more than a hundred and eight thousand whom I've taught for many years; the ultimate heart son-or-daughter disciples, the six to whom I've given the complete teachings; and the ultimate point of my life, at a hundred and fifty years of age. I've received teachings from the Vajra brothers, from Lamas in India and elsewhere, from Vajrabhairava, and more. In various kingdoms, I averted wars and subdued worldly gods.

On the eighth day, after performing a hundred tantric feasts, the four great kings, *nagas* and their leader Madrö, Zurpu king of the scent-eaters of the bardo, and other non-humans[119] gathered to offer me silver and gold and many other things. They asked me not to pass into nirvana, begged me to continue to guide the beings of this degenerate age on the pure path. They promised to provide for all my needs. But this is what I sang in response:

> According to the prophecy of Lamas and yidam deities,
> The ultimate three have been fulfilled at this time.
> To Blissful Pure Land I'll go.

> Where there is widespread pure enjoyment,
> What need have I for the gold and silver of this world?
> If you're devoted to me, pray for the Blissful Pure Land
> And without a doubt, you will be born in that pure land.

> There are as many pure lands on a single atom
> As there are atoms in the universe.

Appearances inconceivable and perfect,
The pure land, the teacher, the Dharma entourage
The realm of infinite light,
All are the Blissful Pure Land.

Therefore, have no doubts on this
And pray for rebirth in the Blissful Pure Land.
As for me, I'll definitely go to the Blissful Pure Land!

After I spoke, deities, dakas, and dakinis intoned mantras and supplications, brought down a flower-rain, and then disappeared.

### The Death of Khyungpo Naljor

ON THE FOURTEENTH day [of the ninth month], Khyungpo came to the assembly and said, "Today will be my last Dharma teaching. Earlier, I taught about happiness and the cause of happiness. But today, the time has come to eradicate all doubts." Hearing this, all the people assembled developed great faith. Lama Khyungpo displayed many bodies in the sky and sang this song:

Alas! All composites are transitory:
Just like clouds in the sky,
They gather
And then disperse.

Although illusory phenomena
Have no true nature,
We cling to them as real
And are deceived.

My body is the Buddha's body.
Never view it
As undergoing birth and death.

My speech is the Buddha's speech.
It is spontaneous sound,
Unborn and inexpressible.

My mind is the Buddha's mind.
It is primordial awareness
Omniscient and non-conceptual.

At these words, the sky resonated with the sound of music and it rained flowers.

After performing a tantric feast, Khyungpo returned to his room and sat on his bed. Rinchen Tsöndrü Mokchokpa was told to go and pick a bunch of flowers, and to call for the local leaders. After Mokchokpa returned with a handful of red flowers, Lama Khyungpo said, "This here is for my practice of the reverent dakini Niguma; that is for the great Dorjedenpa; these stone statues are for Yamantaka and Vajrabhairava; and that there for the practices of Maitripa. To these all, I make offerings." At this, his implements stayed suspended in space and Lama Khyungpo prostrated himself. Then, he told Mokchokpa, "Now it's time for you, disciple, to make offerings!" At that instant, the dakinis Niguma and Sukhasiddhi, all the Lamas, yidam deities and Buddha Amitayus appeared. "And now," Khyungpo said "all you students should pray! You, Mokchokpa, if you practice Illusory Body and Dream Yoga, should you have nightmares, transform them into dakini forms teaching by signs and magic, and you will have no fear. Now I give you my blessing!"

When the influential people of the area had gathered near him, Khyungpo appeared as Hevajra and told them to meditate on Hevajra. Afterwards, he manifested as Hevajra wielding weapons with ninefold entourage. He repeated this display as Chakrasamvara, Guhyasamaja, Mahamaya, Avalokiteshvara, Tara, Akshobhya, and countless other deities, teaching the Dharma each time. He also emanated the Four Blessings Deities above his head, saying, "This is how one should practice!"

Finally, Lama Khyungpo said, "When I was in India and received the four complete empowerments, the wisdom beings actually dissolved into me and since then they have never left me. There is no one superior to me at present. There isn't even anyone equal to me. After my death, don't cremate my body. Place it in a bronze and copper casket filled with gold, silver, and jewels, and present offerings to it. If you do so, this area of Shang will become like a second Bodhgaya and my lineage will flow like a river. Now, I shall go to the Blissful Pure Land and attain enlightenment there. Whatever other prayers you make, always remember to pray to the Blissful Pure Land." And three times, Khyungpo repeated a last exhortation, "Now give up all doubts!"

Eventually he said, "All yogis who do the Transference of Consciousness practice called Wisdom Skylight should practice like this—" and from the aperture at the crown of his head, he shot up in the sky. Transforming into sounds, iridescent lights, and rainbows, he went off into space.

The casket was filled with gold and silver and Khyungpo's body was placed in it. At that moment, monks from Eastern Tibet area arrived and exclaimed, "We'll take the body of Lama Khyungpo to the provinces of Central and Eastern Tibet. We'll place it in a silver-reliquary. Otherwise, let's burn it now!" Under the influence of the monks, a decision was reached to burn the body.

From the vestiges sprung the Five Tantric Deities as well as the Four Blessings Deities. Many sacred relics such as conch shells angled to the right were recovered. For twenty-one days, the sky was filled with rainbows and rains of flowers. After three weeks, a monastery was erected in honor of Khyungpo. Flowers rained continuously. Deities, *nagas*, dakas, and dakinis made offerings and butter lamps appeared from the four directions of the monastery giving a constant glow. Gods and men all gave tributes to the sacred relics.

This brief glimpse into the life of Khyungpo was written by combining individual accounts from Zhangom Chöseng, Lama Meu Tönpa, Lama Mokchokpa, and Khyungpo's attendant Rinchen Dorje. By the virtue of this story—just a drop in the ocean of the masters' lives—may all beings attain unsurpassable enlightenment. This has been a small glimpse into the life of the adept Khyungpo Naljor.

# 5

# Life of Mokchokpa

I, MOKCHOKPA, WAS born in the meadowlands of Lhabu in the Shang Valley of Namling County. I met Lama Khyungpo Naljor early on, but the Lama did not express any interest in me at the time. At sixteen—nearly seventeen—I entered the door of Dharma. For a year, I studied the *vinaya* code of discipline. Then, I requested the Hevajra empowerment from the Shangpa Lama Dubupa [Khyungpo Naljor][120] and he told me, "You will bring great benefit to beings. For now, you need to study. You can go either to Könkarwachen and study the Prajnaparamita, or you can go to Chakriwa and study the Five Treatises of Maitreya. As for me, I have to write some books." I considered what my Lama said and I decided to study with Chakriwa.

In my youth, I studied many texts, including the Prajnaparamita. I met Dromtönpa, the famous disciple of the lord Atisha, who expressed his bitter disappointment with studies and gave me the unequivocal advice to meditate and put aside intellectual pursuits.

At the age of twenty-one, I accompanied the teacher Yorpo Gyamoche to Central Tibet. He said he had to go to Töling and he called out, "I'll see you in Kyishö!" I left for Kyishö. The next day, after crossing a stream, I settled myself in a yard. As the sun set, I

saw a teacher approach, carrying a load of books on Buddhist valid
cognition. He dropped them on the ground next to him. Then he beat
his own breast and cried out, "I may have a lot of knowledge, but I
can't even get fed and no one listens to my teachings, the whole thing
is no good!" He was eating dry tsampa,[121] cramming it all into his
mouth.

"Why do you bother then?" I asked.

But he spat out, "Don't you be smart, young monk! You don't know
a thing! Just shut up." That night, I thought again of the discussions
with Dromtönpa about practicing as opposed to studying. I reflected,
"This man here is carrying a load of Dharma books, yet he under-
stands nothing. And as for me, although I have studied the Dharma, I
understand nothing either!"

While studying with Lama Aseng, I was challenged by sixty scholars to prove my logic. In response, I explained, "There are two truths—
the conventional and the ultimate. In Tibet, there's occasional confusion between the two kinds of conventional truths—the distorted
and the pure conventional truths.[122] As for the ultimate truth, we talk
of both the nominal and the actual ultimate truths.[123] The nominal
ultimate truth makes determinations still based on conceptual elabo-
rations. In the actual ultimate truth, there is no intellect, no causes
and conditions, no fruition, and no good or evil. In the Hundred Thousand Verse Prajnaparamita, it is said, 'In the ultimate truth, there is
no karma, no ripening of karma, no purification, and no afflictive
emotions anywhere.' Confused scholars think that the ultimate truth
can be established!"

I took off for the mountains with the adept Aseng and we vowed
to stay in complete silence for two weeks every month. During those
two weeks, no one was to come visit. We left in the fall and had been
up in the forest for four days when we noticed a small hut hidden
away between the pine trees. I wondered, "Who could be staying
here?"

"It's Lama Burgom Nakpo," replied Aseng. "He is a disciple of the
lord Rechungpa and holds the oral transmission." Hearing this inspired me with great devotion.

Carrying with me all the molasses I had, I went to the small hut to see Lama Burgom. There I saw a white dog known to have killed people, but that dog came to welcome me. Just then, a man appeared from the hut, wearing a yogi's light cotton robe. He looked at me and asked, "Who do you wish to see, my lord?"

"I'd like to meet Lama Burgom Nakpo," I explained.

"Well then, come inside for a hot tea." I followed the man inside the hut but saw no one else there. I asked, "Is Lama Burgom not here?"

"The one called Burgom is myself!" the yogi replied. "I have no attendants." I presented my gift of molasses and told him my story. "I am from the eastern part of Shang," I began. "I have great faith in the instructions of the sage Naropa and have prayed very hard to get these precepts. Please take me as your student!"

"But having dismounted from a horse, would you now ride a donkey?[124] Why leave a great scholar like the Shangpa Lama and get instructions from me, a simple yogi?" I begged him again to give me teachings and he finally said, "Well, if you are truly so devoted, you are worthy of the Dharma." So I spent the winter meditating with Lama Burgom, who gave me both maturing and liberating teachings.

After spending five years with Lama Burgom, I met up with Lama Khyungpo. He said, "Last year your father died and your family performed virtuous practices for him. And you, did you spend last year with Lama Yorpo Gyamoche? Did you get all the teachings on the Prajnaparamita?"

"Well," I replied, "first I went to Dromtönpa and discussed my situation with him. He advised me to concentrate on meditation. Then, on my way to Kyishö, I met a teacher who was carrying a load of books and yet seemed to have no understanding of the Dharma. It looked to me like all his learning was not helping his mind a bit! So I went to get teachings from Aseng and Lama Burgom Nakpo, and practiced meditation. Now, I can recognize my dreams. I have had a vision of the Jetsunma. I have studied intensely with Lama Yorpo Gyamoche for five years. Now I'm on my way to get more provisions."

Lama Khyungpo harshly replied, "Young monk, you *should* know the Prajnaparamita, yet you've got no understanding of it. You *shouldn't* know how to tell lies, but you're sure good at telling them! You say you've practiced Dream Yoga and you've had visions of the Jetsunma—but whether that is the case or not, I don't want you staying near me! Leave at daybreak!"

In the small hours of the night, however, Lama Khyungpo called me. I approached and he said, "Buddha Amitabha has appeared to me, surrounded by dakinis and yidam deities. Amitabha said that I am to give you the instructions of the one-to-one guru-to-disciple transmission. You shall be the Shangpa lineage holder." So I stayed with Khyungpo and received all the Shangpa teachings.

One hot afternoon we were resting under a big sun umbrella when the Lama said, "I've prepared a show for you!" And suddenly on his seat blazed Dranakpo, Vajrabhairava, Vajrapani, and other wrathful deities, teaching the Dharma and dancing in the middle of a fire! From my Lama Khyungpo, I received advice on the Twenty-One Praises to White Tara. I presented an offering of gold and Khyungpo gave me the *sadhanas* of the two wisdom dakinis and said, "You should perform a hundred and eight tantric feasts." After I completed the tantric feasts, he gave me the empowerment of Illusory Body Yoga according to Niguma, and the Blossom Teachings of the Six Yogas of Niguma and all of the dakini's intimate advice. Finally, he said, "On the evening of the tenth day of the month, make offerings and meditate on the Joint Practice of the Four Blessings Deities. The next day, come and see me!"

I meditated on the Four Blessings Deities past midnight and at sunrise I went to see the Lama. On his bed were the Four Blessings Deities making the spontaneous sound of *diriri!* The Lama asked, "Can you see the Four Blessings Deities?"

"Yes I can, Lama." I replied.

"Well then, see if there is any difference between me and the Four Deities!"

On the morning of the eighth day of another month, Lama Khyungpo asked me to prepare tea. When I returned with the tea, I saw the Five Tantric Deities gathered in his room, buzzing *diriri* with the sound of their mantra recitations. At that sight, I realized that the Lama was inseparable from the deities. I thought, "He really is the Buddha." Since then, this vision has never left me.

After refining my practice of Dream Yoga, I gave this advice, "Just as various appearances arise in the context of a dream, so too, various appearances arise at this present time. In their mode of arising, these appearances are equal. During my dream, various objects appear to me, while [at this present time] appearances also arise. There is no difference in the way [phenomena] appear. In the same vein, dream and actual phenomena are equal in their ability to perform functions."

So I was practicing with my dreams in the ways I've described above. One night, while I was sleeping, it occurred to me that I could use my magical powers. All at once, the space in front of me filled with Lamas, yidam deities, Buddhas, bodhisattvas, and more. In the next instant, they emanated all sorts of unusual offerings laid out in a row. With graceful ease, they recited dedications. They gave me wonderful instructions on Illusory Body Yoga.

After Khyungpo Naljor died, I spent two years in solitary meditation. Then, to clarify doubts in my practice, I set out to meet Lama Gampopa whom I found in a cave. Lama Gampopa extended his arm and placed a white scarf in my hands. Leaving his bamboo walking stick on the ground, he turned to me, "You are my spiritual son and we've been teachers to one another for many lives. But this is the first time we have met in this life." As tears flowed down his face, he sang this song:

> In our many past lives
> We have taught one another.
> Because of our previous connections,
> We now meet in this meditation cave.
> Full of faith and devotion,
> You have come here as my son.

Other songs followed this one, and I couldn't help but cry. At that moment, deep calm abiding was born within me. I brought the gifts into his cave and explained, "Since my great Shangpa Lama has passed away, I have continued to practice. I have developed experiences and realizations of Illusory Body Yoga, Dream Yoga, and Clear Light Yoga. But I am not sure if I have all of these in their entirety." I asked Lama Gampopa, "Since my Shangpa Lama has passed away, would you please give me the instructions for the Six Yogas?"

The Lama replied, "Your understanding of the Six Yogas is already very good. What you need now is a teaching to clear away your doubts about the view." He gave me the Eight-Line Mahamudra Teachings as well as five pointing-out instructions to lead me to certainty in the view. Lama Gampopa then said, "As for meditation techniques on the Six Yogas, I myself have pledged not to comment on them or on their *sadhanas*. Since you're empowered in Dream Yoga, however, be mindful of your dreams. You'll get instructions."

So I went off to meditate in a small hut and stayed up until dusk saying prayers. At dawn, I dreamt that I went to Lama [Gampopa] and he taught me the Six Yogas in their entirety. As soon as I woke up from that sleep I remembered the dream and continued with the practice even in the waking state. When I went to see Gampopa, I asked, "The Six Yogas I was taught last night in the dream, are they the ultimate?"

The Lama replied, "Most of them were complete. As for the others—the Transference of Consciousness Yoga and its related practice, Entering the Corpse Projection Yoga, you still need a little more instruction." And he gave me the final words of instruction on these. I received teachings and books from Gampopa and later from the scholar Garpa.

The power of the Lamas' blessings rendered me decisive in the view. In my practice of Illusory Body Yoga, I dreamt one night of transforming myself into a *garuda* and I flew to my friend's house in Lenpa. My friend wasn't there; he was, in fact, a day's walk from the market. I flew again and came to the entrance of a cave. My *garuda* body transformed into the Jetsunma. I could see everywhere at once:

from the nether-worlds to the realms of the earth and the Buddhas' pure lands. I even saw my own body, and reflected on these phenomena. I intoned this song:

> Vast energy of unobstructed expanse beyond birth
> Cannot be encompassed by mind.
> This illusory body, beyond anybody's designs,
> Arises from the vast expanse of yogic awareness.
> Thoughts of this life fade and vanish.
>
> The fully ripened body is the Buddha's body,
> This is the precious lord, pointing-out the essence.
>
> The mental body is the body of reality,
> This is the precious lord, pointing-out the essence.
>
> The habitual body is the Buddha's body,
> This is the precious lord, pointing-out the essence.

Following that dream, I had no more thoughts about this present life. I relied on Lama Gampopa for another year and received all the Mahamudra instructions without exception, which gave me stability in the view.

After a year, it was time to go. I prostrated to Lama Gampopa and supplicated him, "I will move on now. Wherever life takes me, please always hold me in your compassion!" Next, I used my Dream Yoga powers to tame the demon Soksha. I also received visions of Vajrayogini. One day at dawn, I dreamt of jewels and precious articles in the cave of a castle. Men dressed as demons were guarding the valuables, but I saw that none of them was allowed near the treasures. I thought, "My body is like this castle, and my mind, like those precious gems. The five poisons,[125] which prevent realizations, are like these men dressed as demons."

At that moment, the Jetsunma appeared in the space in front of me and said, "O my child, it is just like that." In return, I sang a song of realization for her. Then she disappeared into the sky.

Around that time, I thought, "Well, according to the instructions of the Lamas, I should not leave the mountains until I am either dead or enlightened!" So I stayed in a mountain cave in the Mokchok area.[126] Every month, my aunt brought me five measures of grain. I had been practicing in this way for nearly a year when she came to my cave and said, "Rinchen Tsöndrü [Mokchokpa], I do care for you, but this grain is heavy, and there's no profit in it. From now on, I can bring you only two measures a month."

She did so through the winter. Then one day she declared, "Now look! You come from a fine family. All your brothers have plenty of meat, and butter, and good clothes. You're the oldest one in the family: what are you doing up here in this cave? You have no clothes, no food, nothing. What good is this Dharma to you? I do like you, but I just can't come up here any more. Your poor aunt is old and can't afford to feed you like that." So I walked her out, and from then on, I closed myself up in the cave.

Summers came and went, winters passed, and I could only guess the seasons and the time from the air temperature. Eventually, everything in the cave was covered with a layer of dust, and still I practiced diligently. When I first mastered breathing meditation, I felt weak. But later, as I developed perseverance, my prayers became very powerful. One morning, Sukhasiddhi appeared to me and said:

> When the Dharma itself is not realized,
> When experiences, nourished on human food, grow dim—
> Give up attachment to clothes and food,
> Feast on non-conceptual meditation experience.[127]

This she repeated three times, and at that point I cut all attachment to food and clothes. I had a lucid dream in which I went to Uddiyana

and received the empowerment of the Thirteen-Deity Mandala of
Vajravarahi with this verse:

> This fully ripened body is the Buddha's body
> View it as the union of bliss and emptiness.
>
> This fully ripened body is the body of illusion,
> View it as the union of clear light and emptiness.

One night, I dreamt that thirteen fine horses were presented to me as
an offering. The next day, thirteen disciples of Lama Gampopa came
to me and asked, "Precious Lama, you have a rigorous understanding
of the Mahamudra precepts. Please grant us the Mahamudra teachings which are beyond the faults of conceptual thought." So I sang
this tantric song:

> Where in reality itself, unborn and unobstructed
> Are these 'conceptual thoughts?'
> See the non-conceptual and the conceptual
> As water and the waves in it.

And all those present gained insight into the groundless nature of
mind.

The scholar Gyal offered me eighty measures of gold, saying, "I've
listened to plenty of teachings on the Five Tantric Deities. I've received many *sadhanas* that I've practiced, and yet I still haven't had
any visions of the deities. Could you please give me one yidam deity
practice so that I might get a vision?" To him, I sang the following
instruction:

> Renounce the objects of samsara.
> With a mind free of doubts or second thoughts,
> Meditate on non-conceptual, luminous deity body.

Do not get involved in endless talk
But recite mantras
Which are the union of sound and emptiness.

If you practice like that,
There is no doubt
That you will soon see the deity's body.

The scholar Gyal developed confidence and after three months of practice he saw the face of Tara.

Eventually, I gathered so many disciples in Mokchok that there wasn't enough space to accommodate them all. So, with the intention to benefit beings, a monastery was built in Kuklung.[128] My aspiration was purely compassionate and altruistic: my thoughts were simply of caring for the crowd of practitioners. Yet I longed to cut short distractions and kept thinking of meditating alone in solitude.

One summer, there was a terrible famine. The local people, because they were starving, stole the offerings. They also made away with a yak which was, in fact, the protector's yak and which fought hard to resist, ramming its horns left and right until flames blazed out. I could see that my monks were on the point of taking up arms, so I demanded that everyone assemble. I took a big blanket, loaded my bag with my ritual objects, and I sang them this song:

To ask your Lama for advice
Is the measure of your understanding of the path.

To rely on the holy Dharma with complete faith
Is the measure of your understanding of the instructions.

To cut your mind from the extreme of superimposition
Is the measure of your definitive understanding.

To keep your thoughts in accordance with the genuine Dharma
Is the measure of your progress in practice.

To give the Buddha's words to other beings
Is the measure of your mind training.

To deal with your own mind—and not that of others
Is the measure of your decreasing vanity.

To behave as a guest wherever you are
Is the measure of your decreasing attachment.

To be impartial to either victory or defeat
Is the measure of your physical and mental contentment.

After this song, I took off for the mountains, where I had a vision of
Avalokiteshvara saying:

The flames of anger and attachment
Are quenched by the rivers of love and affection.
It is good, yogi, it is good!

The root of samsara and nirvana is attachment and aversion:
The grasping mind.
Give it up, yogi, give it up!

In the horse year, I entered a solitary retreat, abstaining from human
food, and refraining from giving empowerments. I experienced visionary expansions of the clear-light nature. Soon, I was able to know
the specific practices of my monks as well as their every deed, whether
virtuous or deluded. As a result, I was able to give to each whatever
advice was most appropriate, with great love and compassion.

My practice was culminating in every way: I had many disciples
and was always receiving donations. Yet there were many, such as
Ngomshö Lachö, who didn't really listen to the teachings. I admonished him: if he went back home, he would face death at some not-

so-distant point and would not meet with me again. But he did not take my advice and set out to return to his village. The sight saddened me. I took Ngomshö's hand in mine and sang him this song:

> The Buddha is the predecessor of all sentient beings,
> The holy Dharma is the shared jewel of all sentient beings.
> Since all karma is allotted to men and women—
> Ignoring one's inheritance is meaningless.

> The root of the Buddhas of the three times
> Is the Lama who holds the lineage,
> Fulfilling our wishes and desires in this and future lives.
> Lacking devotion for him, or her, is meaningless.

> For the remainder of this life
> Engage fully in practice with undistracted concentration
> Rather than trying to benefit the ever-dissatisfied.
> Wasting this life is meaningless.

> Immature beings with but a twig of awareness
> Are incited by the demon of death.
> Where they'll be in the future depends on the karma they gathered in the past.
> Doing evil deeds is meaningless.

> In this sorrowful world of contaminated aggregates
> We undergo birth, sickness, old age, and death.
> To hope that this body-bag, a clay pot of sorts, may last forever—
> That is meaningless.

> Since food and wealth are in the nature of an illusion,
> They do not lead to the benefit of self or others.
> Yet you wallow in ingrained miserliness.
> Inability to let go is meaningless.

Drawn off the path by the demon of conceptual thought,
You lose sight of reality,
And fear death, the parting of body and mind.
Mental agitation is meaningless.

You fail to seize the opportunities
To meditate undistracted at the four times of day
On the all-accomplishing tantric practices.
Your ceaseless chatter and dwelling on the past is meaningless.

As for this mind, this wish-fulfilling gem:
If you do not meditate on it as inseparable from the three bod-
   ies of enlightenment,
You are just like a deer chasing a mirage.
Pursuing verbal postulates is meaningless.

Failing to take hold of reality itself as your homeland,
You slack in your vigilance about ego-clinging: wandering aim-
   lessly in samsara
While holding on to the illusion of the citadel of the six classes
   of beings—
That is meaningless.

## The Death of Mokchokpa

As MOKCHOKPA LAY dying, a ghost appeared and begged him to accept his horse. The horse had a brass buckle, a saddle made of small cushions of precious Mongolian silk, ornamented with tassels and dark turquoise stone. Silver had been woven into the fabric on the top and bottom of the cushion, which was studded with five kinds of precious gems throughout. The horse had white pearls on its flanks, stranded like crystalline stripes, and bound by gold buckles. Bridles, made of the finest silver, were flung over the horse and its eyelets gleamed with dark blue turquoise stones. With his left hand, the ghost seized reins of red coral, with bits stamped by silver diagrams, and placed them in the hands of lord Mokchokpa. Mokchokpa replied:

> My child, cut through your doubts on the conventional level.
> You have no need of the conventional Dharma—
> So difficult to learn, yet so easy to forget!
> The eighty-four thousand doors of Dharma
> Are all absorbed into mind itself.
>
> Meditate on phenomena as they are.
> Rest in the unfabricated, innate natural state.
> Recognize appearances as mind
> And mind's true nature as unborn.
> This realization of the unborn is the clear-light nature.
> Allow your mind to experience this.
>
> Since the interdependence of causes and conditions is infallible,
> Get this one meaning, my child!
>
> I am not staying here any longer.
> Now I shall go to the other shore.
>
> I am riding the horse of consciousness,
> So what need do I have for the horses of this world?
>
> I am going with the assistance of bodhisattvas,
> So what need do I have for servants?
>
> I have the wish-fulfilling jewel of mind,
> So what need do I have for these worldly gems?
>
> My entourage is made of all good qualities,
> So what need do I have for crowds of students?

On all the paths, I am guided by the Lamas,
So what need do I have for laypeople?

I am escorted by dakas and dakinis,
So what need do I have for gods and demons?

Keep as a companion the experience of no-fixation.
Realize the view beyond intellect.
Rest in the natural state.

Mokchokpa's disciples gathered around and supplicated, "Lama, please tell us where you will go from here." The unparalleled precious Mokchokpa replied:

After this life, I shall go to the Eastern Pure Land of Joy,
Called Light Brilliance, where I'll attain enlightenment,
And turn a little the wheel of mahayana Dharma.
This Shangpa lineage will be continued by the great Wöntön
    Kyergangpa,
Himself an emanation of Avalokiteshvara.
He will have a disciple of great renown, Sangye Nyentön
    Rigongpa,
Whose disciple will in turn continue the transmission and pro-
    tect the lineage.

The teacher Jotsun supplicated Mokchokpa, "May we never be separated from your compassion!" The incomparable Mokchokpa replied:

Whichever of the four activities you are engaged in
—Walking, standing, sleeping or sitting—
Elevate all appearances to the path, as the Lama.
Pray that you may always have a kind heart.
Then, there will be no separation between you and I, my child.

This, he repeated three times. Then Mokchokpa passed away. May Mokchokpa's qualities, far beyond understanding, steady us along the path.

SARWA DAKALYA BHAWANTU! SHUBHOM!

# 6

# Life of Kyergangpa

BORN TO THE Ba family in the upper reaches of Nang County, I studied and practiced intensely in my teenage years. At seventeen, I joined the retinue of my uncle, Thamche Khyenpa (the All-Omniscient One) and proceeded to Draklha.[129] The sight of a whitewashed little house by the wayside aroused my curiosity. I enquired about it and was told, "It's a great practitioner of Avalokiteshvara, known as Pakpa Chegom, the Sublime Solitary Meditator." I immediately felt intense devotion for this yogi, and went to him carrying three white scarves, my copper pot, flour, and butter with me. I asked him, "Lama, have you had a vision of Avalokiteshvara?"

"I don't know if it's Avalokiteshvara that I actually see or not," replied the ascetic. "But over there in the shadows, a shape always forms."

"Well, would you grant me the Avalokiteshvara teachings?"

"First, you need to receive the Rikte Empowerment," he replied. With two measures of butter, I prepared two butter lamps and celebrated a tantric feast. Next, I presented the three white scarves and three times I received the complete Avalokiteshvara teachings. Then I asked, "Lama, how many years was it before you received a vision of Avalokiteshvara?"

The Lama told me, "For eight years, I begged for alms in the fall, and the rest of the time I practiced in solitary retreat. One warm morning, I felt like going out to look at the sun. Just then, I heard a buzzing noise like *diriri* in the cave where I'd been staying. 'Who can that be?' I wondered. I went back in and there on my meditation seat sat the lord Avalokiteshvara with his two retinues, humming the *mani* mantra and saying the seven-branch prayer as an offering. From then on, I've had continuous visions of Avalokiteshvara."

Then I moved on to Kyergang with a clear mind. "I'm like a yak loaded with salt from the north[130] who either dies or makes it back successfully," I thought. "I now have this precious human body, and either I'll die, or I'll get a vision of Avalokiteshvara. If I don't want to waste my human life with meaningless activities, I had better practice."

I was about to enter into a strict solitary retreat when monks from my monastery in Eastern Tibet arrived and attached their horses nearby. They presented me with fine cloth and white scarves. Stretching out a silk blanket for me, they entreated, "Why spend your youth listening and reflecting? The lineage upheld by your uncle Ba Thamche Khyenpa must be maintained—your duty is to study for a scholar's degree."

I would not hear of it, so the monks discussed the situation and concluded that if no one was allowed to bring me flour or water or wood, and if rocks were thrown against my retreat place, I would soon tire and return to my uncle's monastic seat. I had my mind made up though, and closed myself in my retreat cave to practice Avalokiteshvara. Angered, the monks hurled stones at my door, "You're not going to study and teach? All right then!" they shouted. "Go do your *mani* mantra!" They took off without leaving any supplies for me—which meant that my daily nourishment was just some broth to drink, and some days, not even that. At such times, I would subsist by mixing dust in my water.

One day, I thought, "Sleep is stupidity. Stupidity[131] is an afflictive emotion and has caused me to wander endlessly through samsara." I proceeded with my *mani* mantra recitation without any sleep. Be-

cause of going without sleep, after some time I developed a problem
with the energy flow in my body. My head felt like it was going to
burst. So I tied a sash around my head and continued to fiercely recite mantras for two years. Still, there were no signs whatsoever. I
made an enormous fire *puja*,[132] and although I received signs that some
bad karma was being purified, I still had no vision of Avalokiteshvara.

Four and a half years into this life of practice, I felt despondent and
looked out toward the edge of the cliff below. I could see rainbows
appearing and disappearing in the sky outside. "For the last four and
a half years," I thought, "I have practiced Avalokiteshvara mantras
every day, subsisting only on a daily cup of tasteless broth. Now my
health is shot. Nothing's working! I might as well throw myself off
this cliff." I walked to the ledge, prepared to surrender myself to the
abyss, when a rainbow appeared in the sky before me. In the middle
was Avalokiteshvara, the Lord of Great Compassion, surrounded by
his two retinues. "O Lord of Little Compassion!" I exclaimed. "Why
didn't you show yourself these last four and a half years when I survived on nothing but a bad broth to drink every day?"

Avalokiteshvara said, "My child, three days after you began your
retreat, I was with you, and have been inseparable from you all this
time. You didn't see me before because you had obstacles—your karma
had not been purified for one thing, and you were also overly attached
to receiving a vision."

I praised him and his two retinues:

> Body of compassion pure and perfect,
> Reality itself, pristine as a snowy mountain range.
> Praise to you sitting in full lotus
> On a high throne fashioned with unalloyed gems and water
>     lilies,
> Upon a moon disk that clears away all sorrow.
> Praise to you who subdues the four demons,[133]
> Fruition without limit, enlightened enjoyment-body.

Before Avalokiteshvara stood Red Yamantaka—as visualized in the 'approaching' stage—his right foot pressing down on Mount Takri and his left trampling a peak in Kyergang. In his right hand, Yamantaka held a vajra wheel; his left hand was at his heart, index and thumb touching. His wild hair shot out around him. This was my vision.

Soon my uncle called for me. When I went to see him, he said, "You've had a vision of Avalokiteshvara and Yamantaka. There's no reason for you to study with all the monks from Eastern Tibet. In your case, there is much more to gain by practicing rather than merely listening to teachings. Now in Latö there's a sage known as Tsari Gompa who is skilled in the oral instructions of Lama Rechungpa. Go see him!"

I took six white scarves and a handful of gold and headed west to Lama Tsari Gompa, Rechungpa's student. At noon the next day, I was resting on a hill when a storm gathered. The morning was warm, but hail started to come down. I thought it was weird that hail should appear on a hot day, and reflected, "All phenomena arise from one's own mind. They are the body of reality—mind unborn." At that very moment, I experienced a spontaneous understanding of the unborn nature of mind, the essence of which has remained unchanged all these years.

An attendant carrying water bowed down to me by a stream near the cave in Latö where Lama Tsari Gompa was staying. Surprised, I said, "Why are you saluting me? You must be mistaking me for someone else."

He replied, "This morning, my Lama told me that today, I would meet a great adept from Central Tibet. Now, here you are, and you're the only one I've met. So it must be you! Come along!" And he guided me along a path to a cave. As soon as we arrived, I presented the Lama with my white scarves, and said, "Though I have nothing more to offer, please grant me now the complete instructions of Lama Rechungpa."

The Lama smiled slightly, "You'll receive the complete instructions when you've really given away all your wealth." I must admit, my claim that I was without any possessions was a lie, the only one I ever said to the Lama. In fact, I still had gold. So I went to trade this in and offered the Lama everything I had. Then, I received the empowerments of the Thirteen-Deity Mandala of Chakrasamvara and the Thirteen-Deity Mandala of Vajravarahi. For the next two years, I received instructions from Lama Tsari Gompa in Latö.

After that, I heard that in Öyuk in Western Tibet, Lama Penpukpa Chenpo was giving empowerments and the secret mantra of the lord Atisha. I went to see Lama Penpukpa, with whom I spent five years receiving the instructions of Atisha. At that point, he gave me the heart practice and *damaru* drum of lord Atisha himself.

Next, I heard of a great adept in Lhabu, in Shang. They said he mastered Clear Light Yoga, Dream Yoga, and Illusory Body Yoga, and his name was Mokchokpa. I headed out to see this Lama. On the way, I met a rich man who asked me to take a tantric practitioner's robe to Lama Mokchokpa. That very night, after I'd gone to sleep at the bottom of the mountain pass, a dark being appeared, wearing a brown cotton loin-cover. He said, "Tomorrow every person you'll come across will be helpful. No harm will come to you. Now, think of me as your servant, but don't repeat this to anybody." With these words, he disappeared.

The next day, I made many friends. Finally, I reached Kuklung, where the Lama was staying. As soon as I arrived, the Lama asked me, "Yesterday you met a dark man, didn't you?"

"Yes, I did," I replied.

"Well, that was the protector. He was there to serve you." I practiced with Lama Mokchokpa and my practice grew strong. That's when my Lama said, "My servant went to get tea at the market, but he hasn't returned yet. I wonder what happened to him. Look into it with your Dream Yoga, would you?" Following the Lama's instructions, I prayed until midnight, and at dawn, I had a lucid dream: I saw the attendant at a distance of one day's walk back from the market. He had a package of tea that he was using as a headrest. I could also see that inside the tea package was a bundle wrapped in cotton. The next morning, I approached the Lama and said, "I think your servant has a tea package, and there's a cotton bundle inside the bag."

"I see," said my Lama. "And what is in the bundle?"
"That, I couldn't tell."
"Ha! Well, let me tell you what I saw. The cotton bundle contains some coins. So, this old fox still has a bit to teach you, my young donkey! Now go meditate!" My Dream Yoga practices took me to pure realms, where I obtained precious teachings. One night, in my dream, I went to Mount Potala and faced Tara. She sang:

The essential point of Illusory Body Yoga
Is absence of inherent existence.
Cut through your clinging!

The essential point of Dream Yoga
Is aspiration.
Practice on the path!

The essential point of Clear Light Yoga
Is respect and devotion.
Say your prayers!

The essential point of compassion
Is benefiting others.
Abandon prejudice!

Once, I was preparing an offering for Lama Gampopa when I received the empowerments for the self-generation and the front-generation of the Joint Practice of the Four Blessings Deities. I practiced this for twenty-one days and had an uninterrupted vision of the deities on the crown of my head. When I related all these experiences to my Lama, he said, "Now you have a continuous experience of your yidam deity. Your Dream Yoga practice is very powerful. It's time for you to open the door of Dharma to young, sharp-minded monks. I know that your devotion is very great."

That summer, I engaged others in the Dharma by giving teachings on the *sadhana* of Avalokiteshvara. But I noticed that my practice

was getting less powerful and that things were getting very busy. I
wasn't pleased. I decided to interrupt working for the Dharma in this
way and returned to solitary retreat to meditate. It took me a long
time to regain my meditative powers. I thought to myself, "Until I
have reached the three pure states of a bodhisattva, I may as well
abstain from human food. Until then, I can't really be of any benefit
to beings." Just then, Avalokiteshvara appeared and said:

Worldly affairs and distractions are obstacles.
So long as the various thoughts of anger and attachment re-
    main unhelpful,
Stay always in a hermitage where the conditions are good.
Life is fleeting.
Think of death.

Following this, my practice quickly regained its power.
Before sunrise on the next full moon, I had a vision of the Thirteen-Deity Mandala of Hevajra wielding weapons, his body the size
of a mountain. On the twenty-second day of that same month, I
dreamt that I went to Dhanyakata and saw the faces of the Five Tantric
Deities, all singing in one voice:

If you haven't perfected the four empowerments, how can there
    be maturation?
If you haven't meditated on the inseparability of the genera-
    tion [and completion] stages, how can there be liberation?
If you still long and hope for attainments, how can there be
    fruition?
Natural self-liberation is inseparable from the three bodies of
    enlightenment.

This they repeated three times.
Next, my dreams led me to seek and receive from my Lama the
empowerments, *sadhanas*, and special instructions for the Five Tantric

Deities. At that point, I thought to myself, "Now, I must practice to remove the veil to the knowable." I was practicing diligently one day when I saw three hundred horsemen approach me. They said, "Your uncle Ba Thamche Khyenpa has passed away. Please come and take over the monastery."

"Oh no, I'm not going!" I said, "You'd better look for someone else. From now until death, there's only one thing I'm going to do, and that is practice!" However, my Lama Mokchokpa insisted that I go, enjoining me to keep my practice flourishing, and to remember that the Six-Armed Wisdom Protector, Mahakala, was here to serve me. I had to obey my Lama, so I went to Kyergang and had a monastery erected. (This became my main residence.) The monastery was in need of strong walls. To proceed with the building, I gathered all the construction materials, but people grumbled that the land was not good for laying foundations and prevented me from going ahead with the building. I exclaimed, "Well, I'm supposed to have a protector acting as my servant, and yet I can't even get a single wall built!"

The protector must have taken me seriously because that night the families who had been sabotaging the building fell ill and died. Others were seriously sick. I was filled with regret and intoned the seven-week prayer for the dead, convinced that I should leave all this worldly pettiness behind. It was so distracting. So after spending one month paying tribute to the memory of the previous abbot—my uncle Ba Thamche Khyenpa—I decided to do another retreat.

Every night I made circumambulations from dusk to dawn, never going to sleep. My Dream Yoga and Clear Light Yoga became very powerful. One night, I dreamt I went to the gods' realms after making offerings on the shrine. The relics of the Buddhas were kept in the crystal stupa of a heavenly mansion fashioned out of precious gems, and emitted a five-colored floodlight throughout the ten directions. Devotional goddesses presented offerings to it. The Five Tantric Deities were all within the heavenly castle, one next to the other. Behind the deities were rows of gods, *nagas*, demons, and the scent-eaters of the bardo, all making offerings.

I immediately created imaginary offerings—outer, inner, and secret—and presented these. At this sight, the whole assembly of dakinis
said with one voice, "Such offerings, O noble son! E MA HO!" And
they repeated it three times. Then, light rays streamed from the heart
centers of the Tantric Deities and they spoke thus, "O noble son,
approach, and we will bestow empowerments on you!" I received the
four complete empowerments. When this was done, the gods, the
Five Tantric Deities, myself, and all those present realized union
Mahamudra free of arising or cessation. I sang this song:

> The heavenly mansion is built of precious gems.
> In it stands the most perfect stupa
> Which contains the relics of the seven great Buddhas.
> By presenting imaginary offerings,
> I have realized union Mahamudra,
> The experience of illusoriness free of reference points.

In another lucid dream, I went to Mount Potala. On top of a gem-
embedded shrine, Avalokiteshvara sat bedecked with ornaments, clear
light in nature. He was surrounded by his retinue. On a high throne
was Kasarpani the Great Compassionate One, sitting like an eight-
year old child. He was in the posture of requesting the Dharma, and
said:

> You all, gods, *nagas*, demons, and scent-eaters of the bardo:
> The incarnation of pure compassion
> Will reveal the mahayana Dharma.
> Now ask whatever questions you wish.

All the gods, *nagas*, demons, and scent-eaters of the bardo were seated
on lotus stalks on the peak of Mount Potala, holding tributes in their
hands. They made their requests to Kasarpani who, in turn, repeated
these to the lord Avalokiteshvara and his two retinues.
Avalokiteshvara spoke in the languages of each, "Purify your birth
impulse[134] and perform secret practices."

At that moment, Avalokiteshvara displayed eleven faces. From his three main chakras, three beams of light shone and dissolved into my own three chakras. My body was transformed into the body of Avalokiteshvara. His eleven faces intoned the mantras that purify delusions, gave teachings related to his long mantra, and demanded that the Potala mantra be memorized. Then he added, "All of you who saw this will never again fall into the three lower realms. You will all attain the state of Avalokiteshvara."

Further dream experiences enabled me to see what occurred in far-off places, and to invoke the protectors' help when needed. One evening, I was circumambulating the monastery when I saw the sky gleam with effulgence. Rahula appeared with bow and arrow in his hands. He had eyes all over his face and body, and he breathed out flashes of lightning from his mouth. His body was the color of smoke. The sky, filled with the eight kinds of spirits, was a terrific sight. I cried out, "May the three jewels, Buddha, Dharma, and Sangha, protect sentient beings from such frightful sights!" A white goddess appeared to the left of Rahula, saying:

> My child, look into your own mind.
> You're afraid and mistake your own mind for demons.
> Abandon this clinging and cherishing of the physical.
> It is all illusory, appearance-emptiness, like the reflection of an
>     image.
> So why be afraid? Why fear?
> Pay heed and listen with devotion:
> Extract ink out of sandalwood,
> Use it to write down the names of the Tathagatas[135]
> Use it to write an homage to the Victors—Nagaraja and so on.
> Carry these with you in an amulet,
> And you will be protected from fear.

So saying, she vanished. Further dream experiences took me to different realms. I came face to face with Padmasambhava and deities such as Hayagriva and Avalokiteshvara. The following morning, I was in my cave reciting the seven-branch prayer to Buddha Shakyamuni and was in the process of confessing all my downfalls when, at the entrance to the cave, the dakini Sukhasiddhi appeared. She looked like a beautiful sixteen-year old girl, her body white in color and her hair flowing freely down her back. In her right hand, she held the sword of the three doors of emancipation and her left hand was at her heart with her fingers touching. In a clear, vivid voice, she said:

Listen, O noble son!
The sky is empty and non-conceptual.
Cut the root of this conceptual mind.
Cut the root and relax.

Tara also appeared in my cave while I was praying for the extinction of the three poisons—attachment, aversion, and ignorance. She sang these verses:

If you abandon dualistic clinging,
Attachment will be naturally pacified.

If you recognize all beings as your mothers and fathers,
Aversion will be spontaneously liberated.

If you realize non-conceptual luminosity,
Ignorance will dissolve in its sphere.

The three poisons are unconditioned—
Don't cling to this or that one, and liberation will occur on its
    own grounds.

See your afflictive emotions
As self-arising, self-liberated.

The clairvoyance of my Dream Yoga enabled me to resolve obstacles for scholars and disciples. However, I still created and experienced karma myself.

A man asked me to perform a consecration with the tooth of the Medicine Buddha. The man looked like he came from the Mön region of southeast Tibet.[136] I looked at the tooth and contemptuously declared it deficient. For the next few days, I had to bear a terrible toothache. I became very ill. Jetsunma Tara appeared and said, "You said that the relic was no good. This is the karmic ripening of your words." I confessed then before the relic of the Medicine Buddha. Let us be mindful of even the slightest deeds, because all have karmic repercussions. Also, let us immediately confess and purify our negativities, no matter how small.

I once spoke badly of the man Driwo Gönpo because he was known to kill for food. I called him Murder-Man! On the day he passed away, in my Dream Yoga practice I went to his cremation site. Inside the cremation shrine was Nairatmya with fifteen goddesses, looking at me. I said, "Please let me come inside and see your face, O deity."

But Nairatmya replied, "The deceased whom you once slandered was a great tantric yogi. Now make your confessions!" I made a heartfelt confession and heard Hevajra and his consort[137] making the spontaneous sound of the vowels and consonants. Nairatmya said:

> O noble son,
> The life and attainments of a yogi practicing the esoteric tantras
> Are indescribable.
> If you don't have omniscience, don't pretend to know the minds
>     of others.
> So be mindful of karmic deeds that lead to the Hell of Unceasing Torment.[138]
> Your own mind is still defiled—you must train in sacred outlook.
> Nothing can be accomplished without confession and repentance.

With these words, she disappeared. Through this Dream Yoga practice, it occurred to me that I should, in a dream, ask for the Great
Pacifier Precepts according to the method of Pakmo Drupa.[139] I prayed
fervently for such a dream to take place. The great Padampa Sangye
appeared to me and gave me the instructions for elevating the three
poisons[140] to the tantric path. Then he said, "Sentient beings doing
this secret practice should meditate on me and pray, and they will
receive my blessings."

Jealousy gripped the teacher Lhading as more and more people
came to learn the Dharma from me. He spread rumors behind my
back—that I may be a so-called 'Dharma Lion' but in reality my teachings were just some special Brahmin spirit practices. He also said that
I was deceiving people with supposed supernatural powers, and that
if any merit had been gathered from my actions, it was far from pure!
Such is the maturation of negative karma created in the past. The
fact is, in one of my previous lives I went to India and met the sage
Dharmapala with his fifty monks. I became very clever about the
meaning of Dharma. I thought that in all of India, no one knew the
hinayana and mahayana doctrines better than I did. Although I wasn't
motivated by anger or jealousy, my attitude was improper nevertheless. If you break your *samaya*,[141] you'll have to go through the same
that I've gone through. This is the way karma ripens—in my case,
wherever I am born, I am always being slandered.

I used every incident to develop visions of my yidam deities—
Avalokiteshvara and others. Furthermore, through the kindness of
all the Shangpa Lamas, I was able to practice Illusory Body Yoga and
Dream Yoga. As my sacred outlook became increasingly pure, I gained
understanding and taught for the benefit of others. I also spent more
time with my Lama Mokchokpa before moving on.

A few years later, I had a gnawing suspicion that my Lama
Mokchokpa was about to pass away. On the night of the eighteenth,
I had a lucid dream: I went to my Lama's room and saw dakinis and
non-humans. My Lama said, "Wöntön [Kyergangpa], I'm glad that
you came. I will go soon! Come back tomorrow."

I was crying uncontrollably when the noble Vajrayogini appeared and said, "Your Lama has gone to meet Buddha Amitabha in the Blissful Pure Land and will go to the Pure Land of Joy. Pray that you may go to that pure realm yourself:

> Just as the sky is not born, and does not die,
> So the Lama is not born, and does not die.
> Your strong faith and devotion keep the Lama inseparable from
>     you.
> Don't be sad! Pray to the Pure Land of Joy.

These words made me long for the Pure Land of Joy. But just then, I woke up from my dream.

I spent the next three days secluded in prayer when several messengers from Shang arrived with the news that my Lama had died. I said that I knew my Lama had passed away three days earlier, and added, "I'm going to give everything I own as an offering. You should do likewise." I spent the next month making offerings to the memory of my Lama.

At dawn on the eighth day of the following month, Avalokiteshvara appeared and said, "When you're not in solitary retreat and people request pointing-out instructions or secret practices, you should give them Avalokiteshvara teachings. If you teach such practices in these degenerate times, many will have visions of me." On the fourteenth day of the same month, eleven-faced Avalokiteshvara appeared and said, "Kyergangpa, you and I are inseparable. You are truly in Mount Potala."


### Kyergangpa now concludes


Now, I AM old, and it's better to sit here in Kyergang and sleep than run around everywhere trying to do good things. In Shang, my students have had visions of Avalokiteshvara and seen the faces of dozens of Lamas. I have many disciples and lineage holders who generate such visions. Visions of Avalokiteshvara are particular to my transmission. In fact, Avalokiteshvara himself has predicted that in the future, many more will have similar visions. This should give you conviction! This has been a brief summary of my life written for the benefit of Drakpa Yeshe the scholar and Nakpo Zhöntsul.

*Kyergangpa's last days and final advice are recounted by his students*

LAMA KYERGANGPA TOLD us, "Remember, when you perform your so-called Dharma practice and are mindless of the genuine Dharma, that death may come tomorrow, or the next day. And then, you might just die gasping, like a deer choking on a bamboo shoot. Your face will lose color. Oh yes, when in the throes of death, you'll cry out a late promise: 'If I don't die now, I'll do nothing but practice Dharma, I swear.' So what? You're dying, you die. Be careful, this can happen.

"My disciples, sons and daughters," Kyergangpa continued, "it is in our nature to die. As for me, in the beginning, when it was time to think of the Dharma, I thought of the Dharma. In the middle, when it was time to practice Dharma, I practiced Dharma. And now at the end, when I need the Dharma, I have it!"

"This place used to be peopled with *nagas* and vicious demons but I have subdued them all," he explained. "For as long as my blessings last, this Kyergang is the real Mount Potala. The mountain solitudes in other areas where I have meditated will be happy places for people to sleep in. But in the future, the rural people will gather in a central city; and this place will be covered in dog shit. There will be constant bustle and women with crying babies. Demons and *nagas* will return. The teachings will be scant. At that time, my blessings will be gone and people won't even be able to practice single-pointedly."

This concludes the life story of Wöntön Kyergangpa.

SARWA MANGALAM! SHUBHO! GEO!

# 7

# Secret Lives of Kyergangpa

IN THE HARE year, during the waxing moon, we were performing the Supplication for the Blessings of the White Dakini. On that particular evening, there were only three disciples: Nakpo Zhöntsul, Drakpa Yeshe, and myself, Rigongpa.

I presented Lama Kyergangpa with seven blankets and asked, "Lama, please tell us about your previous lives." But Kyergangpa just said, "There's not much to talk about, and what there is would not be understood."

Still I persisted, "Dear Lama, please tell us a little of what it was like for you, in your previous lives." I insisted so much that he finally gave in, saying, "Very well, I shall tell you. But should it ever be told to others who lack faith and devotion, then may the wisdom protector do his work!"

My Lama Kyergangpa, in one of his past lives, was born on a land bordering India, an area full of deep ravines and prickly thorns, where the Buddha's teachings had not appeared. He was born to the Tritra family, from the man Ralpachen, and his wife Utsuma. Together, they had seven sons, and he was the fifth, named Ziji Drakpa. By the time he was seven, he had already worked for some time as a herdsman and he thought to himself, "This place is beautiful, but I still haven't met with a spiritual guide. I should go to the nearby village." So he left and headed toward the town's marketplace, where he approached a yogi riding a tiger. The yogi threw knives in the air and brought down a rain of flowers. Kyergangpa was very impressed by this, aroused devotion, prostrated, made circumambulations and asked, "Please hold me in your compassion!" The yogi replied:

> All activities are of the relative truth.
> If you realize non-activity, you will attain nirvana.
> And yet—even the Buddhas of the three times
> Actively gather the two accumulations[142] for the benefit of self
>    and other.

The yogi disappeared into the air. Kyergangpa then went to the Mune River to practice. Buddha Kashyapa had erected a temple on its shore. A leper woman standing in front of this temple asked Kyergangpa, "Do you seek the Dharma?" Kyergangpa replied, "Yes, I do."
   So the leper woman sang this song:

> One's own mind is unborn from the outset.
> Its very nature is emptiness.
> Ride the horse of compassion and transcendent union.
> Practice to benefit self and others.

With these words she disappeared. After this, Kyergangpa tried to teach the Dharma to his father and others, but he didn't gather many disciples. Finally, when he was seventy-two, he displayed his passing into nirvana.
   Next, my dear Lama Kyergangpa took rebirth in Ngari in Far-West Tibet. His father was Zhangzhung Tsun, and his mother, Ödenma. He was one of their two sons. When he turned seventeen, he asked his father who would be a good Lama with whom to practice Dharma, but his father replied, "Our lineage follows the Bön tradition, and not the Dharma. You must learn the Bön teachings." And his father

took him to the city to study under three Bön teachers. On the northern slope of Mount Kailash, Kyergangpa stayed at the place of a Shiva-worshipping sage. Kyergangpa gained the ability to exhibit miracles such as walking through the air and so forth.

Shortly after this, he was meditating in a cave by the lakeshore when a great white bird appeared and said:

> Living right by the ocean yet your thirst unslaked,
> Staying on an island of treasures yet leaving empty-handed . . .
> If you can free yourself from the ocean of samsara and renounce
>     evil deeds,
> That would be truly praiseworthy.

The bird then vanished. After this, Kyergangpa decided to return home to his family and think about what had happened. He recalled a line from the Sutra of Advice to the Sovereign,[143] "All birth ends in death. All meeting ends in separation." Keeping this in mind, and entering into *samadhi* meditation as he had in past lives, he perceived that the bird was an emanation of Avalokiteshvara. He gave birth to non-referential compassion toward all beings as numerous as space is vast, and brought great benefit to others.

My Lama Kyergangpa next took a rebirth in China to a rich and miserly father. In this incarnation, he went on pilgrimage and gained visions of Manjushri that induced a profound meditative stability in his mindstream. Later he spent time practicing in Trashigo. There resided a phantom-king called Dharmashri who, in the past, had faith in the Buddhas. However, now he was a heretic. Every day, this king sacrificed a thousand buffaloes. So Kyergangpa took on the emanation of Kartika [Mahadeva's younger son] in order to subdue this heretic king. The phantom-king saw Kartika, and taking him for a god, invited him respectfully, "Deity, you have come. Please take a seat. Let's sacrifice a buffalo for the occasion."

"That's not my kind of food!" Kyergangpa-Kartika replied.

"Oh?" the phantom-king asked with curiosity. "What do you eat, then?"

"I eat only pure food: the three whites and the three sweets.[144] I don't touch food produced through evil deeds."

The phantom-king replied, "But aren't you one of those Mahadeva deities who eats flesh and drinks blood?" At that moment, Kyergangpa sent forth a fire of enlightened activity from his breast. Flames engulfed the phantom-king who cried out, "Please forgive me! Tell me what I must do, I'll do it!"

"Bring the teachings to all who seek them!" Kyergangpa-Kartika ordered. "Practice the ten virtues!"[145]

To the north of Atar was a dense forest in which one of the Buddha's attendants had erected a stupa. This shrine had not been maintained, and thousands of monkeys were wrecking it and urinating on it. Since he had thought deeply about these migrating sentient beings trapped in inferior rebirths, my dear Lama Kyergangpa decided to take rebirth as lord of the monkeys. In that life, he still wore gem ornaments on his head and held a wooden mala. He taught by prostrating to the shrine, circumambulating it, and instructing the monkeys to do likewise, which led them to some understanding of cause and effect. "Now, you monkeys, listen carefully," he said, and sang:

Outside, see appearances as inseparable: this is View.
Inside, maintain awareness free of grasping: this is Meditation.
In between, harbor no acceptance or rejection: this is Action.

Hearing these words, many of the monkeys developed a direct perception of the ultimate truth and gained happiness. This reached the ears of the local people who whispered that in the dense forest of Atar, a single monkey succeeded in making all the monkeys happy. Soon people were coming up to see for themselves. As the news spread, the King heard about it and met with Kyergangpa who was still manifesting as the lord of the monkeys. The King asked, "Why are you all so wise? What makes you so happy?"

"Long life to you, King of the most noble lineage," Kyergangpa replied and sang this song:

Use your undeceiving cognition to cut doubts—
Cause and effect arise interdependently.
Understand that the nature of mind itself
Has always been the great bliss body of reality.

"And if this is a lie," Kyergangpa wagered, "may all the monkeys die right now!" The King and his court were overwhelmed by these words. Tears ran down their faces and in wonder they exclaimed, "Emah!" They prostrated themselves over and over again before leaving. Kyergangpa said:

All of us here are monkeys.
It doesn't matter what appearances arise,
Just know that they are the six consciousnesses,[146] free of fixation.
It doesn't matter what thoughts show up,
Just know that they are mind itself, without basis.
It does not matter which of the five poisons come up,
Just know that they are the clear-light body of reality.

As Kyergangpa spoke, all those present had a direct perception of the true nature of reality. At that moment, the earth shook and rainbow radiance glowed in the sky for all to see.

My Lama Kyergangpa next took rebirth in eastern India. His father was a great Brahmin named Zangpo Pal, and his mother was named Dawa Özer. Kyergangpa was the oldest of seven sons, and was called Zijichen. At seventeen, he took monastic ordination. Kyergangpa received the name Sherab Gocha and studied the Collection of Six Treatises by Kamalashila.[147]

At that time, a demon-faced heretic declared that he would use all means available to cause the deterioration of the Buddha's teachings, but Kyergangpa defeated him in debate. Meanwhile, the learned and skilled yogi Ravigupta[148] engaged a Mongolian sage in debate and was defeated. Ravigupta was required to study with the Mongolian who, in this current life, is Mokchokpa, my Lama's Lama.

In the charnel ground of Kalin in the west, Kyergangpa practiced in front of a self-arisen shrine, when a very small yogi with red eyes and a wooden sword at his side appeared and said, "Life is short and offers no happiness. Listening to the Dharma awakens infinite awareness within. Look into this pristine, unfabricated mirror! Once you abandon samsara, there's no nirvana to be realized!" Hearing this, Kyergangpa perceived all phenomena as one-taste. This yogi, in this present life, is Penpukpa, teacher to my Lama Kyergangpa.

My dear Lama Kyergangpa next took a rebirth in which he devoted himself to studies and debate in his youth. Later, he met yogis in charnel grounds and they advised him to stay in solitude.

In his next life, Kyergangpa went looking for a temple of Avalokiteshvara in Bodhgaya. There was an old lady by the roadside, holding a mala of lotus flowers. She asked, "Where are you going?"

"I'm going to see Avalokiteshvara"

"If you meditate on love, compassion, and bodhichitta," the old woman said, "you, yourself, will become the Great Compassionate One. But without meditation, you will never reach enlightenment. Remember that Avalokiteshvara is intimately united with compassion." With these words, she disappeared. The old woman is Pakpa Chegom in this life, teacher to my Lama Kyergangpa.

In this life, I, Rigongpa, served my Lama Kyergangpa. I asked if he would please concern himself about the expansion of the tradition. He replied, "Sentient beings form plans and designs, but they are just like sand castles, built and soon destroyed—there's not much point to them."

May the merit of our continuous faith and devotion in the Lama— a wish-fulfilling jewel in a stainless ocean—enable us to step on the raft that carries us across the samsaric river. May we find refuge in the inseparability of wisdom and skillful means. Let us set out for the island of precious bodhichitta! With faith and devotion always present in our six senses, may we discover the treasure of spontaneous ben-

efit for both self and other, marked by clear-light emptiness inseparable.

On the night these stories were revealed, Kyergangpa gave the
Chakrasamvara empowerment. Because the teachings are secret, I,
Sangye Nyentön Rigongpa, was instructed to wait twenty-five years
before putting them down on paper. To prevent this transmission from
disappearing, I finally set it down in the ox year. Should this reach the
hands of someone who has neither faith nor devotion, may Heruka
split his or her head in seven pieces!

SARWA DAKALYA CHIWA BHANTU! SHUWO!

# 8

# Life of Rigongpa

BORN TO A family in Yöl,[149] I, Rigongpa, was naturally inclined to the Dharma and sought early on to devote my life to benefiting others. I received a dream vision of a black being, a servant of the protector. Then I met my Lama Kyergangpa and stayed at his side.

One evening, Lama Kyergangpa performed the protector empowerment and torma offering. Once he had given me the entire oral instructions, he said, "This protector is like a servant to you. You will quickly see his face." The next night before daybreak, the Lama said he wanted to go for a walk. We headed out and he pointed to something in the distance, "Look at that big tree trunk over there!" In the darkness, I could make out the wisdom protector, Mahakala, in the midst of an expanse of fire, dancing and trampling on a person with his two feet. I saw his face, his tongue rolling in his mouth, and heard his frightening laughter. Then the protector Kshetrapala tore out the person's heart and presented it to Mahakala. I asked Lama Kyergangpa why this violence was taking place. He replied, "I didn't know that Kshetrapala was going to kill the man. Perhaps this individual is the one who caused damage to the water mill. But take a look for yourself!" I stole another glance at the frightful scene and saw the protector Mahakala grab the man by the neck and hurl him down on the ground a few feet away. The man was dead. So my Lama proceeded to recite the seven-week prayers for the dead and I did the same.

Another time, my Lama said, "Look at the butter lamp I'm holding. See the light falling on this flower? Use it as a point of focus in your meditation and then pray. Now go practice. Good realizations will come from it!" I went to a cave and made fervent prayers. The dakini Sukhasiddhi appeared. Three times she said, "Yogi, place your mind in non-referential awareness." The essence of that realization has never altered.

That fall, after Lama Kyergangpa prophesized about my future, I fetched more supplies and stayed in Kyergang. Lama Kyergangpa transmitted all the secret mantras, leaving nothing out. He then told me, again, about his lives as well as about my past and future lives, but this time in great detail. He also told me how long my present life would last.

He advised me, "You should be a secret yogi—drinking beer, eating the food offerings, and enjoying mixed company [not limited to monks]. People will say that you are not keeping your *samaya* and are acting dishonorably. Pay them no heed! Continue to wear your old rags and even sleep in them. During your exposition of the Dharma, leave out the aspiration prayers at the beginning and the dedication prayers at the end. When you teach *sadhanas* and pith instructions, offer little praise. Teach modestly, as if you were uncertain.

"In general," my Lama continued, "you will establish connections with many students. In particular, you will have ten fully realized disciples who will hold your transmission. I know this because in my dream, ten people asked for the relics of the Shangpa Lamas. Each of these ten individuals carried the relics and when asked who they were, they replied that they were the retinue of Sangye Nyentön—you, Rigongpa. That was my dream. You will become renowned as Sangye Nyentön Rigongpa. Although you will have hundreds and thousands of followers, your ten realized disciples will be better than all the others."

After encounters with Waruna water deities and a vision of my Lama Kyergangpa as Avalokiteshvara, Lord of Great Compassion, I set myself up in a hut in the Rigong region[150] to meditate. Later that day, a shepherd showed up on a hill just above my hut and insulted me. Two days later, Drakshema came at daybreak, riding a lion and holding weapons in her four hands. She tore out the shepherd's heart and dropped it in my hands, commenting, "A couple of days ago, this man insulted you, teacher!"

I scolded Drakshema, "Look, you were not supposed to kill human beings. You shouldn't have killed this shepherd." But it was too late: the shepherd vomited blood and died. I proceeded to recite the seven-week prayers for the dead shepherd and great compassion arose in me.

But my vicissitudes with the protectors were not over. One summer I found stones left at the water mill and was wondering who had abandoned them there. Just then, the wrathful goddess Remate appeared, riding a fat mule. In her four hands, she held a hooked knife, a skull-cup, and a bannered lance as she boasted, "I've destroyed all your enemies at the water mill!"

I exclaimed, "I told you not to go there and kill human beings!"

But she was nonplussed and replied, "It's just too bad. You don't let us go where we want, you don't let us kill whom we want. What misery! Anyhow, about the water mill," she continued innocently, "I couldn't help it! It just collapsed, and your enemies died. Oh, I did obey you, great Lama!" I tried hard to subdue her and make her desist, but it seems that I didn't have much success.

Then, toward the end of winter, Drakshema appeared with Kshetrapala and asked if I would make a Mahakala statue. "Let's strike a deal," I said. "If you don't kill human beings, I will make the Mahakala statue." All these examples show that if I didn't restrain the protectors, they would worsen every time I offered tormas. So in this way, I emphasized the point of restraint as much as possible, hoping to benefit them a little.

I was once exhorting the protector Mahakala in just this way when a daka appeared with a *damaru* drum and a bell and sat himself to the right of the protector while smiling dakinis appeared to the left of the protector. Thus, I was able to admonish both dakas and dakinis at once by saying, "In general, because Six-Armed Mahakala is the wish-fulfilling gem, he leads to the attainment of all realizations and fulfills all wishes. More specifically, because he is the blessings protector, his blessings are swift and his powers great. Since he holds beings dearly, he appears to anyone who prays to him with sincere faith and devotion. He will protect us from all your obstacles. Now, because of obscurations, we do not perceive his true nature. Nevertheless, we should keep faith. From Shavaripa all the way down to me, Mahakala has always been like a servant to our lineage."

Sixteen of my disciples had visions of Mahakala that were as direct as meeting someone face to face. I was on good terms with all the protectors because of their powers and affection for beings. I'm referring to the seventy-five glorious protectors, the Lhamo Remate, the four demons, the protectors of pure lineages, the female guardian deities, and the ten guardians of the ten directions. Nevertheless, I was afraid that these protectors would go and kill human beings, so I never revealed to them where enemies of the Dharma might be, or gave them torma offerings. Furthermore, every evening during the Mahakala practice, I commanded, "Do not kill human beings." I feared their deeds, and held them back.

When I was seventy-three, thunder and lightning burst forth and I was struck on the knees thirteen times. At that moment, my body became self-arising Mahamudra, the stainless deity body, appearance-emptiness free of attachment. Just then, Mahakala himself appeared. I realized that all the phenomena of samsara appear and yet are unborn. I was neither scared nor surprised and the lightning hurt me no more than raindrops falling on a flower.[151] Soon, five wisdom dakinis appeared, red-black, wearing bone ornaments, and throwing blood-colored flowers. They placed me on a rainbow-like cloth, saying, "From there, you will bring benefit to more beings. Come, we'll guide you." I objected, telling them that I would like to stay [in this body] a little longer. Together, they answered:

Lama, Buddha of the three times,
You have disciples in other realms.

If you want, stay here for a few more years
And look upon your disciples with great compassion.

To those who see, hear, or remember you:
No more downfall into the three lower realms.
To those of pure faith and devotion: perfect enlightenment.
And all those connected with you will be your principal dis-
    ciples
In the pure Buddha fields.

"In a few years," the dakinis continued, "we will return to guide you.
May all your disciples be later reborn with special experiences and
realizations." So saying, they threw a rainfall of flowers and disappeared. My desire to benefit my students was the reason why I stayed
here a few more years. This is my song:

When it's time for me to die,
Five dakinis will be my guides.
I will go to the Blissful Pure Land,
Land of banners, land of sounds.
Let there be no doubt at all—
A great yogi I will be!

I traveled to Buddha realms in my lucid dreams and granted
empowerments. A few months later, at dawn on the tenth day of fall,
a dakini appeared, intense blue in color, with red highlights. "What is
your name?" I asked her.

"I am Sukhasiddhi which means Bliss-Accomplishment," she replied.

"Why this name?"

The dakini answered, "Bliss, because my mind is filled with stainless wisdom. Accomplishment, because one can accomplish common
and extraordinary *siddhis* within a year or a month by praying to me."
The dakini proceeded to grant me the four complete empowerments
and the main points of the secret practices, more profound than ever

before. She also transmitted the supreme points on wisdom realizing the non-duality of bliss and emptiness. She gave me very special teachings. Then Sukhasiddhi added, "Yogi, since your body, speech, and mind are liberated, you must bless sentient beings with nectar pills. Anyone who sees you, hears you, or partakes of the nectar pills will never again fall into the three lower realms. Those who get empowerments from you will take rebirth as disciples in the Eastern Pure Land. But why say more? You are Vajradhara himself. Whoever arouses faith and devotion for you will become enlightened and will receive my blessings."

This was Sukhasiddhi's prophecy. Whoever has the empowerments and instructions and seriously engages in the generation and completion stages will definitely attain extraordinary and common *siddhis* within a year or even a month. The swiftness of the practices is what makes them so profound. In conclusion I sang:

> Yogis and yoginis, all you connected to me,
> Abandon erroneous thoughts,
> And always show respect and devotion.

> See my body as indistinguishable from the Buddha's body.
> Hear my speech as indistinguishable from the Buddha's speech.
> Understand my mind as indistinguishable from the Buddha's mind.
> This will blossom into great bliss,
> Self-arising deity body
> Inseparable from the three bodies of enlightenment.

> Yogis and yoginis, if you don't develop faith and devotion,
> You will never see the qualities of your Lama.
> But if you engender complete faith in your heart,
> You will understand that the Lama is himself a jewel—
> The body, speech, and mind of all the Buddhas of the three times.
> You will lead all sentient beings to maturation and liberation.

Of a genuine Lama, this is the life story.
Keep sacred outlook for it,
Don't arouse wrong views even for a second!

Realize that the Lama is the body of reality,
Practice diligently,
And all qualities will be perfected.

The ultimate pith of this story is respect and devotion.
To you all, students, engender sacred outlook!
Yogis, yoginis, always think this way!

This brief account of my life was written at the insistence of the
monk Zhönnu Senge.

SARWA DAKALYA NIBHA WANTU! GEO!

# 9

# Life of Sangye Tönpa

THE DHARMA LORD Sangye Tönpa summed up his life with these verses:

> With devotion I bow down at the feet of all the holy Lamas
> Who, through their kindness, establish us in the pure state.
> Apart from writing a secret story, I've also set down this brief account
> For the benefit of worthy disciples.
>
> In the beginning I studied with great faith and became a monk.
> Next, by listening, I cut through all external doubts.
> In the middle, I relied on my Lama as the actual Buddha,
> And pleased him with my practice and offerings.
> I drank the nectar of the dakinis' ear-whispered precepts
> And received the complete pith teachings of the oral lineage,
> As well as prophecies concerning the future of the Dharma and the future of the lineage.
> Once firm in the view, I realized the Lama as my own mind.
> From here, after death and the transference of consciousness, I shall go to a pure realm.

Of this, as you pray for me, you can be certain.
This brief account sums up my life.
Remember it with faith.


Born to a Bön family in Kharek Tse Silma, I found myself longing to practice Dharma. In all my activities, I spent no time on food or other such mundane pursuits except for nourishment during the planting season when I was digging.

"When harvest comes, what will it yield? And death, coming soon, what will she reap? What to do?" Such thoughts left me melancholy. To free myself from sadness, I would look out at the distant peaks and walk toward them. Then I felt as happy as a yogi taking to the mountains, or a deer running in the wind. I was drinking by the stream one day when I saw an adept. How I wanted to receive oral instructions for meditation! When I told the monk Jangchub Gönpo about this, he replied, "Child, you're too young to bother yourself with such thoughts. Your feelings are either an awakening of your previous karma, or else you're possessed by demons! You'll probably become a great scholar in due time."

I felt an overwhelming sense of renunciation, observed the futility of all things samsaric, and found myself without needs or longings. An impartial, sacred outlook dawned in me. I enjoyed spending my time restoring stupas. My days were colored in such ways, while at night I dreamt only and always of teaching the Dharma, offering flowers, and circumambulating stupas. Thus I entered the door of Dharma, and discerned signs of my obscurations diminishing.

On the thirteenth day of the new year, I turned thirteen and presented myself to the famed Lama Tsarirepa to take monks' vows. When it came time to shave my head in preparation for the ceremony, the Lama named me Tsöndrü Senge, meaning Lion of Perseverance, and explained, "I name you Tsöndrü, or Perseverance, for the tremendous benefit you'll bring to sentient beings through the energy you will devote to the Dharma. I name you Senge, or Lion, for the overpowering brilliance of your realizations." I was able to serve Tsarirepa only for a short time before he died.

After studying with several Lamas, I felt the need for a genuine secret yogi. So, late in the summer, I set out to meet Lama Rigongpa who was recommended to me by both Lama Zhupa Nakpo and the teacher Doktön. That same morning, Lama Rigongpa said to his attendant Kongpo, "I've received a prophecy that today I will meet a great meditator who will be the sole possessor of my oral instructions. This disciple will spread the Dharma from the provinces of Uddiyana and Jalandhara[152] across the ocean to other continents. Today, dakas and dakinis have come to greet him. Now you should sweep the house: this disciple is fond of cleanliness!"

The attendant swept the floor and prepared some offerings. The Lama followed and exclaimed, "Just about now, he should be in the village of Serchikma taking his food. Let's go welcome him!" They set out to meet me. No sooner had Rigongpa and his attendant, Kongpo, reached the monastery of Gangkarda and met me there when Lama Rigongpa said, "For three years, you've been meaning to come. During that time, your two teachers, Doktön and Zhupa Nakpo, who made prophecies that you would meet me, have both passed away."

Hearing him say this, I thought, "This Lama obviously has supernatural powers [he can read my mind and knows my past]."

Lama Rigongpa asked, "Why are you devoted to me? Why have you come?"

I replied, "I heard that you have mastered Dream Yoga and Illusory Body Yoga, realized the clear-light nature of mind, and seen many deities. I also heard that you can see Dharma protectors as clearly as meeting a person face to face and they act as your servants. This inspired me with faith, and I set out to meet you. Please Lama, grant me the Shangpa teachings."

At that, he replied, "There's no difference between seeing me and seeing a yidam deity. Those who differentiate won't see me. All of my pith instructions are encapsulated in the teaching called the Three Bodies.[153] Let it sink in:

By merely imagining the Buddha's enlightened body within
   the fully ripened body,
All aspirations are fulfilled.
Without points of reference, this illusory body simply wan-
   ders, like a vagabond.
This is the teaching of the Lama of one's own mind.

By merely imagining the Buddha's enlightened body within
   the habitual body,
All aspirations are fulfilled.
Without points of reference, this illusory body simply wan-
   ders, like a vagabond.
This is the teaching of the Lama of one's own mind.

By merely imagining the Buddha's enlightened body within
   the mental body,
All aspirations are fulfilled.
Without points of reference, this illusory body simply wan-
   ders, like a vagabond.
This is the teaching of the Lama of one's own mind.

I stayed by Rigongpa's side that night. I saw a frightening cluster of
yogis and dark beings. The next morning, I was convinced of my
Lama's credentials and asked for teachings. My offerings did not im-
press Rigongpa who said that ostentatious objects do not buy the
teachings. After a brief teaching on the protector, Rigongpa promised to grant me the instructions.

   I brought fifty measures of barley which I exchanged for a good
quality knife, and I also placed one pot of molasses and woolen blankets in preparation for the empowerment. On the twenty-fifth night
of the month, my Lama said, "Recognize death, and I'll take care of
you. Now, the protector will always accompany you in your practices. Be confident in all your prayers!" And then he added, "Next

month I'll give you the Illusory Body Yoga empowerment, so remember to bring the necessary objects!"

I gathered many such things, including seventy measures of butter
and barley, gold and other valuables, silk, and woolen blankets. Then
I asked my Lama if I was to get the complete empowerments, and
Lama Rigongpa answered that he would give me two empowerments,
that of Illusory Body Yoga and that of the Path of Means [Inner Heat
Yoga]. I started by performing the preliminary practices. Next, I received the instructions of the Path of Means. After eleven days, I was
able to wear a mere cotton robe.

"At night on the tenth this month," said the Lama, "I'll give you
the actual empowerments."

A while later, I was drawing a mandala when the Lama approached
and said, "You will be empowered for Illusory Body Yoga by all the
lineage masters from Vajradhara all the way down to me. Your practice will be the greatest! You will be guided by the blessings of all the
Lamas of the lineage, mine in particular. Don't make the mistake of
being proud, thinking that you alone have done something special.
Instead, be confident that these are the blessings of the Lamas of the
lineage.

"In my next life," continued Rigongpa, "I'll be reborn in the Eastern Pure Land, called Metok Trampa, and will attain enlightenment
as the Thus-Gone Foe-Destroyer, the perfect realized Buddha, knower
of the world, tamer of beings, unsurpassable teacher of gods and
humans. I'll bear the name Pedma Pal, or Glorious Lotus. At that
time, you will be giving empowerments. When you teach, my blessings will be there. There won't be anyone you cannot reach through
your precepts—even those beings who've committed heinous
crimes,[154] of dull and sharp faculties, young and old.

"In general, at the time of [Shakyamuni] Buddha's complete enlightenment, sentient beings had little of the three veils.[155] But at
present, these three veils are very thick. In his time, Shakyamuni Buddha gave ordination through messages and invitations, and countless
individuals became saints. But once the Buddha is gone, it's hard to
become a saint. The command given to the saints has past, and it is

more difficult to fulfill it now. It is more difficult now to bring forth the Dharma and to receive teachings and commentaries. It is more difficult now for virtuous rulers to appear. Today, people cling to the mere symbols of the teachings. Thus, it is more difficult for authentic practice to take place. Yet, in spite of these difficulties, many disciples will take the bodhisattva vow from you and enter the path."

After I gained experience in Illusory Body Yoga, the Lama ordered me to do without sleep and pray. So I prayed until daybreak when I fell asleep for a short while. No sooner had I fallen asleep than a hundred enormous black dogs showed up, their mouths wide open and fangs bared. "You look like a good meal," the dogs grinned, "we've eaten a lot of humans in the past!" I was petrified with fear but the thought somehow surfaced in my mind that these dogs existed only in my dream. I emanated many wolves that ate the dogs. Then I transformed all the wolves into yidam deities offering prayers to the Lama, and practiced multiplication and transformation within the dream. That's when I thought that it would be good if I were to see the Buddhas' pure lands, but I soon woke up. When I related this dream to my Lama, he said, "Your practice is going well, which is in keeping with your superior faculties. You have managed within twenty-five days [of the empowerment] to perform together the Dream Yoga practices of training, multiplication, emanation, and transformation, a feat even the Lamas of the lineage couldn't match. The black dogs in your dream were the protectors. They assist you in your Dharma practice. Usually they only appear after many years, but they've come to you within a short period of time, which means that you're protected by dakas and dakinis. Be grateful!"

In the fall, I stayed at the monastery to store the salt supplies. Since I was distributing the supplies during the day, I didn't have time to practice. So I performed my practices—reciting the Manjushri Uttering the Names Tantra and the Hevajra tantra—at night. Within the dream state, I could complete my practice in about three hours in the middle of the night. Since I could not possibly accomplish a million recitations in a day, but could easily do so in the dream state, I asked the Lama if this was valid. "What makes one's practice at night so much more powerful than one's daytime practice," my Lama replied, "is its swiftness. The great Shangpa Lama Kyergangpa was getting old and still wanted to do two hundred and fifty recitations of the Manjushri Uttering the Names Tantra. He couldn't have completed this in the daytime, so he practiced in his dreams."

At festivities toward the end of winter, the Lama said, "Be present when I perform the empowerment. Vajrayogini will reveal her face." On the tenth evening of the month, Vajrayogini granted the empowerment and was seen by five disciples when she transmitted the blessings. The following day after the meal the Lama said, "Come to my room and bring torma offerings." I came and he said, "You have Vajrayogini and her four retinues staying by your side. You should present them seven pure offerings." I presented my offerings and the Lama asked, "Now, do you see the face of Vajrayogini?"

"No I don't, Lama."

"Well," the Lama enquired, "do you hear the sound of the Dharma she is teaching you?"

"No I don't, Lama."

"That is because you have fear—an obscuration due to negative karma. The Jetsunma Vajrayogini is here, teaching you the Dharma, yet you neither see nor hear her. Still, there is one instruction for an immediate vision of Vajrayogini, which will dispel all obstacles and redress all transgressions. Pay close attention and write it down." So the Jetsunma spoke to my Lama and he, in turn, passed the instructions down to me. The first two times, I didn't catch it all. But by the third time, I had it written down correctly. The Jetsunma Vajrayogini then spoke, "It is all accurate now." She added, "You don't see me yet but you will soon have *siddhis*—both common and extraordinary. Always keep the vows of secrecy. If you don't, then common *siddhis* will degenerate and weaken. Meditate on this for the next three months and you will have a vision of my face."

I gained the ability to transform foul-tasting barley beer into the finest flavor, multiply its quantity, and change the nutrition and potency of the drink. All those who drank it were cured of illness and evil spirits and their practice immediately improved. Even though I tried to keep my powers secret, friends and other disciples talked about it. As a result, after three years, these powers waned. My Lama remarked, "If you had kept this secret for three months, you would have seen the face of the Jetsunma and gained visions of all the yidam deities. But since you didn't keep practicing in secret, the results have been postponed. Now you see, it's extremely important to keep concealed whatever qualities one has developed."

My Dream Yoga practice became powerful. One particular night, I had the following lucid dream: I was walking toward a great lake when I found myself inside a *naga* palace fashioned out of the four kinds of precious gems. I saw a black nine-headed *naga* with the upper body of a human and the lower part of a snake. He was surrounded by countless other *nagas*. Just as I was thinking that I should try and subdue him, he displayed several emanations at once and made the palace disappear. Then the ocean turned black, rocked by a series of large waves. I manifested into a black nine-headed *garuda*. Immediately, the *naga* began to spew blood from his nine heads. With my *garuda* claws, I grabbed his neck, but his tail began to grow longer and longer with no end in sight. I wondered, "What should I do?" At that instant, the Lama appeared in the sky, surrounded by a host of dakinis. He spoke these words, "The *naga*'s magical apparitions have no end: for months and years, his tail can grow and grow! He is known as the Black Butcher, and he embodies the five poisons. Emanate five *garudas* to subdue this five-sided *naga*! Cut his tails, chop his body, and eat the tails! That's the only way to subdue him." So I changed my nine-headed *garuda* into five emanations, chopped the *naga*'s tails and body, and ate the tails. By then, the *naga* was begging me, "Please, stop this! I pledge my heart and soul to you!" But I woke up without having the chance to accept his pledge. When I related this to my Lama, he said, "If you get the *naga*'s pledge, you'll obtain the three *naga* powers of subduing, casting spells, and bringing down hail."

Knowing that these abilities were connected with the devotion I felt for my Lama, I proceeded with the Dream Yoga practices of training, multiplication, emanation, and transformation. On the tenth evening of the same month, I prepared large offerings and then practiced well into the night. At dawn, I finally went to sleep. No sooner had I fallen asleep than I noticed a big lake right in front of a hermitage on Mount Chuwori.[156] The lake was overflowing. Soon it flooded the whole area, so that even the mountain was submerged. "Ah," I said to myself, "I must have gone to sleep, and this is just a dream. I could do the Dream Yoga practices of emanation and transformation."

At once, in the space above I emanated the Five-Deity Mandala of Chakrasamvara with its heavenly mansions. The whole vision was extremely clear, free of concepts. In front of Chakrasamvara, I manifested my own body into a hundred million emanations covered in wish-fulfilling gems, and performing the seven pure practices.[157] Behind Chakrasamvara, I emanated millions of sons and daughters of the deities covered in jewels, bringing down rains of flowers, dancing, making music, and consorting together. On Chakrasamvara's other side I emanated countless dakinis bearing offerings of *amrita* and the five kinds of meat.[158] In the sky just above the heavenly mansions, I emanated Nairatmya and Jetsunma Vajrayogini presenting pure offerings to other deities. I saw each of these deities, one by one, with perfect clarity, from the five *garudas* soaring above to Vajrapani, and others below. I recognized in them the kindness of the Lama and offered a prayer that resounded in space.

Looking at the lake ahead, it occurred to me that I should now do the Dream Yoga practices of training and multiplication. All kinds of beings—fish, crocodiles, and so forth—appeared on the surface of the lake. Black water birds, lusting for food, dove to catch the thousands of fish. White tortoises plunged left and right by the crocodiles. Black *nagas*, their mouths wide open and fangs bared, sprang out of the water.

Frightened, I decided to emanate as a *garuda* yet again, casting out numerous *garuda* apparitions who cut the *nagas* into bits and ate them. I emanated as white tortoises and annihilated them all. I saw Chakrasamvara standing on the crown of all the fish, water birds, crocodiles, *nagas*, white tortoises, and *garudas*. I meditated on the Lama sitting above Chakrasamvara, while all the creatures recited the seven-syllable mantra of Chakrasamvara. Then I visualized all the fish, water birds, water deities, *nagas,* and so on, praying to the Lama. Again, I could see each of these, one by one, with perfect clarity. But then, the proud thought came into my mind that my power of devotion must be greater than that of previous bodhisattvas or sages. With this thought, a woman approached and said:

> Apprehension of afflictive emotions as truly existing has ceased,
> But you're not free of perceiver and perceived.
> You better not be proud, you better meditate on this.
> Perceiver and perceived: gold perhaps, but still golden shackles!

All my visions engendered by the Dream Yoga practices of training and multiplication vanished. Now, I was ascending a sandy mountain but at every step I only slipped back down in the sand. The woman appeared once again and shouted, "Come up here, show me what you're made of!"

"I can't!" I replied.

She laughed, "And I thought you had grand ideas about your powers surpassing even those of bodhisattvas. So what's the problem with a sand hill?" With these words, she disappeared. This brought me face to face with the pride and attachment I felt for the 'excellence' of my practice, and I concluded that I was certainly not yet a master.

On the first day of fall, I went to the Lama with a liberal gift of honey and white scarves, intent on making a strong prayer of aspiration. I was holding that same thought the day of the full moon, when demons and evil spirits, particularly Karchung Gyalpo, displayed many miraculous exhibitions. To tame all these demons, I took on the appearance of a *garuda.* As for subduing their leader, Karchung Gyalpo, I transformed myself into the wrathful deity, Hayagriva, my horse-head blazing flames. When he saw me thus, Karchung Gyalpo tried to take refuge in the temple and we struggled with each other. The temple fell into ruin and the statues within broke into pieces. Monkeys darted from the debris. So I manifested as a tiger and ate them one by one! But I had hardly finished them off when I felt overcome with love and compassion. At that moment, the leader of the demons, Karchung Gyalpo, came forth in the shape of a monkey wearing ornaments and a garment made of tiger skin. He prostrated himself at my feet over and over again and placed himself under my care. And that's how I subdued the demons and their master, Karchung Gyalpo.

I returned to meditating in my cave when one morning at the crack of dawn, I dreamt that I was practicing passing through the walls of my cave. When I had enough of that, I transformed myself into earth, and then successively into water, fire, and wind. I saw two parchments with the Prajnaparamita writings on them. A woman appeared and said, "Read these!" I recited them and she said, "You've read them. Now use these words for practice!" I practiced training and multiplication with each word on each line, as the Five-Deity Mandala of Chakrasamvara. Next, I practiced training and multiplication without ever slipping between the ink with which the words were written and the page on which they were written. Again the woman commanded me, "Pray!" I visualized my Lama on the crown of the Chakrasamvara deity, and I prayed. I continued my training and multiplication practices without causing any ink stain on the parchment. The woman said:

> The letters lighting up the page,
> Not blurring in and out—
> This is training and multiplication of the Five-Deity Mandala
>     of Chakrasamvara.
> All appear clearly, distinctly,
> Illusion and clarity inseparable.
> E MA AH LA LA!

With this exclamation, she disappeared.

Great devotion swelled in me. I prayed to my Lama for a prophecy that would reveal my own yidam to me. At that moment, a red-brown illumination flashed across the sky revealing a blazing white volcano. A smiling white dakini with a radiant complexion appeared in the center of the volcano. Her nature was sheer luminosity. I presented her with outer, inner, and secret offerings. White light sparkled from her body and dissolved into me. Then she said:

Pure bliss-emptiness inseparable—
Such Pure Land of the Dakini you will reach.

She repeated this three times and I thought to myself, "This is a manifestation of my Lama's kindness." I offered another prayer and the Lama above Chakrasamvara dissolved into my heart chakra. I presented more offerings and emanated many bodies, each one giving unique praises. As a result of the training and multiplication experiences in this dream and the faith and devotion it brought, my practice the following day was more powerful than ever before.

But now Lama Rigongpa told me to develop these same powers during the waking hours. "Daytime practice is so much more difficult than nighttime dream practice!" he declared. "I remember when I went to see Lama Kyergangpa about this. 'I can't do it during the day!' I complained. [My Lama advised,] 'What you have is the ultimate dream practice. Try for a similar experience during waking time.' So I went off to meditate for seven days straight. During that time, I clearly saw the co-emergent arising of even the smallest atom. But the mandala of the deity did not emerge all that clearly from the atoms themselves. I asked my Lama Kyergangpa what I should do about this lack of clarity. He said, 'Stretch night into day, extend your night practice into the daytime. At night you have clear visions. So learn to develop subtle deity body in the daytime as well.' And that, [Sangye Tönpa, my son,] is how you should practice as well. You should habituate yourself to developing the mandala outside of the dream experience. If the principal deity is clear but the rest of the entourage isn't, or conversely, if the entourage is very distinct but the principal deity isn't, you're like a blind man walking in circles with his stick!"

Next, I was taken with the idea of erecting a golden statue of my Lama in Rigong, his native area. This required talking to the craftsmen every day. But other than that, I maintained complete silence in my retreat. Still, one night shortly after midnight, I had a great vision of my Lama in the sky above my cave, his face dark with displeasure. He placed a crystal mala in my hand and said these words:

> A prophecy was made in the boar year.
> That was thirteen and a half years ago.
> Now the time has come for its fulfillment.
>
> Me, I come from the Pure Land of Joy
> To exhort you to practice.
> This golden statue of me is a distraction
> That entangles you in obstacles.
>
> Don't pour this cast body.
> This clinging to samsara and your retreat as having self-entity—
> Put it out of your mind
> And meditate undistracted.
>
> Pray to me single-pointedly.
> With longing, faith, and devotion inseparable,
> Meditate on the mind beyond sickness and death
> And realize the meaning of deathlessness.
> This will set you free from concerns of sudden death.

I spent the fall in the mountain solitudes of Lönkar. At dawn on the tenth day of the month, I dreamt that the surrounding mountains had caught fire. They were blazing but I realized that this was a dream, so I thought, "I should meditate on my own body as being fire." In the midst of the flames burning the mountain I saw the ten wrathful

deities. I also saw Three-Faced Hayagriva, Six-Armed Mahakala, and
Wrathful Vajrayogini displaying one face and two arms, surrounded
by other wrathful attendants. I offered them blessed nectar and all
the hosts of wrathful deities came together to say these words:

To you who seek to spread wisdom and great bliss,
To you with your wild hair going every which way,
To you, perfect enlightened enjoyment-body Vajradhara
In the Pure Land of Akanistha
Who emanates wrathful deities,
To you wisdom dakinis who grant blessings:

When the vajra-word was first transmitted,[159]
Vajradhara himself made a prophecy:
After seven generations of guru-to-disciple transmission
Our one-to-one lineage will open up
To several worthy disciples.
This expansion of the oral transmission
Will greatly benefit confused beings.
That was the first prophecy.

Wise Kyergangpa predicted the following:
One holder of the lineage
Will be a man from the Yorpo region.
The lineage holder Sangye Nyentön Rigongpa
Himself will have ten thousand students.
Among these, ten outstanding students
Will gain great bliss.
Six will gain mastery and tame gods, demons, *nagas*,
Scent-eaters of the bardo, and humans.
Three will guide worthy human disciples,
And will spontaneously experience the enlightened enjoyment-
body.
Only one will subdue the beings of this world

By his emanations in the ten directions.
Whoever hears his name will abandon [the non-virtuous ac-
    tions that lead to rebirth]
In the three lower realms.
And whoever makes a connection with him
Will go to the Eastern Pure Land.
Such was the prophecy made by Kyergangpa.

Sangye Nyentön Rigongpa predicted the following:
To thirty-five disciples
I gave the Avalokiteshvara empowerment.
At that time, the Dharma lord Kyergangpa
And Avalokiteshvara both appeared.
These thirty-five pure disciples and their retinues
Will all go to the Eastern Pure Land.
I come from Yorpo and I'm the best.
I hold the lineage.
My own students will count one hundred and eight adepts and
    secret yogis.
In future lives, they'll guide countless sentient beings
In ways one cannot begin to enumerate.
As for names and specifics,
As Avalokiteshvara has said:
The minds of confused beings cannot grasp it all.
So it is best to keep these secret.

Now the prophecies of the wrathful deities:
Sangye Nyentön Rigongpa was given empowerments
By the illusory manifestation of the yidam deities
    Chakrasamvara, Hevajra,
Guhyasamaja, Vajrabhairava, the Red and White Forms of the
    Dakini, and the rest,
Filling the sky.
Five students drank of the wisdom nectar presented by dakinis.
These, it is prophesized, will go to pure lands.

You in particular, my child [Sangye Tönpa],
Will go the highest realms
And will be the first to teach the mahayana Dharma there,
Enjoying the perfect blossoming of your qualities.
Negative karma accumulated in the past
Ripened in your present life as an illness.
But in this very lifetime, that karma will be exhausted
And you, Sangye Tönpa, will go to the Blissful Pure Land.
Of this, you need to have no doubts.
So stay focused and pray.
There will come a time when you, Sangye Tönpa, will lead con-
    fused beings
As one would a mad elephant.
At such a time, I, your Lama, will send my blessings
From the Blissful Pure Land.
The lowest of beings will be set on the appropriate paths,
For the average ones, the seed of enlightened enjoyment-body
    will spring,
And the best ones will have experience of clear-light
    Mahamudra.
Verily, it will happen in this life.
Don't let your compassion be petty!
Engender the great mind of bodhichitta.
So long as the fruition of blissful peace is not attained,
Engender non-referential compassion.
It takes greater merit to benefit a single being in this life
Than to guide many sentient beings
To the pure lands.
In the beginning, the teachings were expanding,
But in these times of quarrels and increasing degeneration,[160]
When the teachings of Shakyamuni are waning,
It takes inexpressible virtue
To plant the seed of liberation in virtuous beings.

And I won't even mention clear-light Mahamudra or self-arising enlightened enjoyment-body.
Hence the importance of aspiring to benefit others.

I practiced single-pointed meditation at Samten Hermitage. After a
year, I had a vision of the wisdom dakini [Niguma] holding a mala of
one hundred and eight pearls that she gave to me as she spoke these
words:

When it's time for you to depart from here,
After death and the transference of consciousness,
You'll go to the Blissful Pure Land.
You'll have one hundred and eight students
Including secret yogis and adepts.
In their future lives, they will guide countless beings.

She repeated this three times and then disappeared. Such was her
prophecy. To summarize my life, I sing this song:

I've briefly presented my previous lives,
This present life, and all my future lives.
Remember them with devotion.

Once in a previous life in India,
I had doubts during the third empowerment.
In this life, it ripened in a terrible illness,
Which I couldn't shake off.

In my next life, I shall go to the pure land.
This has been prophesized by the Lama-Buddha.

I am bad but my Lama is good.
My effort is small but the teachings are profound.
My possessions are few but my mind is happy.

Awake, I am a sick, ordinary man.
In dreams, I am the actual bliss body of the Buddha

At day, Mahamudra meditation beyond thought and expression
Arises spontaneously.

At night, the clear light of non-conceptual luminous bliss
Arises spontaneously.

The coalescent form bodies appear naturally:
This body is the blissful enlightened enjoyment-body,
This speech is the luminous enlightened emanation-body.
Inseparable, this is great bliss.
See my body, speech, and mind as inseparable
From the three bodies of enlightenment.

O, noble children, train yourselves to perceive appearances as
    pure.
O, noble children, meditate on inseparability.
Pray, O noble children!
Be decisive, O noble children!

This brief story of my life
Was set down for the benefit of the lineage holders,
Who have faith, devotion, and sacred outlook.
May this merit lead all beings to maturation and liberation.

Whatever merit has been accumulated by writing this, may it purify
all the veils and negative karma of sentient beings as many in numbers as space is vast. May this story of the Lama bring lasting protection. May it spontaneously benefit beings. Cutting through concerns
of birth and death, may all attain the body of great bliss.

SARWA DAKALYA NIBHA WANTU! GEO!

# 10

# Inner Life of Sangye Tönpa

*Namo!* To the Lamas who are the embodiment of all the Buddhas, the essence of awareness-holders,[161] and the root of the three gems, I bow down.

Lama Sangye Tönpa was asked by his disciples to tell of his visions of deities. The disciples also beseeched him to reveal prophecies. At first, Sangye Tönpa refused, saying that there was enough written down as it was. But his disciples insisted. So Sangye Tönpa finally assented. Here is the disciples' account of what he said.

When he was thirteen, Sangye Tönpa took novice monk vows from Lama Tsarirepa. At dawn on his fourteenth birthday, he left to hear the teacher Sekpala teach on Manjushri. As he approached the monastery, he saw a white light issuing from within. "In the center," explained Sangye Tönpa, "I vividly saw Manjushri, surrounded by fifty mystical deities."

Later, Sangye Tönpa journeyed to Lhasa, as a servant to Lama Tsarirepa. In Takma Temple, he met an adept from Zangyul. Moved with devotion for the adept, Sangye Tönpa paid homage and offered his services. The adept from Zangyul said, "You're not like the other people in Lhasa. You're actually humble and easy to befriend. To you, I will grant the profound secret instructions of the lineage." The adept

gave him empowerments for seven days, and taught him all the related *sadhanas*. Then he told Sangye Tönpa, "These are the complete
*sadhanas*. Come back in three weeks."

After three weeks, Sangye Tönpa returned. As tea was being served,
the adept from Zangyul said, "The empowerments that Rechungpa
received from Drupe Gyalmo were passed in a one-to-one guru-to-
disciple transmission for seven lineages. It has been prophesized that
after seven generations, there would be an emanation of Amitayus.
This morning, I gained a vision of thirty Amitayus deities: it means
that you are the Amitayus emanation. So listen, Sangye Tönpa—when
you're nineteen, you must take the full vows of a monk. Do not grant
empowerments until you are thirty years of age. All beings who receive empowerments from you, and even those who merely see the
mandalas displayed during the empowerments, will be reborn in the
Blissful Pure Land. You had one major obstacle, but the teachings I
gave you should clear it. Next year, you will see some minor prob-
lems, but on the whole, it will be an excellent year for you."

Later, following the instructions of the adept from Zangyul, Sangye
Tönpa took his full ordination vows before Khenpo Chögyal. He was
headed for Töling but was told that he shouldn't go a certain route
because of the bandits. So that same evening, he left for Lhasa to do
circumambulations and offerings. In Zhönpa, young girls from Töling
offered to guide him part of the way, saying that there were the best
possible guides. Sangye Tönpa and the girls made their way together.
But as soon as they reached the village, the girls were nowhere to be
found.

Sangye Tönpa met Rigongpa and told him about the girls. Rigongpa
replied, "These were the attendants of Tseringma, the great female
protector. According to Kyergangpa's prophecy, our lineage has ten
main disciples—eight men and two women. You are one of these
disciples. You will become a bodhisattva and bring incommensurate
benefit to sentient beings, and among your disciples will be
bodhisattvas on the various stages of the path, who will perceive the
clear-light nature of mind and have visions of deities. You will preserve the teachings and become the greatest practitioner. Even those

who have only a distant karmic connection with the Dharma will become your disciples. Also, the wisdom dakini Niguma has shown a pearl mala of a hundred and eight beads. This means that there will be a hundred and eight adepts in the lineage. However," Rigongpa continued soberly, "in these degenerate times, many beings, upon hearing the Dharma, do not understand it—so it's best to stay quiet!"

Sangye Tönpa practiced with his Lama, Rigongpa. One day, Sukhasiddhi appeared to Sangye Tönpa and said:

> The sky is empty and non-conceptual.
> Cut the root of this conceptual mind!
> Cut the root and relax!

The dakini then granted Sangye Tönpa the ear-whispered transmission. She made several prophecies. She said, "Cut the root of [conceptual] mind!" Afterwards, Sangye Tönpa had repeated visions of the noble dakini.

Once, when Sangye Tönpa was giving an empowerment to the patron Tangkyawa, the protector Hayagriva was clearly seen. Such were some of the visions and prophecies that Sangye Tönpa related to his disciples. They were revealed with the caveat that because of these degenerate times when much evil is accumulated, it is best to speak only few words. By this virtue, may all sentient beings without exception attain unsurpassable enlightenment.

SARWA DAKALYA BHAWANTU!

# II

# Death of Sangye Tönpa

DISPLAYING THE SIGNS and marks of a Buddha, your mellifluous voice like that of Brahma, you fulfill the prophecies of Lamas and dakinis. You guide faithful sons and daughters to the Blissful Pure Land. At your feet, dear Lama, holder of the transmission, I bow down.

The glorious Lama Sangye Tönpa realized the body of reality that benefits oneself. Then, by means of the two form bodies, he acted for the welfare of all beings. His understanding of reality as it is and as it appears enabled him to know every thought of every sentient being, so that in all his activities, he was able to pacify and ease beings according to their individual abilities.

Sangye Tönpa was soft-spoken, his behavior always in accord with the Sutra on Perfect Conduct. When he traveled even just for a day, he took a Buddha statue, a notebook of advice related to his practice, a small book containing extraordinary sayings from the sutras and the Lamas, a pot of ink so he could write, his vajra, bell, and monastic robes. Every day, Sangye Tönpa did three thousand circumambulations and prostrations; he presented food and water offerings. He kept the six-fold praxis of the great Shangpa lineage masters—engendering bodhichitta and avoiding thoughts of [mere] personal liberation; making confessions, vowing restraint, and avoid-

ing transgressions; staying with practitioners and avoiding ordinary
people; accumulating merit and avoiding nihilists; dedicating the merit
and avoiding unskillful beings; practicing all these and avoiding conceptual reference points.

He renewed his vows and engendered bodhichitta at the six times
of day and night. No matter what activity he was engaged in, he recited Dharma sayings, sang vajra songs,[162] and recited mantras with
each breath. He once said to his disciples, "Those who've spent their
whole life in solitude, like me, are rightly called Mountain Men. Now,
I want to die in the mountains, where I can hear the sound of birds."
Sangye Tönpa practiced virtue by reading and writing as much
Dharma as possible. He dedicated all the wealth in his possession to
the three gems—Buddha, Dharma, and Sangha—and to sentient beings, keeping nothing for himself.

One day, there was a wonderful omen: he was sitting on a
mountaintop, and his body gave no shadow. At that instant, he knew
every thought of every being, as well as their past and future lives, all
that had occurred, and all that was yet to happen. Later, when Sangye
Tönpa gave a Chakrasamvara empowerment, he became
Chakrasamvara himself, and all saw him as Chakrasamvara. Likewise, when he gave an Amitayus empowerment, Amitayus could
clearly be seen. When he gave the empowerment of the Five Tantric
Deities, dakas and dakinis appeared with their retinues and helped
him draw the mandala. The sky was filled with the Five Tantric Deities.

Time and again, during Illusory Body Yoga empowerments, lep-
ers, madmen, sick people, those with chronic diseases and long-term
illnesses and so forth, were purified like dust blown off a conch shell.
By merely hearing the name of Lama Sangye Tönpa, good practitioners, neophytes starting on the path, and pilgrims who came to Yöl
and met the Lama, saw their practice improve. In short, many who
came to request the Dharma from him were illuminated [by his pres-
ence]. As more and more disciples practiced virtue, he set up both a
school and a meditation center. To patron men and women, he propounded the *vinaya* code of discipline, the oral teachings, and both

the new and old traditions.[163] His sky-like activity was so pervasive that it touched disciples from the shore of the Chinese ocean to Jalandhara in India.

Although he was approaching death, Sangye Tönpa headed for Shang because of a previous karmic connection there. Once he arrived, he prostrated before the relics of the Shangpa Lama [Khyungpo Naljor] and presented offerings.

Sangye Tönpa continued to practice and give teachings. One day, he told his disciples, "When I die, I'll just be trouble for you!" and headed for the mountains until he came to Yöl. At that moment, magnificent rainbows filled the sky. He was invited to spend the night in a home, and to everyone who came to meet him, he said, "I may have brought just a very little bit of benefit to beings. Now, if I last another year or two, I shall meditate on primordial awareness."

One day, an abbot came in and took the pulse of Sangye Tönpa. Worried, the abbot said, "I can't feel any pulse. He probably won't last more than three months. Anyhow, what kind of yogi is this man? Should we have special ceremonies for his good health, or what?" Sangye Tönpa replied, "It's all the same to me whether there is a ceremony or not. At the time of death, all I need is perfect meditation on the clear-light nature of mind. Nothing else can benefit me."

Many practitioners, old and new, came to see him. To the older practitioners, he said, "I am delighted that you have come. Stay for a few more days; we will talk together." And the next several days, he clarified specific points for them. To his new practitioners, he said, "I am delighted that you, too, have come. If I don't die right away, I would like to finish giving you the precious teachings. But now I am waning like the moon on the twenty-ninth day."[164] To the great meditators of upper Yöl who came to see him with their entourage full of respect and devotion, he said, "The various causes and conditions for our present connection are now fading. Pray fervently that we may all meet again in the future."

And to all the monks, old and young, he gave the following advice, "Generally, in this life one should strive for an understanding of death, impermanence, karmic cause and effect, and the faults of samsara.[165]

In this life, there's not a single useful word to say. The only way to develop qualities is to cut short distractions.[166] Meditate now: death comes to everyone! Give up household concerns, and strive on the path of liberation. Have no attachment for objects or possessions. Recognize the demon of worldly bustle and understand the false lure of wishes and desires. See the activities of this life as the enemy and flee the company of evil men. Genuine devotion for a pure spiritual guide arises through meditation on death and impermanence. If you meditate in this way, you will renounce this life. If you do not abandon this life, it will quickly abandon you! If you don't give it up, then all your actions will only cause you meaningless suffering. All your attendants and servants are like ants, and all your possessions as impermanent as a passing cloud. Stay in the forest, like antelopes. Don't be parrots like the knowledgeable experts—the know-it-alls with their tales. Arouse the proper aspiration, give up this world!

"If you heed my words, if you develop faith and devotion for the Lama, you will naturally experience illusoriness. You will spontaneously have lucid dreams, and clear light will arise naturally. Consider this advice carefully, and practice! Of those qualified to give instructions, I am the best. Others may equal me in intellectual understanding, but I am unparalleled as a meditator. Others may be like me, but none with the same insight as me. Yet even I do not know how much longer I will live! There won't be many more like me in the future. Let these words and their meaning sink in."

In the summer of the ox year, after he taught the Dharma to many monks, Sangye Tönpa told them, "Now I am an old man, I don't know when I will die. I have no wealth to show off. I'm just going to head out into the mountains. After I'm dead, you should take off my clothes and let the vultures and wild animals feed on my corpse." The disciples felt their eyes fill with tears. Sangye Tönpa continued, "Wherever one goes, there is no place that has not been touched by death, neither in the sky nor in the bottom of the sea, neither in the mountains nor in the canyons, nor anywhere else."

Then he spent the rest of the summer on the mountain expounding on the Dharma to a multitude of monks. One day, he went to a monastery in Rinpung and said, "Last night, I received a sign from my two Lamas—omens of death." Now, Sangye Tönpa did know of two or three practices to increase one's life span. But some years earlier, he had concluded that these were just mental activity and so he had set them aside. "Now is the right time for me to move on," he said. "Time for me to die. I don't have any last words, I won't leave any last will."

One evening as winter approached, Sangye Tönpa climbed the ladder leading to his room. He sat on his bed and murmured, "Now, I cannot carry this body anymore. It seems I must go on to another realm, though I could stay here a little longer if I really wanted to." His disciple Tönpa Zhönnu Gön burst in tears and begged him, "O Lama, please don't say that! Please stay for the benefit of beings!"

Sangye Tönpa waved off the plea by saying, "You won't find any state that lasts forever in [this world of] composite things. All composite things are impermanent. But don't let that sadden you. Be happy!"

For the next ninety-one days, Sangye Tönpa presented torma offerings to Mahakala. At the end, he said, "To you, Mahakala, I have given tormas all my life. So I ask that until I reach the pure realm, you guide and protect me." As spring passed, Sangye Tönpa said, "I have been meditating well this last year. If things continue like this, it'd be worth my staying a little longer."

Later, when summer was on its way out, Sangye Tönpa began to show signs of illness. His students suggested performing ceremonies for his good health, but he replied, "I don't care whether you do such a ceremony or not—do as you wish! If I tell you to perform a special long-life practice, you'll develop attachment to this life. If I tell you not to, you'll get attached to all the money you didn't spend on the ceremony!" Sangye Tönpa then said, "You disciples, prepare some fine torma offerings. As for me, I need to go to my Lama's monastery in Rigong. Lama Rigongpa said that I should die near his relics. If I don't, I would be breaking my *samaya*. So I'd better go to the monastery and see his relics."

Sangye Tönpa, some of his visitors, and his disciples left on the full moon, and he gave his attendants several profound pointing-out instructions on the deity generation stage. Once in Rigong, they asked, "Precious Lama, once you have gone to the pure land, how will this lineage expand? What will happen to this monastery in Rigong? What should we, your disciples, do?"

Sangye Tönpa replied, "According to the prophecies of the Lamas, I'll go to the Eastern Pure Land of Metok Trampa. Direct your prayers there. My teachings now extend all the way to Jambudiva and my good students number a hundred and eight secret yogis, of which twenty-one will bring benefit to beings in this life. Others will spread [the teachings] in this and future lives. As for the monastery here in Rigong, my Lama Sangye Nyentön Rigongpa has said things about it. But I won't disclose them.

"If you want to listen to me, here is my advice: do not cling to fame, glory, or happiness either in this life or in future lives. Don't get mixed up in the eight worldly concerns.[167] Instead, go into the mountains and practice. The extremes of mental imputation do not need to be cleared from the outside. Rather, the qualities will arise from within. Remember this well!

> Lamas, yidam deities, dakinis, and Dharma protectors,
> Protect us like your own children with your immeasurable compassion.
> All you faithful monks of Central, Eastern, and Western Tibet,
> Here is how to practice:
>
> Put endless worldly affairs out of your mind.
> Subdue the grasping mind that brings no satisfaction.
> Practice constantly and give up incessant chatter.
> Stop pursuing past and future, hope and fear.
>
> In this short life, endless intellectual pursuits are
> Like a deer chasing a mirage, his thirst unquenched—so drink of the pure nectar.
> If one's own welfare is not attained, one cannot benefit others:
> Begin by practicing single-pointedly for your own sake.

In this and future lives, compassion spontaneously benefits oth-
ers
So arouse it.
Don't be wrapped up in your own selfish interests—not even
for a moment.
In all activities, arouse the mind that benefits sentient beings.

Meditate continuously on death and impermanence.
Be content and renounce this life.
Meditate on this very body
As deity body, appearance-emptiness, free of attachment.

To the Lama, through whom experiences and realizations arise
effortlessly,
Continuously pray with fierce longing and devotion.
In this life, at the point of death, in the bardo, or in future lives,
Rely on dakinis and Dharma protectors to guard you from ob-
stacles.

Outside of one's own mind there are no sentient beings and no
Buddhas.
Whatever appears, know it to be mind.
This mind is deity body:
Like an illusion, it appears and yet is empty.

Illusory clear-light Mahamudra, free of fixation,
Transcends intellectual constructs of creation and destruction,
Birth and death, existence and non-existence.

It is non-meditation, non-mental activity, beyond samsara and
nirvana.
Karma and ripening karmic seeds are self-liberated.

ZHALDRO! GEO!

# 12

# Life of Shangtönpa

WITH OMNISCIENCE, HE perceives the mandala of all objects of knowledge. His compassion establishes all beings in supreme enlightenment.
His great powers annihilate all demons and heretics. I place my head
at the feet of the unparalleled scholar Shangtönpa.

> The tree of leisure and opportunity[169]
> Is garnished with leaves of ethics.
> It blossoms as the flowers of listening, reflecting, and meditat-
> ing,
> Its fruit, vast experiences and realizations.
> At the feet of the great Lama Zhönnu Drup,[170] I bow down.
>
> The flowers—the signs and marks of enlightenment—
> Are sweet with the fragrance of the three trainings.[171]
> Its pistils of omniscient love—the stainless body—
> Are embellished by seeing, hearing, and remembering.
> I bow down before the one who enacted this.
>
> The sky of sutras and tantras with its clouds of scriptures and
> logic
> Trembles in the lightning of oral instructions,

And roars with the thunder of emptiness.
A rain of Dharma falls.
I bow down before this supreme declaimer.

In space—the boundless body of reality—
Shine the sun disks of the unobstructed form bodies,[172]
Revealing the path that clears away the obscurations of beings.
I bow down before this sky-like purity.

From the ocean of the profound classes of tantra
Arises the wish-fulfilling gem of maturing and liberating teach-
  ings
Which fulfill all the needs and desires of fortunate beings.
I bow down before this powerful king.

Down the snowy mountain of the two accumulations
Flow the nectar streams of the two kinds of knowledge,[173]
Gloriously fulfilling the benefit of self and other, and pacify-
  ing samsara.
I bow down before such perfect Buddha activity.


Our Lama is the crown ornament of Buddhas and bodhisattvas and
the two eyes of ordinary beings, the unrivalled lord across the three
pure states, the torch of Dharma which dispels the darkness of ignorance, the wish-fulfilling gem that grants all needs and desires, the
great vessel carrying those who wish it across the ocean of samsaric
attachment, the teacher who sets us on the path and guides those
seeking liberation, the friend of all disciples practicing the pure
tantras—he is the realized and famous Shangtönpa, known beyond
any doubt as Vajradhara himself by all holy and ordinary beings.

His body is birthless appearance and emptiness. His speech is inef-
fable sound and emptiness. His mind is non-conceptual clear-light
and emptiness. Who am I to relate the life story of our great omniscient Lama? I, Rigdor, seek only to humbly present a glimpse of his
life so that my supreme Lama's activity might be remembered. This

story is based on the actual words of my teacher. I shall write it all carefully, and ask that you read it with devotion.

Shangtönpa renounced the world and became a monk with great faith in the teachings. Through listening and reflecting on scriptures, logic, and oral instructions, all doubts were allayed. By relying on his revered Lama and meditating single-pointedly on the profound meaning, his experiences and realizations were brought to perfection. He kept his qualities concealed, and performed the practices of a secret yogi. His teachings established countless fortunate beings on the paths of maturation and liberation. When he went before his Lama, the latter made a prophecy that in the future, Shangtönpa would always bring the highest benefit of beings.

He experienced no physical pain, but in order to dispel the wrong views of those who cling to things as permanent, and for the sake of exhorting lazy beings toward virtue, he passed into bliss amidst omens and miraculous signs at the age of seventy-six and became a Buddha in the Eastern Pure Land. After he was cremated, a stock of sacred relics was found in his ashes, to serve as a basis of inspiration for future disciples.

Lama Shangtönpa was born in the marshlands of Kongyal in Shang, to the Ra family—his father was Wönpo Könchok Palzang and his mother, Joge. When he entered his mother's womb, both his parents experienced bliss and saw many auspicious signs.

Shangtönpa was still very young when the habitual tendencies from his previous lives awakened and, free of any laziness, desire, or greed, he felt great revulsion for samsara. He always reminded himself of the faults of samsara, death, and impermanence while developing compassion and great faith in the Lama and the three jewels.[174] He felt intensely happy looking at solitary places in the mountains and later said it was a sign that in his previous lives, he liked to wander around in solitude. He had a gentle, quiet, and virtuous nature, and at once renounced the games of children.

By the time he was eight or nine years old, he could read and write fluently. At thirteen, he was ordained as a novice monk before the abbot Nyitokpa and the teacher Tsulshe. His attitude was good and his ethics, faultless. He gave attention to the finest points of his training. He studied Engaging in the Bodhisattva's Path and the Prajnaparamita with the teachers Ba and Shakya Bumpa. At eighteen, he presented new commentaries on both of these texts and his teachers said, "Congratulations, you are gaining a true understanding of logic. You should teach it now!"

When he studied, he only needed to hear the first line [of the text] to elucidate on the topic, knowing naturally what came on the next page. This made him renown throughout Central and Western Tibet as Tönpa Zangwa, or Excellent Teacher. He received many teachings, including the Three Bodies Pointing-Out Instructions from the Karmapa. Shangtönpa's actions defied description and his commentaries were in perfect accord with the texts, both in words and in meaning. Everything he wrote was easy to understand and read, and pleasant to listen to. To put it simply, he was graceful in the threefold duties of a scholar[175] as in all other matters.

Shangtönpa had very little attachment to possessions. After his mother's demise, he sold all his estates. On twelve occasions, he distributed presents in memory of his parents. Wherever he went, he delighted the Lamas with his devotion, gifts, and services. He never said a bad word about the Lamas from whom he received teachings, even in jest.

He focused single-pointedly on attainments and kept away from the commotion of samsara, the distraction and longing of worldly possessions, the obsession with leading a monastery, the yearning for fame and approval from others, and the attachment for some and anger toward others. He achieved stability both in the generation and completion stages.

By then, he had already said a hundred million mantras of his yidam deity, Chakrasamvara. The power of the deities' blessings and recitations gave Shangtönpa the ability to purify all diseases and evil spirits. He developed supernatural faculties, gave birth to definitive understanding, and sustained pure *samadhi* within. Still he thought, "All these powers do not really benefit beings. I need to find a realized Lama and meditate."

This he explained to the teacher Tsulshe, who replied, "I, too, have had such thoughts. Let's both go to India: I'll go first. As for you, you should get a measure of gold and join me later. I'll wait for you in Langkor." Shangtönpa did as his teacher said and went to meet him in Langkor. But by then, Tsulshe and his monks had already left and were heading back. So Shangtönpa sold the rest of his possessions, and when he met a teacher, presented him with an offering, which pleased the latter very much.

At this time, Shangtönpa was told that in Rigong in the Yöl area lived Sangye Tönpa, a realized Lama. At the mere mention of Sangye Tönpa's name, Shangtönpa's previous karma awakened and he felt great devotion. He went to meet Sangye Tönpa. As soon as he saw the Lama's face, an uncontrollable, extraordinary faith swelled in him. He began to cry and his meditation experience immediately intensified. Sangye Tönpa proceeded to grant Shangtönpa the general empowerments of Dream Yoga and Illusory Body Yoga. He also gave him the complete instructions for the Six Yogas of Niguma, including teachings on the Path of Means (Inner Heat Yoga). Within seven days, Shangtönpa had mastered this practice so well that he was able to walk around wearing nothing but a light cotton robe.

Next, Shangtönpa practiced Illusory Body Yoga. Within three days of meditating, deity body arose spontaneously, as happens with those of superior faculties. Shangtönpa was aware of his dreams and recognized illusory body. He became able to simultaneously practice training, multiplication, emanation, and transformation within Dream Yoga. As external appearances fused with the experience of clear-light, he saw all things great and small with perfect clarity—stones, mountains, and caves throughout Central and Western Tibet. He related this to his Lama who replied, "Shangtönpa, your practice is even greater than mine. You've achieved the essential meaning of the instructions."

Sangye Tönpa then gave Shangtönpa more teachings. After meditating on these, Shangtönpa realized that appearances are like an illusion, empty of true existence. The experience of the illusory nature of reality arose spontaneously and his dreams became so powerful that he was able to manipulate and transform the four elements,[176] sentient beings, and even objects. He also developed the ability to view clearly and easily all appearing objects, including the pure lands.

Shangtönpa said, "One night during Dream Yoga, a horse rider approached and thrust his spear through my heart. He killed me. I thought, 'Now I'm dead! This is the bardo!' For the next several days, I had a continuous experience of the bardo. When I related this to my Lama, he said, 'The horse rider in your dream was a Dharma protector. He was there to help you seize the bardo.' Thus, although it is usually difficult to seize the bardo in dreams, I found it quite easy."

Engaged in the practices of Illusory Body Yoga with his superior faculties, Shangtönpa obtained a definitive experience and all his doubts vanished. His Lama was delighted and said, "Shangtönpa, your practice is stable, and there's no greater practitioner than you. Both you and Kedrup Zhönnu are advancing on the path. You two really show outstanding abilities!"

One night, Shangtönpa dreamt that the sky was filled with deities. In their midst arose the dakini, Vajravarahi, who embraced him in a tantric union of perfect bliss. He related this dream to his Lama who said, "You have achieved the essential meaning of the empowerment. All the deities in the sky are the pointing-out instructions of the vase empowerment. The embrace with Vajravarahi is the pointing-out instruction of the secret empowerment. The arising of pure bliss is the pointing-out instruction of the *jnana* empowerment. Unobstructed appearances, non-existent and non-conceptual, are the pointing-out instruction of the fourth empowerment." Shangtönpa spent five months practicing Mind Deathlessness, at which point he says that deity body arose spontaneously.

When he was in Rigong one summer, Shangtönpa's practice became somewhat tense. His body was swollen and he had difficulty breathing, so his Lama Sangye Tönpa told him, "You need to do yogic exercises." And he gave instructions on Deathlessness Yoga. After practicing these, his health improved and the experience was physically blissful. His practice was so powerful that it shook his room. He said that the house felt unstable and his Lama responded, "You've been the easiest student to whom I taught these practices! In truth, you are just like a young Virupa!"[177] Shangtönpa later said that he taught these practices to a Dharma friend and that it caused some difficulties in his own practice.

Sangye Tönpa then gave Shangtönpa a series of teachings and was pleased with his student's faith, devotion, practice, and offerings. When Shangtönpa presented himself before his Lama, Sangye Tönpa, the latter embraced him with great compassion and said, "Shangtönpa you are the fortunate one who will drink the nectar of instructions of the lineage. You have been prophesized as the great disciple who will receive the one-to-one guru-to-disciple transmission. You don't need further teachings. You are my finest heart son-disciple and you will effortlessly attain all realizations. The prophecy is that you will reach the fourteenth level of a bodhisattva and bring immeasurable benefit to beings in this and all your future lives. Furthermore, all your disciples and lineage holders will be reborn in the Pure Land of the Dakini."

When Shangtönpa's Lama passed away, the sky filled with rainbows and wonderful displays. Shangtönpa reflected that if he followed the sutras and tantras, and integrated the precepts of his Lama into his own experience, he should be a Buddha in his next life.[178] Later, Shangtönpa stayed in Tsari. Day and night he practiced undistracted and grew very powerful. He dreamt that he went to Mount Potala and received teachings directly from Avalokiteshvara, visited Bodhgaya, Alakavati, and other sacred places.

This dream was so powerful that at dawn the next morning, he had a continuous perception of luminosity and both the earth and the sky made a sharp sound, like the buzz of a bee. He clearly saw every one of the Buddhas' pure lands. At that instant, his body was pervaded by pure bliss and he felt a great surge of power—enough power to subjugate all the beings of the six realms. A deep appreciation of death and impermanence arose in his mindstream

Shangtönpa explained, "In my dreams at night, I went through every one of the six realms of samsara, and unbearable compassion arose in me. I suffered from lice, leprosy, heartbreak, and depression.

I thought, 'There is no one more miserable than myself in this world.' I was insulted. People were angry at me. All I wanted to do was to get away. Milarepa has said that just as everything grows in the summer, so, too, anything can arise in the experience of a yogi. This is very true: observe that in your own practice."

To overcome an illness, Shangtönpa took his Lama's advice and went to meet Lama Genmo Lhepa to receive the Lamdre teachings of the Sakya tradition. After twenty-five days of breathing practices, Shangtönpa spewed out mucus and clots of blood, rinsed his mouth with water, and his terrible pains ended. The Lama explained, "I've helped purify your obstacles. After the special breathing practice, the objects of the six senses,[179] having no true nature, disappear. There's nothing left to grasp to. All your earlier misery and depression etc. arise as the experience of bliss." Shangtönpa practiced day and night until his experiences during meditation were inseparable from those during post-meditation.

Shangtönpa now went with Lama Genmo Lhepa to his Lama Sangye Tönpa, and they meditated together until their breathing was indistinguishable. The Lama was pleased with Shangtönpa and told him, "Your practice of Lamdre is even greater than mine. Experiences and realizations, rather than reliance on books, make for the greater skill."

Next, Shangtönpa was advised by his teacher Sangye Tönpa, protector of beings, to take to the solitudes of Öyuk, "Go meditate, Shangtönpa! This nice, clean place will induce mental clarity. There, the local gods and demons are inclined toward the Dharma." But driven by concerns of food, he went to Jak instead. This is the only time he disobeyed his Lama.

Later, Shangtönpa was practicing by a rock when a new spring gushed. At that moment, Shangtönpa made a vow not to eat any human food.[180] He continued to practice and would not see anybody. He had the sensation that the lower part of his body was ringed by all the villages below, while his upper body was raised high in the sky. Inside him was a red drop about the size of a pea, shifting up and down between his forehead and his secret place. He began to feel extremely cold and the channels[181] in his body shivered uncontrollably. Then all appearances dissolved and only his body was still there, spinning in circles in space, all references gone.

Shangtönpa explained, "Whatever objects appeared in my visual field dissolved to nothing as soon as I looked at them. I turned around but the objects of my focus kept changing into something else. So, I thought that I should look quickly to behold them before they dissolved. After doing so I realized that the experience didn't arise from emptiness alone. Rather, it came from the union [of form and emptiness]."

That's when the wind started to howl and a summer hail fell with a piercing sound. The sky burst with flashes of lightning. For two and a half years, the storm raged every night, like an elemental savage war. Sometimes, for Shangtönpa, it was as though all the knots in his channels had loosened. Other times, earth and sky filled with rows of deities—Chakrasamvara, Shakyamuni, Avalokiteshvara and others—each no bigger than a foot. He heard the lion's roar of the tantric deities—Manjugosha white and gold, Vajrapani, and other unimaginable deities. When Shangtönpa went to fetch water, he saw the deities everywhere and feared he might trample on them. But they parted a path for him. Such appearances were his companions for more than three years.

"First," Shangtönpa explained of these occurrences, "I perceived the central channel and was able to see bodily things, harmful or beneficial. Later, as the experience increased in scope, I saw the three channels of my own body with wheels at the four chakras.[182] Then I felt the million tips of the channels pushing out to the openings of my pores and I perceived the network of channels in the body. I clearly saw the physical condition of the tantric body—the knots in my channels, my breathing, and so forth. I perceived the bliss-chakra of the secret place, and experienced uninterrupted bliss.

"During the torma offering," Shangtönpa continued, "there was a sweet fragrance and flashing brilliance that I hadn't noticed before. I saw signs of dakinis and non-humans. At times, it felt like I didn't have a body. For ten days, I neither inhaled nor exhaled. During that time, my physical condition was excellent and my mind was crystal clear."

Later, he stayed at Bliss Bound Cave. Behind the cave stood a heavenly mansion fashioned out of precious gems. At the top, White Tara appeared with an entourage of female attendants. Shangtönpa was heading toward her when she said, "Your practice has a firm foundation! Now, I shall give you my blessings." The Jetsunma placed her two hands on Shangtönpa's head. At once, all the attendants of the Jetsunma also placed their hands on his head. As the blessings were transmitted, Shangtönpa felt a most perfect experience arise in him. For days, his meditation and post-meditation became one.

Shangtönpa's compassion for sentient beings was so intense that he often couldn't stop crying. However, he has said that this outpouring of compassion can end up causing depression. To overcome this, one should analyze by asking: who is it that experiences the compassion? Toward whom is it directed? And what is the nature of the compassion itself? Such reflections will lead to the experience of profound non-conceptual Mahamudra.

Shangtönpa was once asked by his disciples who his main yidam deity was, and whether he had actually seen the face of the deities. He explained, "First I prayed to my Lama and my central yidam deity. Every day, I did thirty thousand recitations of the seven-syllable mantra of Chakrasamvara. Then one night, I had the following lucid dream: I was meditating on myself as the yidam deity with the Lama on the crown of my head. All sentient beings were saying a prayer together when I called out, 'May my yidam reveal itself!' No sooner had I made this fervent prayer than the Great Compassionate One appeared with his retinue, saying 'I am truly Avalokiteshvara.' So I practiced Avalokiteshvara as my main yidam deity." Thus, Shangtönpa first saw his main yidam deity in a dream. Later, it is said that he saw it in waking life. For a long time after this, whenever he looked at others, Avalokiteshvara appeared. He saw beings with the syllable OM and aroused immense compassion for the suffering of beings who had no protection.

Shangtönpa's reflections on the condition of beings—without refuge in life or death—increased his compassion. Every time he came upon a person, he sought to lead him or her on the path. Every time a person died, he recited the seven-week prayers for the dead. In one particular case, he examined where in the six realms the deceased was reborn and declared with utter certainty that the deceased had taken rebirth in a higher realm.

Some time later, Shangtönpa experienced a sudden sharp pain. His disciples asked about this, and he replied, "Bah, it's just a little pain, a respiration problem. Except for a little discomfort at first, the very nature of pain soon arises as shivers of bliss. The bliss itself remains whether there is pain or not." He spat, drank water in order to purify both illness and evil spirits, intoned many Avalokiteshvara mantras, and blessed nectar pills to be distributed to whoever needed them. Shangtönpa explained, "I stayed focused on the present and I received the blessings of the Lamas and holders of the lineage. As a result, those who came into contact with me were reborn with an inclination to the Dharma and entered the path. Even those who merely saw me developed a spiritual practice. This is what reminds me that teaching the Dharma, even to a single individual, is of great benefit."

Indeed, receiving an anointment from Shangtönpa healed a suffering person from his or her disease, evil spirits, leprosy, wounds, ulcers, and the like. On nights of empowerments and instructions, disciples did all they could to assist Shangtönpa, even carrying the earth, stones, water, and wood that he requested. Many disciples gave birth to genuine devotion and some even attained realizations. As part of the teachings, Shangtönpa set up dedications to the deities and began the traditional monthly and annual offerings, the organization of a religious community, and the repetition of the *mani* mantra. He did everything for the sake of virtue, saying that it is important to dedicate oneself entirely to the benefit of beings.

He and Kedrup presented themselves to Sangye Tönpa. Sangye Tönpa, teacher and protector of beings, turned first to Lama Kedrup and advised, "Kedrup, cut short distractions! Benefit others!" Then he looked at Shangtönpa and declared, "Meditate, Shangtönpa! Meditate! You must meditate!" So Shangtönpa vowed that from that day on, until his death, he would only meditate. No more granting of requests; only retreat! He went into solitary retreat and did not allow anyone to come and see him.

But in the bird year, many scholars and spiritual friends came from all over the land to pay their respects. They begged Shangtönpa for teachings. From his retreat place, he taught the scholars the Six Yogas of Niguma as well as the Mahamudra Reliquary, Mind Deathlessness and Non-Deviation, the Three Ways of Integrating the Path,[183] the Instructions on Dharma protectors, Body Deathlessness, Chö practice, and so on. He ended with the advice, "Now go into solitary retreat. Practice until you have realized these teachings. Some of you have brought offerings here. Give them away to monastic centers; keep nothing! Or make offerings in memory of Khyungpo Naljor, Mokchokpa and Rigongpa. So—that's enough Dharma teachings. I'm off to meditate!"

All those present gained confidence that the great Shangtönpa was inseparable from the three bodies of enlightenment, stable in the sphere of non-activity, beyond coming or going. As death approached, Shangtönpa showed no attachment for his place of residence, his clothes, whatever gold there was, or even his ritual implements. He kept only his meditation seat and a change of clothes. It was really quite marvelous.

His state of no-returning[184] was obvious in his ability to see the beings of the six realms as pure. His own body was stripped of impurities and he took on a brilliant glow. Just looking at him made one feel clean. Because of this incredible quality he had, our Lama, protector of beings, became known as Tsangma,[185] the Immaculate.

On the eleventh day of the third month, the Dharma lord Shangtönpa said, "Ha! I see an obstacle coming up: this morning, a man in white came and stared at me. He told me I was always in his heart and warned me of an impeding obstacle. To solve it, I had to recite the long version of the Prajnaparamita."

"Can this obstacle be cleared? What is it?" asked the disciples.

Shangtönpa explained, "The man in white was Avalokiteshvara. His instruction to read the Prajnaparamita was an injunction not to waver from [the realization] that the nature of all phenomena is emptiness." It's true, Shangtönpa did experience an obstacle in the form of an illness; but it was very minor and the fatigue left him after a prayer was said. When his disciples asked about his experiences and realizations, Tsangma Shangtönpa said, "I have unobstructed experiences. I witness the exhaustion of all dharmas.[186] I recognize the Lama as my own mind. I always dwell in the Mahamudra state of reality."

To summarize: Shangtönpa, in his life, received the Lama's blessings; practiced Clear Light Yoga and Illusory Body Yoga; attained actual realizations; and was naturally freed of the eight worldly concerns. He had many prophecies and visions of yidam deities. He became a great adept of vast supernatural powers. However, since it is important to conceal one's inner qualities, he kept his own counsel and remained a secret yogi of great abilities, a protector guiding beings through degenerate times. He established fortunate disciples on the paths of maturation and liberation. Many of his students gained experiences and realizations, had lucid dreams, were able to follow the path, received pointing-out instructions, and made auspicious karmic connections.

As for the prophecies on the succession of the lineage, Shangtönpa himself spoke thus, "I shall go to the Eastern Pure Land, where, as was first prophesized, I shall be the principal disciple of Sangye Tönpa. In the future, I will accomplish the vast benefit of beings. I shall perfect qualities on the path and after attaining unsurpassable enlightenment of the fourteenth level of a bodhisattva, I shall turn the wheel of Dharma. If a meditator—even a mediocre one—comes before me, that alone will be enough for him or her to practice easily."

Shangtönpa was approaching death and became ill. Yet, except for the fact that he hardly ate anything, there was no overt evidence of physical pain. The essential nature of pain arose as bliss. He was very easy to care for. When the attendants in charge of nursing him performed their work, they experienced perfect clarity of mind, received blessings, and perceived hosts of dakinis wearing bone ornaments.

One day, his disciples told him they should get him to a doctor. But the great Shangtönpa replied, "If I can't improve my own health, a doctor won't either!"

"Please," the disciples insisted, "for our own peace of mind, let us get a physician for you." So they brought the physician Rinchen Sönam. After taking his pulse, the doctor became alarmed. "What is it?" the students asked. "Is he about to pass away? Let there be auspicious connections now!"

"Bah," Shangtönpa replied, "there's no need for all that!" So the students now asked which pure land he would go to, and what prayers should be said. Shangtönpa replied, "My Dharma brother, Kedrup,[187] has gone to the Blissful Pure Land. I myself shall hasten to my Lama Sangye Tönpa in the Eastern Pure Land. You should pray to go there as well. When I have reached this Eastern Pure Land, I will lead many fortunate disciples to maturation.

"As for my body made up of these aggregates," continued Shangtönpa, "burn it out of the prying eyes of impure people. When my body is burnt, look for relics in the cremation shrine, make *tsatsas*[188] with them and dispose of them in the Shang River. Don't bother with outer or inner shrines for me. Wipe your tears and go off to meditate in a hut! Emulate me, so that people will remember Shangtönpa as they do the great Jetsun Milarepa. As I said, collect my relics after cremation, and most important, practice, practice everywhere you go, practice for realizations! If you don't give up the activities of this life, you'll never get anywhere!"

After several days, gods and demons came to receive the Dharma from Shangtönpa, but he gave strict orders that no one disturb him. After performing a ritual for his Lama Sangye Tönpa, Shangtönpa declared, "Don't get carried away with pilgrimages and all that. Simply abide in the clear-light nature of mind."

He spoke not another word, recited not another prayer: he shifted on his mat and gestured that he would remain seated there. After a glance, he entered into meditation. It was dawn on the fifteenth day of the fifth month in the bird year.[189] His breathing stopped. He dissolved into bliss and entered a state of brilliant clarity. Thus, in order

to dispel the wrong views of those who cling to things as permanent
and for the sake of exhorting lazy beings toward virtue, Shangtönpa
passed into nirvana at the age of seventy-six. For three days following his death, his face kept a radiant glow.

> The radiant sun of his immeasurable compassion
> Shines the bright rays of his kindness
> That mature and liberate.

> Darkness is dispelled
> And the blossom lotus of mind unfolds.
> Even the way a sun sets is displayed out of kindness for dis-
> ciples.

> In the sky of great knowledge,
> The clouds of skillful means gather.
> The lightning of understanding flashes.
> The roar of thunder resounds vast and deep.

> Just as rain from the clouds of compassion ripens the harvest
> of disciples,
> So he demonstrates the nirvana of passing into the space of
> reality.

After Shangtönpa passed away, all who served him and all who sat by
the side of his dead body or held him experienced a mental clarity
more perfect than ever before, and going without sleep for days, had
dreams of dakas, dakinis, and Dharma protectors from the Eastern
Pure Land, carrying precious umbrellas, royal banners, prayer flags,
and medicinal powders in offering to Shangtönpa. They wore various ornaments (jewels, bone ornaments, diadems, and silk clothes),
presented offerings, and led Shangtönpa on a scintillating trail across
the sky to the Pure Land of the Dakini. During this vision, many
miraculous signs occurred. The sky was filled with a sweet fragrance
and the sound of music and dancing deities. Rainbow paintings shone

day after day and everyone present experienced primordial awareness free of obstacles and unmoved by the waves of confusion. Definitive understanding arose deep within.

After the cremation at dawn on the eighth day, all kinds of sacred
relics appeared out of the bones to serve as a basis for the devotion of
future disciples. On the tenth month in that same bird year, the disciple Rikpe Dorje transported Shangtönpa's skull to Swayambhu in
Nepal. That very night, in Nepal, the remaining relics multiplied sev-
enty-fold and an adept from Yerang declared, "Your Lama was an excellent sage. I had many signs foretelling all these outstanding relics!" Impressed, the adept placed some of the relics in the stupa of
Swayambhu. Other relics were entrusted to devoted practitioners in
Central and Western Tibet.

Our Lama's life, meditation experience, supernatural faculties,
magical emanations, body, disciples, and activities are all too vast to
be ever fully comprehended. Nevertheless, using his own teachings
as a basis, I have faithfully put some of his words in writing.

This short story of Shangtönpa, refuge of all beings, was written
from memory in the hare year. At the time, I remembered many other
wonderful stories about the great Shangtönpa and always said that I
should write them. But now, I have forgotten some of the details.
Also, I was not given permission to give the specifics on certain things,
so I have refrained from elaborating. But the essential point is that
faith and devotion for the Lama are alone enough for definitive knowledge to arise.

> Above the golden ground pure from the beginning,
> Swell the ocean depths of inexpressible clear-light,
> Where our Lama, precious gem of no-fixation, clear-light and
>     emptiness, is born.
> How can one measure the oceanic depth of the Buddha activ-
>     ity
> Of our Dharma lord, the spontaneous three bodies of enlight-
>     enment?

Faith and confidence quench our thirst and pacify our clinging
and grasping.
Though it quenches our thirst, this ocean neither increases nor
decreases.
That is its value.


This life story is but a drop in the ocean of vast teachings. May the
readers not arouse wrong views for a single word of this story. By the
devotion of seeing the excellence of whatever the Lama does, may
his blessings touch the minds of all mother-beings as numerous as
space is vast. May the iron hook of the Lama's compassion draw beings from the lower realms to the higher ones. May all beings develop
perfect meditation experience. May all beings attain nirvana and enjoy the state of Mahamudra.

In all my lives, may I not be separated from the perfect Lama,
And so enjoy the splendor of Dharma.
Perfecting the qualities of the paths and levels,
May I swiftly attain the state of my glorious Lama.

Great Lama, whatever your body and your entourage,
Whatever your lifespan, pure land,
And sublime name,
May I achieve just the same.

Glorious Lama, Kedrup Shangtönpa,
When you are a Buddha in the Eastern Pure Land,
Please guide me and all sentient beings, as numerous as space
is vast,
Until we too attain enlightenment.


This is a brief extract in the life of the realized Lama Shangtönpa.

SARWA DAKALYA NIBHA WANTU! ZHAL DRO! GEO!

# 13

# Life of Zhönnu Drup

To the precious Lama,
To the yidam deities,
And to all the wisdom protectors,
I bow down.

I bow down to Zhönnu Drup, unchanging great bliss,
Supreme in the spontaneous benefit he brings to both self and
    others,
The undisputed son-disciple of all the Kagyu Lamas,
Whose time has come to guide beings through his activity.

Since this glorious Lama's secret body, speech, and mind
Are just like those of the Buddha,
His qualities cannot be grasped by ordinary beings.
How could I, of low intellect, claim to understand them?

Inseparable from the Buddhas of the three times and ten direc-
    tions,
The very essence of the five Buddha families,
In nature Vajradhara—the sixth Buddha and the main deity of
    all the mandalas—

Such is my dear Lama, Zhönnu Drup, whose life story shall be
   told.

Whatever small merit there may be in this paean to the Lama's
   life,
May it be an inspiration for beings.
All [that I write], I have heard from the Dharma lord himself,
Having had the honor to spend just a little time in his presence.
Please treasure what I say with clear faith.

Mighty Vajradhara in the form of the Lama,
Your qualities cannot possibly be grasped by mind,
Yet as limited as my faith and understanding may be,
I praise those qualities I can see,
And supplicate you: please protect me with your great compas-
   sion.

The mighty lord of great bliss, whose body, speech, and mind are
inseparable from the truly realized Buddha Vajradhara, was perceived
by the Buddhas as the body of reality free of the two delusions,[190] by
the bodhisattvas of the three pure states as the enlightened enjoyment-body, and by ordinary beings and those of the lower levels as
the enlightened emanation-body. To me, he appeared as the embodiment of kindness, a genuine Lama who gave blessings and achieved
the full grace of empowerments and oral instructions. I know with
absolute certainty that he was truly Vajradhara.

   Zhönnu Drup was skilled and omniscient. He merely had to teach
for *samadhi* meditation to dawn, illnesses and demons to disappear,
and disciples to gain realizations. His clairvoyance was unobstructed,
his attainments stable, his compassion tireless, and his activity beneficial. Who can ever conceive of the ocean of qualities of this special Lama whose life was so immaculate? Even though one cannot
describe his mind and aspirations any more than one can use words
to explain the natural state, I shall still try.

In the beginning, I was fortunate enough to have the rare opportunity to meet with Lama Zhönnu Drup, and felt as though I had come across a wish-fulfilling gem. In the middle, I stayed with him for a long time. He looked after me with great kindness, as a mother would after her child. In the end, through his compassionate blessings, I understood the wonder of his complete liberation.

Although Zhönnu Drup developed all qualities, he kept them mostly concealed for reasons elucidated elsewhere. He always acted in ways most suitable to the different aptitudes of his disciples. Whatever he did was done well. Whatever he taught was marvelous. I write this eulogy with the most profound devotion: may our Lama's non-referential compassion be a source of refuge for all sentient beings.

LAMA ZHÖNNU DRUP, you were only four years old when,
Seeing the places where great adepts had meditated in the past,
Effortless *samadhi* was born within you,
Awakened from your practice in previous lives.
I supplicate you: please protect me with your great compassion.

Out of compassion, this glorious holy Lama took rebirth for the benefit of beings. As for his birthplace: the Nyang River flows from the north and is said to nurture purity of mind. The whole area of lower Nyang, in fact, is renowned for its fabulous properties as the praise of numerous scholars and Lamas confirms.[191] To the east, the landscape is dotted with mountain peaks. The land is so flat and spacious that the harvest and fruit it produces surpass any other. The Nyang River Valley was the birthplace of such beings as the great translator Vairochana, the scholar Tsang Nakpa, and others. All over the land, people are happy and joyful. They saturate the fertile ground with an intricate lattice pattern.

The inhabitants of the area included the Ding family on the male side:[192] A household of farmers who, although lay people, maintained the ten virtues in all their acts. Zhönnu Drup's father was Gyalpo Tsepel. His mother, Gyamo Kedren, was known for her faith, compassion, and devotion. My Lama himself said, "When my mother was alive, our relatives and the local people enjoyed good health and were on good terms with her. Every word my mother uttered was meaningful. However, I found myself smothered in affection, so I fled to Kyong Cave and was brought up by the woman practitioner Majo Chökyi."

When Zhönnu Drup was four, he returned to his village and stayed in the fields while weeds were uprooted. He was especially content when he looked up at a mountain cave. One day, he asked Majo Chökyi about it. She said, "Up there lives Hungbar the adept." For a long time after that, he derived great joy from looking at the mountain, and would stare at it continuously! Sometimes he thought that he might like to stay up there. At other times, the mere sight of the mountain cave led to perfect meditative stability. Thus he gave birth to the *samadhi* of clear-light without center or limits.

Later, my dear Lama Zhönnu Drup studied extensively and remained in solitary retreat, thinking, "The time of death is uncertain, and the nature of samsara is nothing but unbearable suffering, so now I must meditate." In addition to the *samadhi* meditation he had already developed, he also gained direct knowledge of his own true nature—the naked luminosity of mind beyond objects. With this meditative attainment, he developed definitive understanding. Homage to Lama Zhönnu Drup whose pure karma from the past awoke naturally.

LIVING IN THE great monastic institution of Narthang,[193]
You took the vows of a monk and kept good ethics.
You trained in sutras, tantras, *shastras,* and oral precepts.
I supplicate you, great and authentic scholar.

When Zhönnu Drup turned ten, he became a monk in Narthang before the abbot Chimpa Yidzhin Norbu. He observed the precepts of a novice monk. At twenty, he took full ordination, studied with the teacher Lokyawa, and maintained perfect ethics. "I became very learned," my Lama related, "and for a few years, I acted as a scholar."

At twenty-one, he thought to himself, "It is time for me to stop my intellectual studies and aim for actual attainments. For that, I should study the tantras and oral precepts." So, he went to the Sakya Lamas to get tantric teachings, which he put into practice. "With all my teachers," he explained, "I considered both the words and the meaning they expressed." Homage to Zhönnu Drup, Dharma lord, who grasped the words and their meaning without contradiction. Homage to this great authentic scholar of perfect ethics.

YOU ENGENDERED REVULSION for the faults of samsara,
Showed no attachment for friends, money, or this life,
Which are no different from grime on the palm of the hand.
I supplicate you, master of renunciation.

Zhönnu Drup had a general revulsion to the intense suffering of samsara. He developed a particularly strong sense of renunciation when strife began to develop within the Sakya community and everyone took up weapons. "All the people talked of taking up arms," my Lama related. "They had no time to listen to teachings, practice, or meditate. They were not maintaining their *samaya* commitment[194] to their teacher. They knew the preciousness of this human body. They also knew that virtuous deeds lead to happiness and evil actions to suffering, and still they engaged in actions that would result in a rebirth in the three lower realms. I thought to myself, 'I've got to go! I don't want to hear another word about this war. I need to get away from such sights.' So I gathered up my possessions, books, and statues, and entrusted them to the faithful few who were still like disciples to me. I gave away the land that provided sustenance for my Dharma practice and left unburdened, with nothing at all."

As a final visit before leaving, my dear Lama Zhönnu Drup went to see Jangsem Kungzhön in his chamber and explained, "From the beginning, I wore the armor of one who practices renunciation. I came here with great faith in the Sakya teachings, but it's been difficult to deal with the hierarchy to receive teachings from the Lamas! In a future life, I hope to meet a simple Lama who really knows the

Sakya teachings, a yogi of authentic meditation experience." He and
Jangsem Kungzhön discussed this at length.

Jangsem Kungzhön later related that Zhönnu Drup truly wore the
armor of a renunciate, and was strong in his ascetic determination.
Jangsem Kungzhön told my Lama to choose any object that might be
useful in creating an auspicious connection. He then provided Zhönnu
Drup with some men, and said, "Now you must meet the great ascetic master Dampala."

It so happened that Dampala had started his solitary retreat that
very day. As Zhönnu Drup approached, he saw the last of the clay
wall go up that closed off the practitioner for retreat. My Lama
knocked on the wall, approached the attendant, and explained his
situation. At that moment, Lama Dampala himself came to an opening by the wall and said, "I had a dream of a white man who told me
not to go into retreat as long as he didn't have my teachings. That
must be you."

The Lama proceeded to give Zhönnu Drup several ascetic practices such as Cutting the Thread. Then he explained, "These ascetic
practices can overcome all your obstacles. But if you don't follow my
instructions, you won't benefit from them, even if you teach them to
others. Take these precepts to heart, and these ascetic practices will
be advantageous for you."

Zhönnu Drup considered the happiness and pleasures of this world
as putrid as staring into one's own vomit. Thus, having no attachment, he developed mental renunciation. During the harvest season,
he repeatedly told himself, "It doesn't take much intelligence to observe people and see that they don't know what kind of harvest they
will reap. And what about consideration for their own deaths? What's
there for them, after this endless, thankless labor?"

These thoughts made him feel very sad and great compassion effortlessly arose in him. Zhönnu Drup needed no reminders about
death and impermanence because he naturally mused on such meditations. He used this power at night. Always sleeping lightly, he got
up several times between dusk and dawn to practice. Once, when he
was going to Lhasa to do circumambulations, his friend and fellow
traveler told him, "Kedrup, you're a really good practitioner. You even

practice at night. I, on the other hand, sleep like a corpse. It's embar-
rassing! Maybe we should sleep in separate places!"

Zhönnu Drup truly took to heart the meaning of death and impermanence and found no satisfaction in the joys of samsara. Homage
to this great renunciate for whom worldly pleasures held no lure and
whose life was pure and unrivalled.

RESIDING WITH MANY Lamas and adepts,
Your mind mixed inseparably with theirs, fulfilling all inten-
    tions,
And receiving predictions. This is undisputed.
I supplicate you, holder of the victory banner.

"My feelings of melancholy, first born when I saw the armies of Kunga
Zangpo[195] prepare for war, grew to sadness and revulsion for samsara,"
my Lama said. "Once I was approaching a mountain when the thought
occurred to me that I should go to Zar.[196] So as I headed toward the
mountains, I thought, 'I need to escape the many snares of samsara,
and practice until I reach enlightenment for the benefit of beings.' I
knew that the only things I needed to achieve this were food and
clothes. As for clothes, decent old rags would do. But food would be
more difficult: I needed at least something in the morning and evening.
Still, I took an oath to devote myself to practice."

While Zhönnu Drup was wandering in the mountains, he heard a
voice and turned around to meet Lama Lopön Gelong of old, from
whom he received several cycles of teachings. Next, Zhönnu Drup
met Lama Kamchenpa who related the life of Sangye Tönpa, and
Zhönnu Drup was immediately inspired with an intense faith. Feeling an urge to meet this precious Sangye Tönpa, my Lama set out for
Central Tibet.

In Rigong, Zhönnu Drup heard that Sangye Tönpa was staying
nearby. So, he spent the night with his head pointing in the direction
of the Lama. He prayed and fell asleep after midnight. That night,
Zhönnu Drup had an auspicious lucid dream as he described: "I had a
most auspicious experience of the illusory nature of reality. In front

of me were three yogis wearing cotton robes and singing songs. The one in the middle, whose skin was a pure blue, said these words, 'Go to Rigong, there's real Dharma there!' He spoke with a radiant smile."

The following morning, my dear Lama Zhönnu Drup met Lama Sangye Tönpa. As soon as he saw the face of Sangye Tönpa, all conceptual thoughts, coarse and subtle, became of one flavor. A sense of patience and forbearance naturally brought happiness to his mind.

Zhönnu Drup requested the empowerment of Illusory Body Yoga, and began practicing the Six Yogas. He thought, "Mere listening is not enough, now I need to develop experiences." After meditating for forty days on the practice Empty Enclosure Resounding with A, an experience arose, at which point he requested further visualization instructions. My Lama practiced these while maintaining all his previous practices as well.

At dawn following a teaching on the Dharma protector, Zhönnu Drup had a dream omen. He reported it to Lama Sangye Tönpa, who said the dream signaled that he was about to see the face of the protector. Sangye Tönpa gave him the complete instructions on the Six Yogas and then ordered, "Come back tonight." When Zhönnu Drup returned that night, Sangye Tönpa said, "I've given these instructions to all your Dharma brothers and sisters. But as for other profound teachings, one must carefully consider whether to reveal them or not, and teach them gradually, when and if one does.

"You know," Sangye Tönpa continued, pleased, "the sight of a bodhisattva like you gladdens the heart. So I've decided to give you all the instructions of the lineage. You are the right person. To you, I shall teach everything. I won't keep anything secret. This will be of great benefit to beings. You may pass them on to any of your Dharma brothers and sisters. Keep your *samaya* practice and show diligence in all the teachings and oral advice."

During that period, Zhönnu Drup was told to meditate in the mountain solitudes while preparing to receive a series of teachings—including the empowerment of the Five Tantric Deities, Chakrasamvara, Amitayus and other empowerments, the Six Yogas of Niguma, Mind Deathlessness and Non-Deviation, Mahamudra, oral instructions of the Dakpo Kagyu, Drikung Kagyu, Drukpa Kagyu, Tselpa Kagyu, and the Sakya school as well as the [Chö] teachings of Machik Lapdrön, etc. The most important of these teachings were given several times.

Zhönnu Drup steadily practiced all the teachings he received. Through the blessings and compassion of his precious Lama, conducive practice conditions provided by dakinis and Dharma protectors, and his faith and devotion, the pith experiences arose in his being.

One winter while practicing in Kharak, my Lama headed out to receive teachings when he slipped just outside his cave and very nearly died. Just then, two dakinis, Drutön and Trashidrup, appeared. "Where are you going?" asked Zhönnu Drup.

They replied, "Lama [Sangye Tönpa] sent us to look after you," and they helped him up. Later, when he related this to his Lama Sangye Tönpa, the latter replied, "Yes, yes, two dakinis. I had a feeling you might face a little obstacle, so I sent them out last night to go and help you." This is just one example of Zhönnu Drup benefiting from the blessings and unfailing kindness of his Lama.

On three occasions, Lama Sangye Tönpa reminded Zhönnu Drup, "You must labor for the welfare of all beings and, you must especially benefit those disciples who are worthy vessels for the teachings." But my Lama objected, "I want to entirely give up this world rather than expound on the Dharma."

Lama Sangye Tönpa returned a fourth time and emphatically declared, "You shall be the holder of the precious Dharma. I've taught the rightful owner." With these words, he blessed Zhönnu Drup. The latter prostrated, placed his head at the Lama's feet and cried out, "I'll do whatever you ask. My practice is poor. There's not even a trace of virtue in me! Please hold me in your heart."

My Lama later related, "I felt enormous devotion [for Sangye Tönpa]. On my return from Kharak, I went to see my Lama but he was in poor condition—insomnia and no appetite. I was so affected that I couldn't stop crying, and I placed my head at his feet to receive his blessings. After that, we talked. His health improved immediately [after my return]. He actually slept better that very night. He told me to come back the next day. When I went to see him the next morning, he looked much better. His complexion was positively radiant and he declared happily, 'Teacher Zhönnu Drup, you have taken my illness away!'" This—and other such stories which I've not had the chance to write down—illustrate the lives of the 'father and son,' Sangye Tönpa and Zhönnu Drup, Dharma lords.

Zhönnu Drup went to see many teachers from whom he obtained teachings, including Lama Tropupa, Lama Zhankun Pongpa, Lama Dakjarwa and others. "Great benefit arises from perseverance and renunciation," my Lama explained. "Whatever the teachings and experiences, you need perseverance to bring them to life. Perseverance cuts through even the strongest physical or mental hesitation."

My dear Lama fulfilled the wishes of all his teachers, manifested their qualities, and received their blessings. Thus his mind and their minds became one and inseparable. Homage to Zhönnu Drup who, by the grace of his teachers' enlightened actions, held the victory banner.

> WITH INTENSE COMPASSION for the suffering of beings,
> You showed no attachment to your own happiness.
> You practiced diligently, abiding within the body of reality.
> I supplicate you for whom meditation and post-meditation are
>     forever one.

Armies from Mongolia approached when my Lama was practicing virtue in the wilds of Je. The sight depressed him and he sent [the attendant] Geshak to find out more. Geshak returned with the news that the central battalion was planning to attack the Drikung armies. "Well now," Zhönnu Drup thought to himself, "both the Sakya and Drikung monks are going to form into battalions. They'll be fighting, arguing, taking sides. I foresee more death."

My dear Lama was intensely concerned for the suffering the monk-soldiers would surely experience in the lower realms, where their lifespan and physical situation would be dreadful. He stopped sleeping, and without any concern for his own happiness in this life or peace and quiet in future lives, his unbearable compassion inspired him to practice with undistracted diligence. This effort blossomed into quintessential Mahamudra.

When Zhönnu Drup stayed in a guesthouse in Je, west of Shang, he saw a leper there with stumps covered by blood and pus. Zhönnu Drup bent down and sucked the legs of the leper to ease the pain. The act stretched the limits of his compassion and mental training.

"During the great famine in the sheep year," Zhönnu Drup explained, "I thought that I should practice in Kharak, so I took a bag of tsampa and left. Along the way, I saw an old couple atrociously emaciated, and noticed that no one gave food to the old people. Unable to stand their suffering, I gave them all the tsampa I had with me. Later, I met the monk Tarpapap in Yuri[197] and I said, 'Please don't get distracted on my account. Just practice!' On the way back from Yuri, I stopped to rest. You see," my Lama explained, "all appearances are but the clear-light nature of the mind. Oh yes, they are!"

During his retreat in Samding,[198] Zhönnu Drup asked a student to read him the Mahamudra Golden Rosary. The student began to read, then looked up and saw Zhönnu Drup apparently sleeping. So he thought, "I'd better stop the reading for now."

But from Zhönnu Drup came these words, "Please do continue!" There are many other such examples of my dear Lama's mastery of both gross conception and fine discrimination unimpeded even by sleep. Any person who has studied with him will tell you this, and Zhönnu Drup acknowledged, "Sleep is not an impediment for me."

My Lama's songs in Zabulung and elsewhere came across as the sound of realization itself. Homage to this great master, whose every action was imbued with the flow of meditation experience.

WHEN YOU STUDIED the various aspects of Dzogchen Expanse,[199]
You reached the highest pinnacles.
Upon that, the experience of no-self blazed.
I supplicate you who reached the peak of all the vehicles.

For five years, our precious Lama Zhönnu Drup stayed in the forest
of Jomonak, living in the most austere ascetism with nothing but a
thin cotton robe. He subsisted on water only. He had many extraordinary experiences and realizations connected with the ocean of oral
precepts and tantras of both the old and new traditions.

After perfecting the secret Dzogchen teachings, he studied the
Dzogchen Expanse by Garab Dorje,[200] and progressing on the path,
succeeded to the highest level at which point he thought, "Experiences and realizations shine within the unshakable body of reality,
mind itself. Such are the signs of Atiyoga realization coming true.
Homage to this supreme being who reached the peak of all the vehicles and manifested all qualities.

> WHEN YOU STUDIED oral precepts,
> The clear-light nature of your mind intensified.
> You perceived pure lands and nether-worlds alike.
> Omniscient all-seeing one, I supplicate you.

Very special prophecies were made by my Lama, the virtuous adept
who knows past, present, and future. He requested instructions from
Lama Gelong, a worthy son-disciple of enlightened mind refined with
love and compassion. Lama Gelong actually experienced his principal yidam deity and possessed supernatural faculties. He gave Zhönnu
Drup numerous instructions including the Four Verse Gangama
Mahamudra teachings of Tilopa, the expanded and concise versions
of the secret practices, and the Mahamudra Golden Rosary. Zhönnu
Drup's realizations greatly increased by meditating on the cycle of
teachings of Lama Chegom.

One night, having entered the Clear Light Yoga in sleep, he looked
around and saw all external objects with absolute clarity. The radiance of appearances was enhanced and he clearly saw the Buddha
pure lands, the realms of gods and humans, as well as the three lower
realms of hell-beings, hungry ghosts, and animals. Such sharp, clear
experiences occurred more than once. He perceived the radiance
manifest in all things, but always kept concealed his experiences and

realizations and carried on his life with modesty, never making any claims. Homage to this omniscient Lama whose Clear Light Yoga perceptions were unimpeded.

> DURING YOUR STAY in Kharak, you practiced in your sleep.
> The precious mantras and teachings of Lamas
> You received in their entirety, and have condensed them here.
> I supplicate you, holder of the treasury of oral teachings.

In Kharak, Zhönnu Drup strictly maintained his practice in spite of physical and mental obstructions during meditation. He exerted himself in the Lamdre practices, but felt still unclear about the words and their meaning.

One night, he dreamt that Trelungpa gave him the complete, condensed, and concise versions of the Lamdre, including both the words and their meaning. Later, he received the pith practice that brings together all the Lamdre teachings in a single word. He asked Trelungpa about his birthplace and Trelungpa replied that he came from Menlung. But Zhönnu Drup woke up before he had time to ask details about Trelungpa's father and family. At such reflections, all his previous obscurations and discomfort dissolved. Remembering the kindness of this Lama, he offered a prayer to the Lamdre lineage. Homage to Zhönnu Drup of peerless qualities, who brought us these teachings.

> NEAR THE TOWN market place,
> Trouble began to show up.
> At that time, your body took on the proportions of a wrathful
>     deity.
> I supplicate you, whose body was the Buddha's body.

My Lama Zhönnu Drup put on the armor of mental renunciation. For the next twelve years, summer or winter, he stayed alone, wandering to new places every two or three months to escape inclement weather. He vowed to move on and never accept more than a handful of food when it was offered to him. He wandered like a hermit in the wild.

Once, in the charnel ground of Naga Kuri near a town market, he settled himself to practice Chö and overcome *nagas* and demons. He was sleeping when he heard someone approach, brown-black in color, wearing layers of goatskin turned inside out. "I was in deep sleep," Zhönnu Drup explained. "I transformed my body into an enormous Hayagriva deity, stuffed the demon in a big bag and shook and shook! He was fuming inside. So to pacify him, I explained the visualizations involved in the Six Yogas of Niguma. I shook again, and the demon let out an awful gasp! When I opened it up, his bluish liver was quivering, and I felt great compassion." In that way Zhönnu Drup pacified all obstacles and demons by employing Chö, Dream Yoga, and Illusory Body Yoga in such a way that they complemented one another. In Naga Deity Cave, Zhönnu Drup had hostile visions for several weeks. After forty nights of this, he dreamt of four men pouncing [on him] with knives, and at that point his practice was freed of achievements or obstacles, and profound awareness arose in him.

Another time, he was sleeping in the forest by a monastery when around midnight, a horse rider appeared saying he had seen a blazing fire. People say that Zhönnu Drup replied to the horse rider, "It was me you saw! Now prostrate yourself and make an offering!" That was my dear Lama's life, and gods and demons came from all over to pay him homage.

Yet another time, he fell asleep in a cave. Toward midnight, he felt dirt trickling down from the ceiling of the cave. "What can this be?" he wondered, and took a closer look. From a fissure in the ceiling, he saw that dirt and rock were falling. When a stone the size of a fist detached itself, he ran off, frightened. But then, he thought, "Ego-clinging is just an unceasing torrent of suffering and must be cut!" He returned to his cave and slept there for two days and two nights, without provisions, keeping his head facing the exit. Then he left for Chelong. Later he returned to the cave and saw that a big stone had fallen right where he had slept.

During a retreat in Kharak, a problem with the energy flow in his body returned to plague him. Neither warm clothes, changes of diet, breathing exercises, nor anything else seemed to help. Although he had various methods—visualizations, oral precepts, and techniques to overcome illness—none of them brought him any relief. Zhönnu Drup concluded, "It must be time for me to die, then." He gave away all his books, clothes, carpets, and other objects. My Lama advised, "If you really want to reach enlightenment for the benefit of beings, then look into death. That will turn your mind to the Dharma."

Zhönnu Drup left for a charnel ground, but he was so weak that he stopped by the Tsang River.[201] He settled himself between boulders along the shore, but the combination of the water washing in and the wind blasting through made it intolerably cold. He shifted his position. But even while meditating, he felt as though his head would explode, so great was the pain. Finally at midnight, he went to sleep.

In short, Zhönnu Drup lived through every conceivable sickness and infectious disease, from nausea to leprosy. Stories of the obstacles he had to overcome during Chö practice were heard by myself and others. Perseverance through these obstacles enabled Zhönnu Drup to abandon ego-clinging and meditate until his body was deity body, and his mind was the actual body of reality. Homage to him whose body was the Buddha's body.

WHILE DOING SECRET practices in Nyeka,
You saw Chakrasamvara, clear as ever,
In an ocean limpid and blue.
I supplicate you who beheld his yidam.

Zhönnu Drup went to Nyeka and practiced tantra. There, he found many fish washed up on the beach. He made a considerable effort to place them all back in the Tsang River. His practice greatly improved and his awareness shone with clarity.

One morning, he sat by the clear blue water of the lake, pure as a reflection in a mirror, and saw in the water the co-emergent body of the Buddha ornamented with all the signs and attributes of enlightenment, victorious, virtuous, and transcendent. He saw this as clearly as meeting someone face to face. He dwelt in the natural state of unborn mind, happy and free of fixation. As of that time, his generation practice became perfectly clear and he understood his own mind as the deity. His realizations expanded.

Zhönnu Drup once prostrated and performed the Six Practices of the Kalachakra in a dark room, when he saw a limitless number of deities. And when performing secret practices in Zabulung, he had a visionary experience: the whole valley filled with countless deities. Homage to him who saw the face of his principal yidam deity and received the blessings of Lamas and yidams inseparable.

> MAKING GREAT PRAYERS of aspiration
> In the presence of the Dharma lords of times past,
> You were graced with the blessings of the Kagyu Lamas.
> I supplicate you, wondrous blessed one!

Zhönnu Drup spent time in Rigong to receive teachings. One night, in a dream, a horde of Mongols came after him to take the gold he planned to offer for teachings. He was chasing them when he realized that he was attached to the gold, and became hesitant. When he woke up, he thought to himself, "I should have seized the dream, I should have practiced lucid dreaming, but I didn't. Seems that I'm still bound to this gold I have here!"

The following day, he presented a half measure of gold. When he saw that others were short of offerings to present for the teachings, he gave them his gold. He had hardly anything left to offer, so he made a private prayer of aspiration for the teachings and looking up at the sky, he aroused devotion. "I felt graced by a shower of inconceivable blessings," Zhönnu Drup said. "The deities must care for me very much to bestow blessings so great. These great blessings came because all the Kagyu Lamas of the past were answering my requests." Homage to this marvelous son-disciple of the Lamas of the lineage.

> IN THE SOLITUDE of Tingpo,
> Your mind became inseparable from space, yet

You saw it all and retained the echo of a prayer.
I supplicate you.


Zhönnu Drup wished to go south on his own. He gathered up all his attendants from Eastern Tibet, gave them his few vestigial possessions, and entered into solitary retreat in a cave in Tingpo. He practiced, isolated, and did not sleep at night. His mind became inseparably mixed with space, without even a trace of physical appearance. Within this meditative stability, he perceived all things, coarse or subtle. At the same time, clearly imprinted in his mind was a prayer of faith and devotion. My Lama savored a deep joy. I've heard a stock of stories connected with his experiences, but I've not set them all down. Homage to Lama Zhönnu Drup, stable in the clear-light nature of mind beyond coming or going—the unchanging natural state.


JUT AS YOU woke up one morning,
Countless deities appeared, proclaiming teachings on compassion,
Amidst an array of countless *amrita* drops.
I supplicate you to whom appearances spontaneously arose as deity body.


The great meditator Zhönnu Drup said that he once saw deity body arising by itself. "At dawn one morning," Zhönnu Drup explained, "I was performing the practices of Emptying the Channels and Purifying the Energy Winds, when all objects disappeared and the cave filled with an array of countless *amrita* drops. In their midst, deities displayed various mudras, expounding teachings on compassion. My experience was beyond achievements or obstacles; dualistic clinging was completely purified." Homage to this great adept to whom appearances arose as illusory clear-light deity body, the twin dimensions of enlightenment[202] forever as one.


IN A GATHERING of great meditators, your realizations stood out.
Amidst scholars, your Dharma was like a lions' roar.

Even among peerless beings, you shone as the supreme crown
    jewel.
I supplicate you who held the banner of the teachings.

After my dear Lama gained proficiency in the three-fold duties of a
scholar, he meditated diligently with ethics untainted by any wrong-
doing, and gained experiences and realizations. He stood like a lord
far above agreements or contradictions. His mental sharpness in understanding and training has already been explained in detail. Homage to him who held the banner of the precious teachings and was
unmatched in his abilities as a scholar, monk, and meditator.

MAKING A CONNECTION with you was always meaningful.
Saying a prayer to you always led to a glorious state.
You were my sole comfort, my only safeguard—
I supplicate you whose kindness was incomparable.

Since Zhönnu Drup filled the measuring scale of the two accumulations of merit and wisdom in the past, he [now] found it easy to provide food, clothing, and teachings to whoever came to see him,
whether there were many or few. Even when he stayed in desolate
valleys without people nearby, his connection with the sublime jewels of Buddha, Dharma, and Sangha enabled the fulfillment of all his
needs. He told his devoted patrons that they would experience no
hardship in their present life, and that their [generosity] would benefit them in the future, as befits the infallible law of cause and effect.
    Many came to see him and receive his blessings. Just offering a small
measure of flour to Zhönnu Drup led to good karmic connections
with him. Merely hearing him speak aroused heartfelt respect for,
and certainty in, the Dharma. Those who offered a prayer with sincere devotion were established in a glorious state. Others beside me
can vouch for the truth of this from direct experience. Zhönnu Drup
held in his great compassion any practitioner who saw him, heard
him teach, or had devotion for him. Homage to the Lama of unparal-

leled kindness who, like a true friend, guided and cared for us with Dharma, food, or clothes, no matter whether we were of superior, average, or mediocre faculties.

ESSENCE OF THE three sources of refuge, glorious spiritual friend,
Grant us the blessings of your infallible compassion!
This account, written in the forest of Yuri in the bird year,
Is but a drop in the ocean of life stories of the Lamas.
I apologize for any errors in presenting this, and dedicate all merit.
O Zhönnu Drup, may I find refuge in your great compassion!

In the bird year, Zhönnu Drup stayed in profound meditation in the fields of local protectors, the palaces of dakinis, and the valleys of gods and demons.

This account of the outer, inner, and secret liberation of Zhönnu Drup's body, speech, mind, qualities, and activities was set down during a stay in the forest in Yuri in Western Tibet. Although my intelligence is no greater than a hair's width, I decided to write these lines of praise. They are just brief verses and by no means cover everything. They shift between the past and the future, are covered in colloquialisms, and probably include some mistakes. I was concerned about stifling the story with too many words, so I've tried to keep it short. For the sake of easy understanding, all the verses of praise assembled here are followed by a prose commentary inspired by the words of my teacher, Zhönnu Drup. May holy beings forgive these inferior explanations!

This has been an account of the immaculate life of the lord Zhönnu Drup. It was written from memory by the Sakya monk Bodhi Prajna in Samding monastery in Yuri, Western Tibet. By this merit, may all beings, as numerous as space is vast, quickly attain the level of our Dharma lord, Lama Zhönnu Drup!

# 14

# Death of Zhönnu Drup

*Namo Ratna Guru!* REALITY ITSELF, LAMA Zhönnu Drup, your body, speech, and activity are always commensurate with the aptitudes of your disciples. You teach with perfect insight into the future. In your behavior, whether it relates to food, wealth, or possessions, you maintain three-fold purity. You bring down a shower of Dharma instructions to those who gather around you. Your Dharma activity continues through your glorious son-disciple, Gyaltsen.

Recognition of one's mind as inseparable from the Lama appears to the devotee as the pure realm of compassion. You give detailed teachings on the transmission to disciples of the lineage. To those who cling to things as inherently existent, you demonstrate the truth of impermanence. You satiate disciples with your miraculous displays. We supplicate you who passed into the Blissful Pure Land: may we find refuge in your great compassion.

In the winter of the male earth horse year, Zhönnu Drup, the very essence of the Buddhas of the three times, stayed on Mount Sinpori[203] doing winter practice. Zhönnu Drup explained, "Evil spirits caused an obstacle. Demons, gods, and cave spirits of Latö came to meet with me." When we asked Lama Zhönnu Drup whether [the gods and demons showing up] was a good sign or not, he related the story of Sangye Tönpa who met with gods and demons at the time of his death.

After the winter practice, Zhönnu Drup spent twenty days teachings the Dharma and giving empowerments. All those assembled performed many long-life services. The Lama's health was good and he decided to go to his monastery of Samding after telling his attendant, "Döndrup, bring me donations and cushions, and most of our cooking utensils!" He turned to us and declared, "Any of you can stay and sleep here in my bed." And the party set out.

Once in Samding, he requested that no one have access to him, and went into retreat. Nevertheless, more than four hundred people—scholars, influential figures, and locals from the mountains—gathered near the Lama's place. They lined up to pay homage, arranged rows of offerings, and waited for teachings. But Lama Zhönnu Drup dismissed them, saying, "Right now, my health is poor and my body feels heavy. I cannot grant you the teachings you want. Let each one of you return home. Perhaps in the future, we will meet under more auspicious conditions. For now, it's best for me to stay at the Zhalu monastery."[204] And, to improve his practice, Zhönnu Drup gave away the last of his wealth. Then he continued with the following advice, "Even great meditators exert themselves. So I, too, will spend a year in retreat out here, and purify those delusions that cause harm to beings. Those of you who are good practitioners can stay here and spend the year practicing, and if you can't get the support you need, I'll help you. The rest of you, go wherever you like. What's most important is that you do not harm one another."

The following month, Zhönnu Drup's health seemed to improve. He intensified his practice and admitted about seventy practitioners. Soon, men and women filed as if on a pilgrimage procession, hoping to catch a glimpse of Zhönnu Drup or just hear him teach. After straining himself to give individual instructions to each person, he finally declared he couldn't stay any longer. As a final teaching, to suitable students he transmitted such teachings as the Six Yogas of Niguma, the Mahamudra Reliquary, Mind Deathlessness and Non-Deviation, the Four-Word Mahamudra teachings of Tilopa, the Five-Deity Mandala of Chakrasamvara, etc.

Due to his sickness, Zhönnu Drup spoke much more slowly than normal. He blurted out words that were quite striking, resulting in questioning expressions on the faces of the older scholars—these unconventional teachings seemed rather different from those in the past. But none of the scholars dared ask for further elucidations!

In the fifth month of the year, many people came to Zhönnu Drup to request the Dharma. It's said that some even came all the way from Mongolia. But Zhönnu Drup was not well. He had no appetite and felt drowsy. Except for granting a few pointing-out instructions, he remained in solitude. And once again, his health appeared to improve.

On the eighth day of the following month, older scholars requested the Lama's permission to perform a concise long-life practice for him. But Zhönnu Drup replied, "Up to now, I've never done any kind of long-life practice. It's always seemed to me to be an excuse [to gather donations]. But there's nothing wrong with these practices as long as we use our own funds for the expenses and don't go around asking for contributions like taxmen! I'll admit that right now I feel as terrible as an elephant sinking in mud!" The older scholars proceeded to perform the *sadhanas* of Medicine Buddha and Avalokiteshvara, the hundred-syllable mantra, and Guru Yoga. They also presented offerings, intoned mantras, read three times without a break the Hundred Thousand Verse Prajnaparamita, and offered more than three million tormas.

On the fourteenth day, Zhönnu Drup drank a little tea and said, "At first, I was hoping to leave without a trace. But it seems like that's not going to happen. There will be good, devoted disciples. In particular, the practitioners of this Zhalu monastery were hospitable to me and wanted me to leave something behind so they would not feel too sad when I passed away. They're sincere people, not like some who seem so white and turn out to have a very dark side indeed.[205] Zhönnu Drup had men load the offerings he received and told them to place the tributes at the Lamas' monasteries, the foot of the Buddha statue in Lhasa, and any monastic institution of good repute where the monks' ethics were genuinely good.

The next evening, Zhönnu Drup said, "Last night, I wanted to move on, but a white man appeared and would not allow me to go just yet." Gods, demons, and many ordinary beings wanted to see Zhönnu Drup and ask for teachings. But he was weak and specified that no one was to come in, adding, "Nothing can stop me from going now. When all my tasks are accomplished, in my next life, my body will be the form bodies and my mind, the body of reality."

One particular night, an individual asked to do a special service for Lama Zhönnu Drup, but the Lama replied, "Just leave it! There's a point when, no matter what one does, one's health just won't recover. Let me tell you of my Lama Sangye Tönpa—he was very ill in his meditation cave and he said, 'The sole, continuous focus of concentration should be the clear-light nature of mind.' These are the words of my holy master."

Lama Zhönnu Drup said he'd be going around the eighteenth day of the month. So on the given day, one of his disciples told him, "Lama, today is the eighteenth." And Lama Zhönnu Drup ordered, "Gelong Tregön, prepare a large offering!" At noon that day, five men, including the teacher Tratön, asked Lama Zhönnu Drup if a practice to prolong his life could be performed. "Ha! Sure, sure!" Lama Zhönnu Drup laughed, but he didn't go ahead with it.

Understanding that the end was near, the men prostrated before him, begging him to hold the students and lineage holders in his compassion and to reveal which pure realm he would go to and what prayers should be made. Lama Zhönnu Drup stretched and then explained, "I've already given advice to every person. Surely that's enough. If you've received pointing-out instructions, you won't need to say anything else.

Supreme yogi Heruka,
Whichever your land,
That is where I'll be.

Wherever I am,
That is the Pure Land.


And Zhönnu Drup added that he'd always be one with those gathered around him. But some students protested, "This is advice for superior students. What about those of us who are average, or even mediocre? Please provide meditation and visualization instructions for us, too."

Zhönnu Drup simply advised, "All those who make sincere prayers to go to the Blissful Pure Land will get there. Now stop worrying about me and pray with single-pointed concentration."

On the evening of the nineteenth, Lama Zhönnu Drup warned, "My breath is getting very weak." His attendant asked, "Lama, you've been inhaling and holding your breath for long spells, and then you don't exhale. Why is that?"

Zhönnu Drup explained, "Well, my breath is entering my principal channel."

As death was close, the attendant asked some final questions, "Lama, are there non-humans? What are they like? We know so little. Please give us some clear, direct advice!" But Zhönnu Drup kept his answers vague.

On the twenty-fourth evening of the month, the Lama did not allow any more visitors. He neither accepted nor gave any presents. Then he advised his retinue, "There's no reason for you to come along. You know that all great meditators go into retreat when they are dying. There is no better assistance than one's own spiritual practice at times of illness and death." The monk Gelong Gyalwapal led the others in chanting while three men prostrated repeatedly. They prayed for the Lama's good health.

Zhönnu Drup's monks asked him to leave some miraculous signs and relics for the sake of all future disciples. Lama Zhönnu Drup answered, "There won't even be that much. After I'm dead, wash my body and scatter my bones in the Nyang and Tsang Rivers. There's no need for outdoor or indoor relic shrines!" But his disciples begged again and again, so that finally Zhönnu Drup relented, "All right then, since your prayers are so sincere, I'll do as you wish. But there'll only be a few relics. And you're not to make any indoor or outdoor shrines bigger than a few inches. You'll be breaking your *samaya* if you make bigger ones."

That night, his speech became slurred and he expressed himself with a few hand gestures. The following day, he could hardly speak at all. He would not eat or move from his bed. His body took on an extraordinary glow as if he'd never been ill. At that very instant, all kinds of miraculous omens appeared near and far. Dakinis, there to guide Zhönnu Drup, could be heard in the sky. On the twenty-ninth day of the late summer month, the sun rose above the mountain and amidst rain, sun, and stars, Lama Zhönnu Drup passed into reality itself.

This account in homage of Zhönnu Drup has been pieced together from the words he spoke to his attendants.

SARWA DAKALYA NIBHA WANTU!

# 15

# Life of Gyaltsen Bum

WITH RESPECT, I bow down at the flawless lotus feet of the holy Lama!

Your precious human birth is adorned with the three trainings.
By listening, reflecting, and meditating, you perfect experiences
   and realizations.
You give fortunate disciples [the teachings which enable] en-
   lightenment within a single lifetime,
At your feet, Gyaltsen Bum, I bow down.

Having perfected enlightened activity in previous lives,
You entered the realm of reality beyond birth.
Yet, propelled by your compassionate aspiration,
You [chose to] display the form of a human being, lord of all
   bipeds!

You awoke to the Dharma due to pure past karma.
You cut external doubts at the root with the sharp knife of lis-
   tening and reflecting.
You removed internal chains of darkness with the lamp of medi-
   tation.
Genuine Lama, you fulfill the two benefits [of self and others].

Glorious protector of all beings in this deluded age,
We prayed that you would stay here for a long time.
But caring for the disciples of other pure realms,
You've left for the Blissful Pure Land amidst miraculous omens
At dawn on the twentieth day of the summer month in the dog
    year.

In order to guide devoted beings in the future,
You leave behind many relics—a basis for our devotion.
May we treasure this brief account of your life.

Our Lama, renowned as Gyaltsen Bum, the essence of the Buddhas
of the three times, quickly traversed the five paths and the ten levels.
Although inseparable from the birthless body of reality, he manifested
the two form bodies and worked extensively for the benefit of sentient beings, training his lineage disciples on the pure path and making vast aspirations that the ship of the Buddha's teachings may endure.

These earlier compassionate aspirations aroused in Gyaltsen Bum
a heartfelt concern for the sentient beings of this deluded age and led
him to take birth as a human in Konglam Tsatang, to the Shuje family. His father, Chökyong Tsen, and his mother, Yangmote, were both
wealthy. As soon as he was capable of conscious thought, Gyaltsen
Bum always and only recited the *mani* mantra. His father, realizing
that this must be the awakening of previous karma, went before
Drinchen Riwa and asked him to inform the boy about the lineage of
Avalokiteshvara and teach him about the *mani* mantra.

When he was six or seven, Gyaltsen Bum went to a teacher to learn
how to read and write. Soon, all the other children learning to read
were fighting with him because they were envious of his skill. Once,
they tore up the pages on which the Sacred Golden Light Sutra was
written in Sanskrit. Concerned that the teacher, Rinchen Dze, would
get angry at the torn pages, Gyaltsen Bum rewrote them all. As he
expected, the teacher now demanded to see the work the boys were

doing. Picking up [Gyaltsen Bum's] book, the teacher asked, "What is this? This wasn't in the book before. Who wrote this down?"

"I did. What was there before got torn," replied Gyaltsen Bum.

"But this is written in a language I haven't taught you!" exclaimed the teacher, Rinchen Dze. "Yet you seem to instinctively know it. You must be a reincarnation! I know that there have been many adepts among your ancestors—Senge Drak, and others. You must be along the same lines." Indeed, with a single glance at the Manjushri Uttering the Names Tantra, the Heart Sutra, or the [Twenty-One Praises to] White Tara, Gyaltsen Bum knew what would follow without missing a beat.

At fifteen, Gyaltsen Bum took monks' vows before Lama Sharpa Kunga Senge and Lama Tengkangpa. He maintained an impeccable attitude and faultless ethics. He gave up what should be abandoned and cultivated what should be developed. So, in the stage of cutting through external doubts through listening, he studied the Prajnaparamita with Lama Tengkangpa and the teacher Kunga Bum. He absorbed both the words and their meaning for three years, and developed new elucidations. After this, he studied the Hevajra Tantra and learnt the songs and practices of the Sakya school. He became so skilled that he even gave new explanations on the subject.

He went once to a tantric feast. Just as he was setting foot through the door, he saw the face of the protector Gurgyi Gönpo[206] huge in size. He immediately invoked his Lamas, Tengkangpa and Kunga Bum, and was bestowed a series of teachings.

On his way to Bokdorchöpa, he saw Lama Shangtönpa practicing alone in the grass. Gyaltsen Bum thought, "I'd like to receive the Dharma from this Lama and become just like him." Inspired with faith, Gyaltsen Bum approached the Lama and asked, "O Lama, please give me the instructions of Niguma, the wisdom dakini!" Lama Shangtönpa replied, "First we'll have to create a connection."

This convinced Gyaltsen Bum to practice and meditate on what he'd been studying. However, Lama Tengkangpa and Sharpa Kunga Senge both told him, "Look, we need you to come and take care of the education and upbringing of our young boy, Khenpo Lodrö Gyaltsen."

Gyaltsen Bum explained, "These two insisted and I could not refuse. I went to the Sakya monastery where I educated the young boy. The highest Lamas were pleased with my good work. After a couple of years, they said, 'Now go and give the same kind of education to another young boy, Kunga Lodrö.'

"But I was tired of studies, explanations, and entourage," continued Gyaltsen Bum. "I explained that I wanted to go to Lama Shangtönpa and become a good meditator while there was still time. They tried to hint that it was important, in these times of civil upheaval, for future abbots to have qualified teachers. I replied, 'Don't ask me to do that! Don't pressure me.' And I adamantly refused.

"Leaving the Sakya institutions, I presented myself to Lama Shangtönpa and asked for the Six Yogas of Niguma, a teaching few men intuit. I felt such a vast faith in both the teachings and in this particular Lama, Shangtönpa, that I had an extraordinary realization. I thought to myself, 'All I need to do is practice.'"

In Tredzong Fortress, Gyaltsen Bum received Mahamudra instructions and was able to dwell for a long time in the natural state of Mahamudra. In this [meditative] stillness, mind itself is molded like space—evanescent, ephemeral, and insubstantial. At times, his mind seemed to exist in the sky. Other times, Gyaltsen Bum felt like his body did not even exist. For the next three years he had such experiences, fluctuating and flickering. At the end of three years, a definitive understanding of emptiness and impermanence had arisen in his mind.

At that point an illness returned, which he interpreted as the result of evil deeds committed in the past. In spite of his sickness, Gyaltsen Bum received a series of teachings from Lama Shangtönpa, including Mind Deathlessness and Non-Deviation. Following this, Gyaltsen Bum practiced for three years in Kuklung.[207] During that time, all kinds of experiences and realizations arose in his mind.

The learned Gyaltsen Bum now went to perform the seven-week prayers for a deceased man. Through her Clear Light Yoga, a great woman meditator saw him eject the consciousness of the deceased and told him, "Such Transference of Consciousness Yoga[208] confirms that you are enlightened. When I die, please perform this practice of transference for me too." She presented Gyaltsen Bum with one and a half measures of gold. Gyaltsen Bum realized that the woman had true confidence.

He spent the next three years in Tokar.[209] One day, he was thinking of going to a nearby spring when the local people advised that the spring wasn't reliable. Gyaltsen Bum replied, "I dreamt of a white being taking care of the spring." Indeed, after the dream, water had returned to the spring. No matter where he stayed or went, Gyaltsen Bum was always sought out by the local deity who never failed to provide conditions conducive to practice.

As students of Gyaltsen Bum, we wanted to hear anecdotes of his life. We once asked him, "What kinds of miraculous experiences did you have when you practiced Chö?"

Gyaltsen Bum replied, "I once went to Monak Dingma Lake. It was covered with a sheet of ice, so I went to sleep there. Halfway through the night, I heard some noise and wondered if the sheet of ice covering the water was breaking. Out of the ice arose a being with the wings of a bird and the body of a man. I could make out a knife in his hand, and saw him coming from behind with the knife pointing toward my back. He stabbed me once and I said, 'Go on, scratch my back a bit, scratch it, would you?' He wavered, uncertain. I knew if I showed fear he would have stabbed me, but when I made it clear that I knew what he was up to, he didn't dare touch me again. I said to the creature from the sea, 'You know, you won't get any-where like this!' And the creature disappeared back into the lake depths. It was a miraculous experience! However, it should be under-stood that all miracles, great or small, are one's own mind. Neither gods nor demons have any real impact."

Curious to hear more stories about our dear Lama Gyaltsen Bum, we then asked, "People say that you had even more awesome experi-ences in Zangra. Now what was that about?"

Gyaltsen Bum answered, "What happened is that after the experience at the lake, I decided to head for Zangra, where I spent the rest
of the night. Five days later at dusk, I was falling asleep when a cav-
alry of black horsemen shot forward. They struck me with their
swords and spears even as I collapsed. Injured, I rolled down into the
water. Fish, frogs, and other creatures passed by me. My body was in
agony. Actually, I was asleep and the moment I realized that I was
dreaming, I transformed myself into Vajrabhairava with three faces
and six arms. The horsemen vanished away. It was a fine experience
of the illusory nature of reality. Other than that, there were no further miracles!"

Still we wanted to know more. Gyaltsen Bum graciously elaborated, "At one point, a hunchback woman fell ill and was paralyzed
on one side of her body. She could hardly stand on her legs. I did a
special practice, then I whipped her and she was cured. But the evil
spirit was now in me, at the level of my back. I went into a cave and
was practicing Chö when a man wearing the clothes of a Mongol
took a great leap over me. Well, right then, I chased him with a spear.
I don't know where he went, he was nowhere to be seen—but all my
pains disappeared. If you practice Chö and tame the great evil spirits,
the small ones are naturally subdued.

"So you see, wherever I've gone, I've cut through everything with
my Chö practice. In the end, I've never been hindered by either gods
or demons, and the reason for this is that, day or night, I recognize all
obstacles as self-arising, like those that appear in a dream. Such are
the signs of mastering Chö practice."

"One night, I had the following dream: I was staying in a house
which had many doors. There were lots of people in the house asking me to grant them the empowerments of the Five Tantric Deities.
I thought that I should open the doors. No sooner had this idea popped
into my mind than the doors opened of themselves, and in the frame
of each one, I clearly saw the Five Tantric Deities. This was the dream
in which I granted the empowerments of the Five Tantric Deities."

Following this, Gyaltsen Bum went into retreat in the upper cave of
Jak, vowing not to eat any human food. He spent thirteen years prac-

ticing in solitude. At one point, he felt more and more sleepy, when he heard a ringing sound: "Gyaltsen Bum, practice! You shall bring great benefit to beings." It was the prophecy of dakas and dakinis. Gyaltsen Bum said that as of that time, he perceived visions of the yidam deities. His dreams were powerful and he clearly saw the Buddha lands, the citadel of the six kinds of beings, and all inner and outer phenomena.

Lama Shangtönpa, to whom Gyaltsen Bum related all this, said, "Now that you are liberated from obstacles, keep your practice grounded. You'll become learned, pure, and wise.[210] You are the rightful owner of these teachings. So bring about the happiness of beings!" And Shangtönpa gave Gyaltsen Bum several books.

Three years later, Lama Shangtönpa displayed his passing [into nirvana]. The attendant who had served him during his last days brought some outer and inner relics. The attendant also presented Gyaltsen Bum with a ceremonial crown made of the five precious objects,[211] "so that the tradition may continue uncorrupted," as Shangtönpa had said. Gyaltsen Bum confirmed, "Lama Shangtönpa appeared to me in a dream: he took my hand in his, and told me to take over for him and protect the Dharma. Moreover, he predicted many things regarding the pure Buddha lands, the samsaric realm, the lifespan of people, and so on."

Taking an oil lamp, Gyaltsen Bum left for Lhasa, Kyergang, and the high mountains. On his way, he met the Dharma lord Rangjung Dorje,[212] who gave him the Three Bodies Pointing-Out Instructions, advice on placement meditation, Mind-Energy Inseparable, the Dzogchen Heart Essence, and the Approaching and Accomplishing Practices. Shortly after that, he met Lama Sangye Yeshe from Lari, from whom he received the Red Yamantaka Tantra and other teachings. Thus, receiving large numbers of tantras, authentic teachings, oral instructions, and specific explanations from an unbelievable large numbers of teachers, Gyaltsen Bum developed great qualities of mind.

Following his Lama's instructions, Gyaltsen Bum spent a long time in Jak acting for the benefit of beings. This, however, was not fulfilling and he decided to go to a quiet, solitary place like Tsari.[213] He spent a night in Kharak when a host of dakinis and Dharma protectors appeared and said, "You left your residence, Lama. Where do you think you're going? Go back, look after your monastery, take care of your disciples, and protect this lineage! There's no greater merit than to benefit beings!" Gyaltsen Bum compromised, "I'll just go on a pilgrimage to Lhasa and then I will come back."

Gyaltsen Bum said that another night, while staying by a spring in Zabulung, dakinis appeared and said that if he didn't stay in his monastery, it would be the end of it—the blessings of the Dharma lineage would run out. So he wrote down and memorized the commentaries on the Six Yogas, the tantras of the Five Tantric Deities, as well as secret oral teachings, and profound instructions. Gyaltsen Bum granted empowerments and teachings for the benefit of beings. He also received prophecies by Lamas, dakinis, and Dharma protectors, in dreams and in actuality, about his beneficial influence.

In short, he was graced by the blessings of the Lamas, received the authoritative one-to-one guru-to-disciple transmission of the lineage, and obtained all kinds of prophecies from dakas and dakinis. All the students who asked him for the Dharma, even those who had just entered the path, were able to develop a strong practice and behold the clear-light nature—so out of mind's reach that writing it down cannot do it justice.

At this time, his practice in the generation stage[214] in the visualization process of his yidam deity was so stable that people merely had to look at him for all appearances to transform, demons and diseases to be pacified, and experiences and realizations to arise effortlessly. In short, his mastery was so pervasive that merely thinking about him brought the self-liberation of all obstacles and hindrances. When disciples with sacred outlook received empowerments from Gyaltsen Bum, they had visions of him as the central deity of the specific mandala: the teachers Zhönnu Drup and Tsulteng saw him as Chakrasamvara with four faces and twelve arms. Lama Drup Senge saw him as Hevajra holding weapons. The Sakya Lama Sögyalwa saw him as the Three-Faced Solitary White Vajrayogini. During the empowerments, dakinis appeared to assist him.

His mastery of the completion stage was also powerful. It was so great that his practice stayed unaffected by the worldly bustle going on around him so that he was able to enter a thousand different *samadhi* meditations. He had no attachment to either samsara or nirvana. Merely receiving instructions from him led even those disciples who had no meditation experience to a powerful non-conceptual meditative state. They experienced lucid dreams and saw the arising of the clear-light nature of mind. Therefore it can be said that Gyaltsen Bum had perfected his body, speech, mind, qualities, and activity.

One morning just before dawn, the teacher Gyaltsen Gön was reciting his prayers [with Lama Gyaltsen Bum] in a cave in Öyuk. When he finished his devotions, Gyaltsen Gön saw a hundred horsemen cloaked in thick woolen cloth galloping, bearing gifts of silk and satin brocades. They reached him and said, "We've come to meet the Lama from Jak. Can you please introduce us?" Lama Gyaltsen Bum heard the riders' request and immediately stepped out of his cave. The horsemen saw him, presented their gifts, prostrated, and asked for blessings.

Later that day, the teacher Drupseng Chen came by and exclaimed, "I heard something going on this morning! There were oblations and prostrations that sounded like *diriri*. I heard it from down there." And turning to Lama Gyaltsen Bum, he asked, "Did someone come here today before sunrise?"

The Lama smiled and replied, "Yes indeed, they were non-humans. You can't see them when the sun is up. But the nights are filled with non-humans." The teacher Drupseng Chen became vividly aware that Lama Gyaltsen Bum was indeed the Buddha. This is only one of many such episodes: it's simply impossible to put them all on paper!

Thus listening, reflecting, and meditating, Gyaltsen Bum perfected all experiences and realizations. He fully mastered Dream Yoga and Illusory Body Yoga, and gained actual understanding of the clear-light nature of mind. He could see all the realms with perfect accuracy—from the Buddha's Pure Lands to the six samsaric states, down to the nether-world.

He also read the minds of others: the teacher Zhönnu Drup wanted to borrow the Aspiration Sutras from Gyaltsen Bum who was staying in Zabulung. But hesitant to make such a request, he sat for three days without daring to go and see the Lama. Eventually, Lama Gyaltsen Bum handed him the book he'd wanted to borrow, saying, "I believe you didn't dare ask me for this, but here it is." The teacher Zhönnu Drup turned to the people walking by and shouted, "People, watch out! This Lama really has unobstructed clairvoyance! All of you staying nearby had better watch yourselves!"

Gyaltsen Bum said, "These qualities that you attribute to me are the fruit of concealing my tantric realizations." And he added, "When the great Lama Shangtönpa was alive, he always practiced tantra secretly and advised me not to teach it to others. A few years after he passed away to the Blissful Pure Land, a dream came to me: I was going south toward Dongkar when Shangtönpa appeared in the sky before me. He spoke these words:

> Perform as always the tantric techniques.
> Casting away one's ties to the fatherland
> Enables men and women to practice Dharma.
> Ah, think before you speak.
>
> In death-bound life, the Lama provides shelter.
> This precious life then gains perfection.
>
> In reality or in dreams,
> Keep secret your experiences and realizations.
> On this basis I've refrained from expounding to others.

Lama Gyaltsen Bum was a Buddha—of that there is no doubt. All sincere students said as much. Even an abbot meditating in a cave at the time heard three times the distinct words, "This Lama is indeed the Buddha."

On the tenth day of summer in the dog year, Gyaltsen Bum showed signs of illness. As his students, we asked if he wanted remedial or long-life services performed. Gyaltsen Bum declined, "Old age and death are part of being human. Your remedies and ceremonies wouldn't do the slightest good."

"But Lama, please," we protested, "stay for a few more years. Have compassion for us!"

Gyaltsen Bum was not moved. He said, "You see, I was originally told that I may die in my twelfth year, but I survived, thanks to my Lama Tengkangpa—who had obstacles himself. Then I was told that I would die at age sixty-two. Yet another time, I was told I would die when I reached my seventy-third year. Well, I am seventy-three now, and it's time to move on! After my death, Jampa Pal will look after this monastery. He'll protect the lineage. So go and practice well!"

Thus, thinking of all the disciples in other realms, turning away from their wrong views those who believed in permanence, and exhorting those who were lazy to practice, the Lama passed away on the twentieth day of summer in the dog year, amidst wonderful omens, sounds, effulgence, rainbows, rains of flowers, and perfumes of sweet, distinctive scents. Gyaltsen Bum, great light of this world, was welcomed to the Blissful Pure Land by dakas and dakinis. All who witnessed his passing away—his attendant, his disciples, etc—experienced perfect mental clarity. They spontaneously entered into profound non-conceptual *samadhi*.

When it was time to cremate the body, a dazzling brilliance scintillated from the east and penetrated the cremation shrine. Soon, rainbows colored the sky in all directions and were absorbed into the cremation shrine. For the duration of the [funeral] prayers, sacred relics from the body, statues, miraculous signs, and omens came to life as a basis of devotion for future disciples.

May all future faithful disciples be confident that the great Gyaltsen Bum went to the Blissful Pure Land. May these future disciples go there as well. Here is proof that Gyaltsen Bum did go to the pure realm: Gyaltsen Bum's death was kept secret at first. Just days after Lama Gyaltsen Bum's passing away, the teacher Gyaltsen Gön was meditating in a small hut when four women appeared with bone ornaments and turquoises in their hands. They danced and said to the teacher, "Lama Gyaltsen Bum died three days ago. His death was not immediately revealed to you. He has gone to the Blissful Pure Land. We're on our way there ourselves."

Shortly thereafter, this same teacher had a dream that Lama Gyaltsen Bum displayed several bodies at once. After showing the practice for pure and impure illusory body, Gyaltsen Bum said, "I've gone to the Blissful Pure Land. Direct your prayers to that quarter!"

Also, at dawn on the day after the monthly offering rituals, the teacher Jamdor dreamt that many dakinis wearing head jewelry and bone ornaments were present while he was staying in the room of the late Gyaltsen Bum. A young dakini approached. With a sweeping gesture she said, "We're all dakinis." Well, Jamdor was about to go back to sleep when he thought, "I could ask these dakinis where Lama Gyaltsen Bum has gone." So, Jamdor grabbed the young dakini by the hand and asked her. "Pray to go to the Blissful Pure Land," she replied simply, "for that is where he is."

Jamdor's dream continued: Gyaltsen Bum was sitting on top of a pile of barley. He held a tankha and said, "Unfold this tankha of Chakrasamvara!" Jamdor unfolded it and Gyaltsen Bum said, "Now I shall sing a song!" Which he did, but Jamdor could only recall the first part of the first recitation, praising the Aspiration of Manjushri. It ended with:

> In an age of polemists arguing the degeneration of the path,
> You, with no clue how long you have to live,
> Better exert yourself on the path.

At this point, Jamdor awoke from his dream and longing for Lama Gyaltsen Bum, he made a sincere prayer to meet him again.

Then Jamdor sadly thought to himself, "I looked after him when he was sick and stayed by his side; even received advice. And now he is gone to another realm." He prayed intensely and that night, he had the following dream: Lama Gyaltsen Bum came to him displaying the symptoms of the illness he had before his death. He was sitting naked, his head slouched over his left knee. [Attendants] tried to hold him up but he slouched back down. Jamdor asked the Lama about his posture and Gyaltsen Bum said, "Straighten me up and I'll go!"

Jamdor asked, "Lama, must you go now?"

"Yes, now," said Gyaltsen Bum.

"How can you hold us in your compassion, if you're in the Blissful Pure Land?"

"Pass me that turquoise box!" answered Gyaltsen Bum. Jamdor saw an amulet box tied with a green ribbon and handed it to the Lama. "Now open it and look inside." Inside the box was a silver mirror, which Jamdor showed to the people outside. Next Lama Gyaltsen Bum said, "Now replace the mirror and the green ribbon back with the box." At that moment, Jamdor woke up from his dream and thought, "This is a sign that one should look into one's own mind as one would in that white silver mirror. The green ribbon tying the box is a symbol of one's perseverance: it holds the practice together." Definitive understanding arose as a result of the previous night's experiences.

These lines are but a drop in the ocean of Gyaltsen Bum's inexpressible qualities, written by combining the accounts given to Lama Wönpopa, Drupseng Chen, and Jamdor. May the Lamas forgive any mistakes made here. By this merit, may all sentient beings attain enlightenment.

> At all times,
> And in all places,
> May the Lama hold us
> In his great compassion.

# 16

# Life of Tsultrim Gön

*Namo Guru!* THE FAMED SCHOLAR, Khyungpo Tsultrim Gön, was born in the Shang area, in the female fire bird year, to the Khyung family. His father was Wönpo Gönne and his mother, Chukmo Kunden. He was named Pedma Gön, Protector Lotus.

His previous karma awakened and he showed no attachment to the objects of samsara. He heard the great practitioner Örgyenpa (on a visit to Shang) giving bodhisattva vows to his parents and the people of the area, and felt an intense yearning for the Dharma. He had a pure heart.

But when Tsultrim Gön was four, his parents told him, "Since you are the first-born, you'll be the head of the household, and your younger brother will be a monk." Preparations were made accordingly. But that night, when all was ready, Tsultrim Gön picked up his younger brother's supplies and escaped. He reached Jak the next day, and fenced himself into a small retreat place.

One day, a person carrying water came by and asked Tsultrim Gön, "Where are you from?"

"I come from far away and all I want is to meet a Lama and practice Dharma. Can you help me?"

"Well," replied the man hauling his water, "the Lama is now in strict retreat. It's not possible to meet him." But Tsultrim Gön begged that he would do anything to meet a Lama, so the man relented, "All right. Look, stay here and I'll go see if an audience with the Lama can be arranged." The man soon returned, saying, "The Lama normally doesn't grant audience to anyone. But he's invited you. Go!"

Tsultrim Gön went to the Lama's white hut and immediately prostrated, presented offerings, and requested blessings. The Lama [Shangtönpa] told him, "Last night, I dreamt of Khyungpo Naljor and of your arrival. Your Dharma practice is pure and steady, so I will give you teachings."

Lama Shangtönpa became his spiritual guide and gave him the name Khyungpo Tsultrim Gön, saying, "You will be a venerable scholar. Now, I have given you this name, don't ever abandon it! It is the same name as that of the great Khyungpo Naljor." The Lama then granted him empowerments and Khyungpo Tsultrim Gön practiced the Six Yogas of Niguma. He was also given the complete instructions for each of the Six Yogas and many other teachings. Great experiences and realizations arose in the mind of Khyungpo Tsultrim Gön. The Lama next told him to take monastic vows from Tsultrim Pal, the abbot in charge of the Jonang[215] monastic seat. Next, he went to the abbot Gendun Gyamtso and to the abbot's delight, proved himself to be a monk of good attitude and flawless ethics.

Later, when Shangtönpa passed away, Tsultrim Gön made strong prayers to fulfill the intention of his Lama [Shangtönpa]. He went to practice in Jak where, in addition to all his previous practices, he vowed to never lie down again. During this time, Shangtönpa came to him in a dream, his body displaying the signs and marks of a Buddha, ornamented with bones and precious jewels. He appeared on a throne of gems of wonderful and indescribable beauty and gave Tsultrim Gön the Shangpa Kagyu teachings that spark auspicious connections for the benefit of beings.

At that time many obstacles arose. So Tsultrim Gön headed for Lhasa to receive blessings to help him overcome them. On his way, he stopped at Tsurpu and met the lord Rangjung Dorje. As soon as they met, Rangjung Dorje asked, "Have obstacles arisen for you?"

"Yes indeed, they have," Tsultrim Gön replied. Realizing that Rangjung Dorje was really clairvoyant, Tsultrim Gön felt a tremendous faith well up in him and his obstacles cleared away.

Tsultrim Gön then decided to take full ordination. The principal Lama was Zhönnu Jangchub, abbot to Gendun Gangpa; the action teacher was Jangchub Gön; the secret preceptor, Sönam Rinchen.[216] Tsultrim Gön took his vows amidst ten members of the Sangha whose faith was pure and perfect.

That same year, the harvest was bad, so Tsultrim Gön stayed practicing in Lhalung with only a few measures of tsampa. With or without nourishment, his practice held strong. Tsultrim Gön then remained in the area of Upper Shang for twenty-five years. In his tenth year there, the locals brought Tsultrim Gön an old, sad couple, saying, "See the old people? They had two sons. Both died within the last two months and the parents are mad with grief. Whenever they look at anyone, they think of their boys." Tsultrim Gön saw that the old people's sorrow was so intense that they didn't care whether they drowned in a lake or fell off a cliff. He felt great compassion, and within a month, the suffering of the old man and woman had lifted and their realizations improved. Tsultrim Gön also gave instructions for other people who suffered from diseases and demons, all of which benefited a great many beings.

For the next fifteen years of his retreat in Upper Shang, Tsultrim Gön went alms-seeking in the fall. The rest of the time, he practiced single-pointedly. Once, as he was crossing a stream, he felt something or someone pull the sheepskin off his back. When he turned to look, he saw a human skull with a tooth, which transformed into the Sixty-Two-Deity Mandala of Chakrasamvara with multiple hands and faces. This image stayed a long time before disintegrating.

Once, he was staying with Bijir the Mad Teacher, making torma offerings. With his clairvoyance, Khyungpo Tsultrim Gön was able to see that in the valley below, a girl was milking a female yak. In her carelessness, the girl spilt the milk and all the people around began to laugh. Tsultrim Gön quietly laughed as well, which set off the Mad Teacher, "What's so funny? Why are you laughing at me?"

"I'm not laughing at you!" Tsultrim Gön replied. But with these words he burst out laughing again and Bijir the Mad Teacher turned angry.

"Look," Tsultrim Gön explained, "I'm just laughing at something funny down in the valley."

"What a lie!" the Mad Teacher fumed, "there's nothing down in the valley."

The weather was balmy and the next day, the patron Gyene came up from the valley with his horse and rolls of cotton cloth as an offering. Bijir the Mad Teacher used the opportunity to question the patron about what, if anything, had happened in the valley. "Actually," the patron Gyene related, "something funny did happen there yesterday. Our son's bride slipped and spilt the milk. Oh, everyone was laughing!" Bijir was filled with regret for his earlier doubts and with renewed faith, he turned to Tsultrim Gön, "Yesterday I didn't believe you and thought you were teasing me. I'm sorry." That's when Tsultrim Gön gave the Mad Teacher many teachings. Bijir the Mad Teacher, as well as all his relatives took Tsultrim Gön as their root Lama.

Later, hearing that the rebirth of Rangjung Dorje was in Tsurpu, Khyungpo Tsultrim Gön went to meet him. It was the time of year when rivers swell, and many individuals were staying by the river shore, unable to cross. So Tsultrim Gön took a big slab from the boulders on the mountain slope and placed it across the stream to form a bridge. He stepped across it just in time because in the next instant, the slab collapsed, carried away by the current. In Tsurpu, Rolpe Dorje [the rebirth of Rangjung Dorje] gave him empowerments and numerous teachings.

Disciples said that when they had the opportunity to request mind training teachings from the precious bodhisattva Ngulchu Tokme,[217] who was an emanation of Avalokiteshvara, he replied, "My own teacher is Tsultrim Gön, who is an emanation of Khyungpo Naljor. You should get the Six Yogas of Niguma from him." The praise is echoed by [the Third Karmapa] Rangjung Dorje himself who once said, "The great lord Tsultrim Gön has absolute control of the channels and energy-winds. He is my spiritual guide."

One day Tsultrim Gön said, "A great meditator doesn't need wealth. A great meditator doesn't need a fine house. He or she can die fulfilled in a small hut, a solitary place, or a cave. Give up fixating on a self, this area of Dechen, or anything else, and go to a solitary place." At this hint [of Tsultrim Gön's approaching death], disciples and patrons begged the Lama not to move on, but stay with them. Tsultrim Gön replied, "Within seven days, I will have abandoned these physical aggregates. At that time, my body should either be cremated or given to the birds."

Thus, in the tiger year, amidst loud noises, sheets of light, earthquakes, rains of flowers, and rainbows filling the illuminated space, Tsultrim Gön passed into the Pure Land of Joy, in accordance with his aspiration. Those in charge said that the blessings would be greater if his body were placed in a copper casket. This was done, and immediately a strong earthquake erupted. During the special ceremonies, it rained flowers and the sky dazzled and glistened. These phenomena lasted a full year.

After a year, an outdoor and an indoor shrine were built in which to insert the relics of Tsultrim Gön's body. Out of the blazing fire consuming his body, the sound of *Om Hri Ha Ha Hung Hung Phet!* exploded and could be heard throughout the region accompanied by many apparitions. When the cremation shrine was opened, many sacred relics and other marvelous signs were present. A vajra, wheel, lotus, sword, and precious jewels, appeared from his bones. Rainbows shone. People brought their sick animals and made them circumambulate the shrine to Tsultrim Gön and the animals were cured of their diseases immediately. The custom has remained to this day.

This brief story of the life of Khyungpo Tsultrim Gön, compiled from various sources, was put in writing in Dechen.

May virtue increase! GEO!

# 17

# Life of Ridrö Rechen

*Namo Ratna Guru Ye!* I, THE MIGHTY yogi Ridrö Rechen, was born in Eastern Tibet, the oldest of five children. Both my father, Ayul, and my mother, Ngag Kek, behaved like a yogi and a yogini and practiced the special [long-life] teachings of Red Avalokiteshvara. Our whole family lived in the mountains and was sustained by nuts, fruit, and whatever else was available. We were so virtuous that as soon as we children could speak, we would recite the *mani* mantra, and when one of my siblings died, rainbows and precious relics appeared.

In my fourth year, my father made me a pair of colorful long boots. I put them on, and with a whole group of other children, went up the top of the mountain to play. But there, I tore my boots. Just then, my father arrived. As soon as he saw the torn boots, he gave me a good beating!

That night, I had my first auspicious lucid dream. I dreamt I was sleeping at a neighbor's place and had my boots, good as new, with me. When I woke up, I understood that something [a torn boot] can change into something else [a boot in good condition, as in my dream].

Throughout my childhood, I only cared for the light of Dharma, but was not free to do as I wished—my parents had arranged a marriage for me. Then one day when I was six, I went to get some water with one of my brothers. I carried the pitcher and he, the ladle for scooping the water. My brother made a sling, threw a stone, and accidentally hit me in the leg. I was laid up for a long time, and have suffered from a limp ever since. But at least the family of my prospective bride cancelled the marriage plans! And so, in my ninth year, I took the lay vows of a monk. I was given the name Ridrö Rechen. Soon after, I received instructions from Senge Dra and practiced them in my dreams.

I spent time in retreat in the plains below the village. During that time, in addition to my leg injury, I fell ill and dreamt of frogs exiting my body. Then I heard a voice say, "Be firm and courageous." For the next month, I practiced alone, and gradually grew stronger. By the time I was twelve, I was able to teach the Hevajra Tantra. At age eighteen, I gave commentaries on Engaging in the Bodhisattva's Path and knew the Prajnaparamita teachings by heart.

At nineteen, I began practicing Chö and spent about a year in Tsurpu. Next, I studied the Sakya branch of Buddhism with the Sixth Kenchen abbot. He was hospitable and warm. We conversed about many topics. I also became famous for my study of the philosophical treatises.

When I was twenty-eight, I expounded on commentaries and traveled to monasteries throughout Tibet. But in my mind the thought recurred, "There is no essence to the activities of samsara. What I need is to practice and prepare for death."

After I left Drikung, I met Lama Lozangwa, a disciple of Zhönnu Drup. He gave me special instructions for seeing Maitreya face to face and advised me to meet his own Lama, a great Shangpa adept named Khyungpo Tsultrim Gön.

So I did, and practiced the Six Yogas of Niguma under the guidance of Lama Tsultrim Gön. After six years of such practice, I asked for further meditation instructions and the Lama said he would see about that. He eventually gave me some teachings, and within seven days of practicing Inner Heat Yoga, I was able to stay warm with just a cotton robe.

Niguma said that enlightenment is achievable within six to twelve months of practice, and her instructions are the easiest means for achieving it. With this aspiration I practiced and studied the Lives of the Shangpa Kagyu Masters, such as that of the sage Khyungpo Naljor. But reading their lives only made me think that they were not that extraordinary. Frankly, why write their lives down at all?

A year and a half went by. Despite my repeated aspiration to attain enlightenment, I wasn't getting there! I began to wonder about those Shangpa Kagyu masters, from Khyungpo Naljor to Shangtönpa. How did they achieve enlightenment so quickly? It then dawned on me that my failure to achieve enlightenment within six to twelve months was the price I paid for the negative thoughts I'd had about their life stories. That's when Lama Khyungpo Tsultrim Gön told me more about the Lives of the Shangpa Kagyu Masters, from Khyungpo Naljor down to Shangtönpa, and passed on many teachings.

On the fourteenth day of the fourth month in the monkey year, my mother died. The following day, I went before my Lama and dedicated all virtue for my mother's benefit. In dedicating my practice that day, I particularly thought of my mother. About a year after this, my younger brother came to see me with his entourage, urging me to return. "Mother's well, everybody is fine," my brother said, "but if you don't come back, mother will be so sad."

"Your lies aren't working!" I replied. "I know that mother died already. She passed away the night of the fourteenth in the fourth month in the monkey year. I also know that you didn't even wait an appropriate length of time after her death. You cremated her the day after she passed away, which is much too early. You've committed a great evil." And I recounted the exact deeds of all my siblings, adding, "I'm not buying your deceitful stories now!"

I left for Shang, and through the intensity of my Inner Heat Yoga, I traveled as fast as if I were riding a horse. The time I lived in was a period of upheaval and power struggle; and now the local faction heard that a messenger was conveying information to the enemy in Taktsang.[218] The locals decided to capture and execute him. The messenger escaped, but his pursuers caught up with him and stabbed him once. At that point, the messenger began to bleed profusely [but he got away] and begged me to help him. A breeze arose and soon it was night. I hid the wounded messenger nearby. The following day, the people returned, keen to find and kill the man. They asked me if I knew where he was, and I replied, "Oh, I don't know. He's probably moved on already."

One winter it felt rather warm and I decided to go see what was causing the heat. I saw one of my main disciples taking a yak blanket and soaking it in the water. The disciple then wore the damp blanket through the night, practicing Inner Heat Yoga visualizations and yogic exercises. By dawn, the blanket had completely dried. When the student explained his practice to me, I confirmed, "That's what one needs to do with Inner Heat Yoga." And the blanket was displayed for everyone's amazement.

Later, I presented myself to Lama Zhönnu Drup. This was a time when many sought responsibility for the lineage teachings here in Dechen, but all were turned down every time. "I've kept the transmission for you," my Lama Zhönnu Drup confided. "You will hold my lineage." Bending down, he touched his head to mine. "Yes," he mused, "your head is just like mine! Beware that no tradition survives when disciples don't listen to their teachers." So I took over in Dechen and maintained the teachings there.

## Death of Ridrö Rechen

IN THE SEVENTH month of the boar year, Ridrö Rechen showed signs of illness but kept his condition hidden for a long time. When at last it became known, he did not allow any remedial or long-life ceremonies. He was lying in bed when his attendants tried to readjust his pillow. But Ridrö Rechen waved them off, "No need for all this!"

"But you're ill!" the attendants protested.

"Yes, and I'm not going to get better!"

The attendants made a final attempt, "Lama, when we pray, which pure realm should we direct our prayers to?"

"To the Blissful Pure Land in the west!" All his attendants stayed with him through his illness. When they asked for more Dharma, Ridrö Rechen said, "You don't need more teachings at this time."

At sunrise on the twentieth day of the seventh month in the boar year, at age sixty-nine, Ridrö Rechen entered into deep meditative clarity and passed into nirvana. His body was cremated and all his disciples made prayers and donations. The sky filled with a rain of flowers, rainbows shone, and sacred relics appeared from the bones.

This has been the story of the realized lord, Ridrö Rechen.

SARWA DAKALYA NIBHA WANTU! MANGALAM!

# 18

# Life of Shangkarwa

*Om Soti!* SHANGKARWA RINCHEN GYALTSEN's mother was Jösema Palchen, and his father, Wönyig Zangpopal, was a respected secretary. Shangkarwa was born in the female water snake year. When he was three, both his parents passed away and he was placed under the tutelage of two monks, Shakya Senge and his uncle Rinchen Ödzepa. Before long, Shangkarwa was able to read and write.

At the age of eight, he took monks' vows. At twelve, he went to a large temple in Zamtsar and took further vows before the abbot Dzepa Gyaltsen. Also present were Shakya Pal, holder of the *vinaya* code of discipline, and several Sangha members. At that time, he received the name Shangkarwa, Precious Royal Banner.

When he was twenty, he took full ordination. He practiced conscientiously, remained mindful in body, speech, and mind, and studied extensively with several teachers. In his study of the Prajnaparamita, Shangkarwa found a few slightly different versions. So he went to the great library of the monastery of Narthang and found that the commentaries of Arjangchub Yeshe[219] corresponded exactly to his own conceptions on the topic.

One day, his uncle told him, "The great scholar Khyungpo Tsultrim Gön is staying nearby. Go study with him." Shangkarwa went to see

Tsultrim Gön and requested the practices of Clear Light Yoga, Dream Yoga, and so on, which delighted Tsultrim Gön.

Next, he went to receive empowerments from Butön who transmitted to him his wisdom mindstream, and Shangkarwa generated great realizations. He received—more than twenty times—various tantric commentaries.

Shangkarwa had not been begging alms and found himself short of food. Since there was just a little bit left to eat, he drank his soup and went to get more water. While he was gone, Rinchen Gyamtso arrived. He had been sent by Butön who was worried Shangkarwa might run out of provisions. Rinchen Gyamtso reached Shangkarwa's place but found only a little tsampa. Moved by the destitution in the room, he sat on Shangkarwa's bed and wept. Just then, Shangkarwa returned and Rinchen Gyamtso exclaimed, "My friend, such hardships you have endured!"

That fall, Shangkarwa found an abandoned house in Narthang and stayed there in retreat. Soon, there was no more tsampa to eat, so Shangkarwa went to the dump and in the middle of the garbage, he saw some yellow felt. He picked it up and found two measures of gold in it. Since nobody claimed the gold, Shangkarwa decided to use one measure for food and to offer the other measure to his Lama. He thought that, perhaps, the protectors had left the precious gold there for him to find.

Shangkarwa was to receive teachings on the Guhyasamaja Five Paths in a Single Session in Chumik, from the great teacher Jangchub Tsemo.[220] That very morning at dawn, a white man appeared at the head of his bed saying, "Ask Avalokiteshvara for the empowerments." Soon afterwards, someone came to get him and he went before the Lama [Jangchub Tsemo]. He received the four complete empowerments of Guhyasamaja. During the ceremony, he realized that the Lama was, in fact, Avalokiteshvara. He saw the realm of appearances as the experiences of Illusory Body Yoga, Dream Yoga, and Clear Light Yoga. He enlarged the scope of his sacred outlook.

Later, Lama Tsultrim Gön passed away. Shangkarwa had hoped to receive the entire Shangpa teachings from him, but now this seemed impossible. However, in upper Dechen he met Ridrö Rechen Sangye Senge who gave him the entire cycle of teachings of the Shangpa lineage. Ridrö Rechen was very pleased, saying, "Not even Shangtönpa kept such a powerful practice." Ridrö Rechen presented him with books of the Shangpa teachings, entrusted him with responsibility for the lineage, gave him a bell and the like, and gave his blessings.

During the days devoted to the Medicine Buddha, Shangkarwa sang with great devotion and his blessings blazed and set everything alight. All the objects presented as offerings multiplied and all the water bowls overflowed. When people tried to count the donations, they doubled in quantity. They were displayed for all to see and everyone exclaimed how wonderful they were! The attendant Paljor Zungdrup was preparing mantra rolls to be placed inside statues when he saw water spout from one of the bowls.

When his Lama Ridrö Rechen passed away, Shangkarwa made continuous prayers and offerings. He also agreed to take over the monastic center and established religious festivals and accomplishment ceremonies.[221] He kept butter lamps continuously lit and made uninterrupted oblations to the statue of his Lama. Shangkarwa mastered *samadhi* meditation. Such a practitioner is as rare as a star in broad daylight.

Shangkarwa was physically pure. He had no blemishes, dark spots, no internal or external infections. When he bathed, the water that washed off him was like dew drops, clean and free of dirt. He exuded the sweet scent of ethical discipline: his room and his clothes smelled of this fine perfume also, and all who experienced the fragrance found their senses satisfied.

Shangkarwa once said that some scholars are boastful but such pride will only bring the Dharma lineages to an end. Their prideful activity causes the essence of the teachings to disappear, and there is no greater enemy to the Dharma than just that.

In the first month in the tiger year, Shangkarwa's pulse weakened. His students asked whether they should do special prayers for him, but he merely replied, "Now, I will go before Maitreya and, like a young god-child, listen to his teachings. I came to this place hoping to do the practices of Niguma, but my patrons lacked resources and my students lacked understanding—no, I have not been completely satisfied."

In the seventh month in the tiger year, Shangkarwa lost his appetite. Toward the end of the month, he got sick. He was entering his eighty-second year when, at the first light of dawn on the twenty-fifth day of the twelfth month in the tiger year, Shangkarwa's emanation-body dissolved into the realm of reality. In the sky, a five-colored rainbow appeared through the clouds.

Winter soon came but Shangkarwa's area of Dechen saw neither hailstorm nor dust. A wandering Lama said that Shangkarwa's realizations were powerful enough to control even the external elements. As for Shangkarwa, it is said that his body remained in the meditation posture for twenty-five days after his passing into nirvana.

A large cremation shrine with offerings was prepared. When the fire was lit, the flames dazzled like white crystals, swirling counterclockwise. A rainbow glowed to the west over Shangkarwa's room and many sacred relics were found. When the cremation was over, the practitioners opened the door of the cremation shrine in order to collect the ashes and relics with which to make *tsatsas.* At that moment, more rainbows appeared and the air became fragrant with sweet smells.

This has been a brief account of Shangkarwa's life.

SARWA DAKALYA NIBHA WANTU! GEO! GEO! GEO!

# 19

# Life of Palzang

THE DHARMA LORD Nyame Sangye Palzang was born near Taktsang in the mountains west of Lhasa, to the Be family. His father was Wön Rinpoche Zang and his mother, Tsebum Pal. These two had first had a boy who died in infancy. After their boy died, the parents invited the hermit Ridrö Rinchen to perform the seven-week prayers for the dead and to consecrate a clay *tsatsa* containing relics and the like. The hermit placed inner offerings into the *tsatsa*, breathed a blessing onto it, and said to the mother, "Soon, I assure you, you will have a special child."

Soon afterwards, all the local people went to see the scholar and translator, Jangchub Tsemo, and the bereaved mother approached the great man, saying, "I've lost my only son. Please have some compassion for me."

"Well, tell me what you want," replied the scholar. She pointed to her breast. Discreetly, Jangchub Tsemo sucked it. Then he said, "Same time next year, you will have a boy. Be good and protect him well." That very night, the woman had a dream that many young girls were carrying pots of water to wash her and all the impurities within her body were cleansed at once.

When Sangye Palzang entered the womb, his mother experienced great physical bliss and perfect clarity of mind. She dreamt of the sun and the moon rising together, so bright that one could not look at them directly. After nine or ten months, she painlessly gave birth to Sangye Palzang.

While still of breast-feeding age, Sangye Palzang had already mastered meditation. As soon as he could talk, he began to teach. He was given stones to play with, and he used them to create practice objects—a vajra or, alternatively, a bell. He always placed his vajra in front of him and held his bell as if to ring it.

When people came to the house, they saw Sangye Palzang playing with his toys, with wild rabbits resting at ease by his side. Sometimes, he would hold the rabbits, and at other times, he would let them go. Seeing him release the rabbits, a man called, "Hey, hold on to them!" But to the man's annoyance, Sangye Palzang didn't.

Sangye Palzang repeatedly destroyed fox traps until the locals hid them better to prevent the boy from purposely setting them off. At harvest time, about sixty pails of hay had been bundled and brought into the barnyard. Sangye Palzang walked into the barnyard and saw three sheep tied there. Fearing that the sheep might be butchered, he untied them and led them to a stream. There, he came across the butcher who shouted, "Hey you, what are you doing with these? That's our meat!" They began to fight and Sangye Palzang ran off to hide in the woods, where his father eventually found him.

"You're just trouble, boy!" the father shouted angrily. "You're no son of mine. You're as bad as my own enemy!" Sangye Palzang prepared himself for a serious beating, but in the end, his father went no further than words. "What in the world are we going to give the workers in the field, now that you've let our meals go?" asked the father. Sangye Palzang said, "We'll have to make do with butter and tsampa!" All these adventures led the family to make a rule that any animal slaughter should be kept from Sangye Palzang's eyes.

Sangye Palzang was only ten but already he helped the villagers by writing letters on their behalf or reading documents to them. In short, the young child was acting as a secretarial representative. The villagers insisted that he wear all sorts of jewelry. There were no finer letters in the whole province than those written by him.

Sangye Palzang was skilled and highly intelligent. Yet, when he asked to be made a novice monk, his request was denied. So he decided to have his family meet the monk Uktsang for a meal. At the meeting, the monk said, "Your son has great devotion for the Dharma and can only affect your reputation positively. Allow him to become a monk. Send him to a monastery!" But to no avail—the parents still refused the boy's request. The Dharma lord Shangkarwa now intervened with a personal plea to the parents, saying, "I know of an adept of supernatural powers in the upper monastery. See if your boy can go there to practice."

The boy presented himself to the adept who said, "Do me a little drawing!" Now Sangye Palzang had never seen before what a five-point vajra looked like, but that's what he drew. The adept said Sangye Palzang's drawing indicated tantric activity. Yet, his parents were still opposed to him becoming a monk. At that point, Sangye Palzang was ready to run off. But his father caught him and finally agreed to allow him to become a monk. In fact, his mother aroused devotion and became a Dharma friend to her own boy.

On the fifteenth day of the royal month in the dragon year, Sangye Palzang turned fifteen and took novice monks' vows before the abbot Kenchen Gyalwa Zangpo. Sangye Palzang studied with Shangkarwa, and by age eighteen, was able to give new explanations on the texts. In his nineteenth year, Sangye Palzang took the full vows of a monk with Shangkarwa as his abbot, Lopön Kunzang as the action teacher, and Lama Sangye Dorje as his secret preceptor.

At first, Sangye Palzang trained in the two kinds of bodhichitta.[222] In the following months, Shangkarwa taught the precepts of Niguma to a hundred people near the Gungtang pass. Shangkarwa also taught Sangye Palzang a new visualization every fortnight so that within nine months, he had perfected them all and could teach meditations, visualizations, and recitations to others. He had wonderful experiences. His meditation practice was naturally superior.

Sangye Palzang listened carefully to the instructions leading to liberation. His Lama Shangkarwa declared, "My child, you come from a rich family and you could be quite arrogant and mean-spirited, but you are not. You will be the lineage holder. Later, you will go to the Blissful Pure Land."

Following this, Sangye Palzang received the instructions for the Yogas of Niguma, including teachings on Inner Heat Yoga. After a year of practicing these, he experienced the blazing heat of bliss and the realization of illusoriness arose in him. He gained a clear understanding of the Dream Yoga practices of transformation and uncovering objective appearances, as well as a continuous experience of the clear-light nature of mind. One night he dreamt he went to the Blissful Pure Land. The next day, he was able to explain in detail what he had seen.

Sangye Palzang summarized his experience: "I met Shangkarwa when I was fifteen, and relied on him without interruption for seven years, practicing everything I was taught. In our family, we originally received a lot of support. But after my father died, my uncle made off with most of our belongings. However, I never tired of the Dharma and never gave up trying to create the right conditions for practice. I recalled the words of my teacher and instead of entering into an argument with my uncle, I wholeheartedly renounced fixation on possessions as having inherent existence.

"I prepared my Lama's tea and was his attendant. I wrote and read books. I prepared offerings, big and small, of colored sand, vases, medicine, incense, and anything of use. The day before my Lama Shangkarwa was due to perform a ceremony, I laid out everything in advance and learnt all the necessary rituals so that I could assist him without making any mistakes."

During a stay in snowy Lhabu, Shangkarwa told Sangye Palzang, "Now I shall reveal it all to you, my child." For the next five months, Lama Shangkarwa gave him the Six Yogas of Niguma, the teachings of the Six-Armed Wisdom Protector, and so forth. By then, Shangkarwa was advancing in years, and his sight was diminishing. He now needed someone to care for him and handle his books; someone who could be his eyes. Before long, the lord Shangkarwa showed signs of illness, and medical attendants were called. The illness broke out at once. Lama Shangkarwa was grimacing from the cold. Sangye

Palzang became afraid that his Lama might pass away. Nothing seemed to stop the condition, not even wrapping scarves around him. One night, Shangkarwa became dizzy. Sangye Palzang was preparing tea for his Lama when he heard words as if from a distance. He soon recognized them as his Lama's voice.

Shangkarwa had regained consciousness, called back by the smoke produced in making tsampa. He now said to Sangye Palzang, "You're worrying yourself sick! You've endured so much for me. Remember: in all our lives, you and I, teacher and disciple, are inseparable." With these words, Shangkarwa passed away into the clear-light realm of reality. It was the twenty-fifth day of the twelfth month in the tiger year. Sangye Palzang prayed continually for the next forty-nine days. Then he made a statue of his Lama in a reclining posture. As it was consecrated, Sangye Palzang said, "From now on, I shall present monthly offerings to it and set it out at all of our great festivals."

Shortly thereafter, during a stay in Lungtang Valley, Sangye Palzang had a dream that he was blowing into a white conch shell toward the south. Then, when he was practicing in a cave, he had another dream in which there was a crumbling old white conch shell and a great monastery. "These represent my perceptions," he thought, still in the dream. He saw that mold had gathered everywhere: on the conch shell, inside the monastery, and around it as well. He proceeded to dust off every bit of mold with the greatest attention.

Just two days after this last dream, Sangye Palzang left his retreat cave and arrived at the monastery of Kuklung,²²³ full of relics and sacred writings. Looking around, he saw that it once sheltered many adepts. But it was clear that the monastery had been neglected for a long time. He took this to signify that the precious oral transmission of the Shangpa would have few descendants and little power. These sad thoughts brought tears to his eyes and he vowed to restore the monastery and the lineage. Then, he went to sleep right there in the monastery. While Sangye Palzang was sleeping, many Dharma protectors approached and expressed their approbation. Over the next ten years, Sangye Palzang built strong walls around the monastery, strengthened the foundations to withstand the cold, and established separate sections for monks and nuns.

Sangye Palzang gave the Bell Empowerment of Chakrasamvara to one of his great female practitioners, Drungdrup Chenmo. As the ceremony got under way, Sangye Palzang told her that she should think of the Lama as Chakrasamvara. Just then, she saw her Dharma lord as the actual Black Chakrasamvara, empty of inherent existence. In all of his chakras were dakas and dakinis sitting in perfect union. She prayed that she might develop such qualities. At this point, the Dharma lord Sangye Palzang said to her, "Meditate on mental activity as deity, and on verbal activity as mantra."

On the twenty-fifth night in the winter horse month, Sangye Palzang gave Drungdrup Chenmo the Red Vajrayogini Empowerment, and told her, "Our skull-cup of inner offerings has frozen into ice. You do a visualization, and I shall perform a special practice." After some time, the Jetsunma appeared on top of the skull-cup of inner offerings, her body the size of a thumb, blood-red and so beautiful that one never tired of looking at her. Before their eyes, the Jetsunma dissolved into light, which was absorbed in the inner offerings. A wheel the size of a spindle appeared from within the inner offerings and melted in a dance of red flames, boiling over and spilling in a whirl on top of the small table.

Taking the skull-cup of inner offerings in his hands, Sangye Palzang placed it on top of his head and requested empowerments from the deities. After blessings and offerings had been granted, the vestiges were formed into nectar pills to be given to those with fortunate karma. Then the empowerment proceeded, and while it was taking place, the sound of lutes and flutes could be heard. If one listened toward the east, then it seemed the sound was coming from the west. But if one listened toward the west, then it seemed the sound was coming from the east. Remember, this was at the height of the winter freeze, yet a lotus flower blossomed in the vase of inner offerings.

At dawn on the eighteenth day of the summer month in the female bird year, Sangye Palzang showed signs of illness and said to his disciples, "I'm a little weak now. Yesterday, Lamas and yidam deities gave me prophecies. For the last year or so, I've stayed here intending to benefit beings. But I am tired of the actions of degenerate beings. At present, the obscurations and defilements of beings are such that I don't see any reason to continue on." On the nineteenth night of the month, his pulse weakened considerably and he said to his disciples, "There's no reason for you to get worked up! Go back to your homes now and practice Guru Yoga."

The following night, all the great female practitioners of Namling, north of Zhigatse, came to say their farewells to Sangye Palzang, and he repeated his words from the previous day. The Lamas of the lineage, as well as dakas, dakinis, and Dharma protectors all appeared around him and Sangye Palzang declared, "These evil times are nothing but sorrow and misery. I'll be moving on now."

The next night shortly after midnight, Sangye Palzang said, "I see many goddesses bringing gifts." Indeed, they could be seen before the disciples, and soon the room was filled with a sweet fragrance. The students asked, "Lama Sangye Palzang, what pure land will you go to? What prayers shall we make?"

"I will go to the Eastern Pure Land known as the Pure Land of Joy," said Sangye Palzang. "Pray that you may also go there." His great female disciple, Drungdrup Chenmo, begged him for a heart practice and Sangye Palzang replied, "You must say, 'Subdue the mind!' That is best."

At the first light of dawn, on the twenty-second day of the month, at age sixty-eight, Sangye Palzang's emanation-body dissolved into the clear-light realm of reality. Five days later at sunrise, white and red bodhichitta spilt from his nostrils, and with a radiant complexion, he moved beyond meditation. Sweet smells and a clear radiance filled the room. When his body was cremated, rainbows shone in the sky and the letter 'A' appeared on his bone relics.

This life story of Sangye Palzang was compiled from many sources.

SARWA DAKALYA NIBHA WANTU! GEO! GEO! GEO

# 20

# Four Lamas of the Shangpa Tangluk Transmission

## *Life of Shangtönpa*

KETSUN TSANGMA SHANGTÖNPA was born in the marshlands of Kongyal, in Shang. At thirteen, he became a monk before Lama Nyitokpa and proceeded to study the Prajnaparamita and Engaging in the Bodhisattva's Path. He also studied several sutras and tantras. Soon Shangtönpa was a great scholar with all kinds of experiences and realizations.

As soon as he met his Lama, Sangye Tönpa, in the Rigong area of Yöl, Shangtönpa had visions and felt an extraordinary faith. Realizations occurred spontaneously. While studying the entire cycle of the profound Shangpa teachings, Dream Yoga and Illusory Body Yoga dawned effortlessly. In brief, Shangtönpa was graced with the blessings of the Lamas, practiced Clear Light Yoga and Illusory Body Yoga, and displayed great realizations. The eight worldly concerns were liberated of themselves, in their own sphere. He saw the faces of yidam deities and received numerous prophecies. Although he had unobstructed clairvoyance, he kept his inner qualities concealed and used his teachings to lead countless fortunate disciples to maturation and liberation.

When death approached, Shangtönpa gave away all his possessions: his cushions, his robes, his furniture, and whatever gold he had. At dawn on the fifteenth day of the fifth month in the bird year, when he was seventy-six years of age, Shangtönpa passed away into the Eastern Pure Land, known as the Pure Land of Joy. There, he returned to his Lama, Sangye Tönpa, protector of beings, amidst many wonderful signs and omens, and manifested as a fourteenth-level wisdom bodhisattva.

## Life of Müchen

MÜCHEN GYALTSEN PALZANG came from a family of adepts in the Nyak region. His father was the teacher Dorje Nyingpo. At the moment of conception, his mother, Könchok, had a wonderful omen of Avalokiteshvara entering her womb. When she gave birth to Müchen, the local village was shaken by an earthquake and covered with a rain of flowers.

At age twenty-six, Müchen took the full vows of a monk before the abbot Chöje Gyaltsen Palzang and the action teacher Rinchen Sönam. These and others taught him the Kalachakra, the Lamdre teachings of the Sakya school, and so on. His careful study earned Müchen the respect of all.

The Mongol King, Ayuwara, invited Müchen to his imperial palace in Taitu, where he brought immeasurable benefit to beings. When he returned to Tibet, he stayed in meditation and practiced asceticism. His experiences and realizations defy description.

When Müchen heard about Lama Shangtönpa, he decided to meet him. At the same time, Shangtönpa received a prophecy from the wisdom protector that foretold he would have a great disciple and lineage holder to whom he should pass on the transmission. Once they met, Shangtönpa taught Müchen all the instructions without exception. Müchen continued to study and practice with the greatest respect for his Lama, and developed the ability to transform himself in dreams. Clear light arose in his mindstream. He gained Mahamudra wisdom and dwelt in the essence of meditation. Soon the new Mongol King, Genpa Chenpo, insisted that he come, so Müchen went to Taitu again.

He brought immense benefit to Mongols, Tartars, and Siberians, as well as the people of Nyak, his native province. In Tibet, Müchen organized large festivals and greatly spread the Dharma. In a mountain cave of the Mü Valley, he taught practices and *shastras* to great crowds.

On the twenty-sixth day of the seventh month in the fire boar year, an earthquake exploded and amidst loud sounds, iridescent lights, and rains of flowers, Müchen passed into the Blissful Pure Land.

## Life of Kedrup

FROM A YOUNG age, Kedrup Dorje Zhönnu had a spontaneous renunciation for the suffering of samsara. He learnt sutras, tantras, and the philosophy of emptiness. He studied in depth the entire Shangpa doctrine from his Lama, Müchen, and by practicing it diligently, he quickly traversed the path.

During the cold season, Kedrup's Inner Heat Yoga was so great that heat steamed off his pores. He experienced the joy that arises from the union of bliss and emptiness, and found it easy to perform the Dream Yoga practices of emanation and transformation. Supernatural faculties dawned within him. His Deathlessness practice enabled him to live long without showing any signs of aging. Kedrup did nothing but practice undistracted, and was deeply respected by many Lamas.

His Lama, the Dharma lord Müchen, gave Kedrup the entire cycle of Shangpa teachings. Loaded with the responsibility of the oral instructions, Kedrup showed the path through both his practice and his commentaries.

## Life of Namkay Naljor

NAMKAY NALJOR WAS born to Lama Dorje Sönam, a scholar well versed in both the old and new schools of teachings. His mother was known as the Avalokiteshvara Yogini of a Hundred Thousand Vajras.

Early on, Namkay Naljor revealed faith, knowledge, and supernatural faculties. He took the vows of a layperson before the abbot Shakya Penpa, and received the name Namkha Gyaltsen. He studied sutras and tantras at great length and made wishing prayers vast in scope. In particular, with his predecessor, the great Lama Müchen, he studied the entire practice path laid out by the dakini Niguma. After a month spent meditating, the experience of blissful heat arose effortlessly in him. With his perfect teacher, Lama Kedrup, he studied from beginning to end whatever other teachings of the Buddha were available. At age twenty, Namkay Naljor took full ordination before Kedrup.

Apart from the time he spent studying the Dharma, Namkay Naljor always practiced in mountain solitudes. He meditated in single-pointed concentration. Definitive understanding and non-referential compassion arose in him. He obtained Mahamudra realization and was safeguarded by yidam deities such as Avalokiteshvara. The meditation known as Many Doors of Samadhi encouraged the development of Namkay Naljor's supernatural faculties and revealed his inconceivable qualities. Dharma protectors were at his service. He also established, helped mature, and liberated countless disciples, including the Fifth Command Holder, Paljor Sherab, as well as Rongtön Sheja Kunrik, Sempa Zhönnu Chok, Müchen Könchok Gyalsten, Tangtong Gyalpo,[224] and Kedrup Gelek Palzang, all of whom had great experiences and realizations, vast knowledge, perfect discipline, enlightened activity, mastery of the Buddhist teachings and set alight the noble teachings of the Shangpa Kagyu.

On the twenty-sixth day of the second month in the mouse year, when Namkay Naljor was ninety-three years old, his mindstream entered the sphere of great peace amidst rainbows, ravishing radiance, loud sounds, sweet smells, and streams of flower blossoms. Those with pure karma saw Namkay Naljor go to Uddiyana and the Blissful Pure Land. When the cremation shrine was opened after the ceremony, many relics and sacred signs, too wonderful to be put into words, were found, and aroused profound faith in his disciples.

SARWA DAKALYA BHAWANTU! SHUBHO!

# 21

# Life of Gyurme Dechen

HOMAGE TO THE great bilingual translator, Kalzang Gyurme Dechen!
On an auspicious fall day, amidst wonderful signs and omens and
following connections established over many past lives, a boy was
born, as prophesized, to the Chakzampa family known for its many
sages. He was named Ratna Bharapa Lotsawa, or Gyurme Dechen,
Unchanging Great Bliss.

When he was ten, he received the Vajrapani Empowerment from
the tantric teacher Lhundrup Palden, and learnt mantras. After he
turned thirteen, Gyurme Dechen took ordination and served Lama
Sönam Tsemo.[225] Under the guidance of his Lama, he studied the ocean
of oral instructions, the Lamdre, and other great Sakya treatises, as
well as the profound instructions of Niguma.

At age twenty, he took the full vows of a monk under the great
translator Ratna Bhadra, and studied the Six Practices of the
Kalachakra, which he then practiced for four years and eight months.
He planted the victory banner of practice, received blessings, aroused
faith, developed strong renunciation, engendered compassion, experienced the dawning of the clear-light nature of mind, and achieved
mastery. Moreover, with the tutor Chökyi Lodrö, the great translator Ratna Bhadra, Jamgon Kunga Drolchok, Chödar Drakpel, Chökyi

Drakpa etc., Gyurme Dechen studied the ocean of vast and profound instructions, chief among them the Shangpa teachings, the
Lamdre of the Sakya school, and all the vast, profound, and ocean-
like instructions of the Kalachakra. With Shenyen Namgyal and the
bilingual Rapchö Dawa, he learnt lyrical works and studied the four
common sciences,[226] which he mastered to perfection. Gyurme Dechen
eventually joined the ranks of noble beings.

May virtue flourish! GEO!

## 22

# Life of Taranatha

*Namo Guru!* HERE IS A brief account of the first four years of the omniscient Jetsun Taranatha's life. Jetsun Taranatha is unrivalled in the three realms, and the greatest guide to those beings who see, hear, remember, or come into contact with him. The moment this master first entered his mother's womb, and again when he was born, were crowned by vast and amazing wonders that cannot be put into words. The local people who were there at the time, as well as those who have heard the story since, can vouch for the truth of these accounts.

Jetsun Taranatha's birthplace was the Drong foothills, near a place now called Chökorling,[227] an area protected by Dorje Yudrönma—one of the twelve female Dharma guardians—traditionally depicted to the left of the central female Dharma guardian.[228] The lineage of Ra Lotsawa[229] had originated in that area, and was held at the time by a tantric master named Tsultrim Gyamtso. This elder had four sons who shared a wife by the name of Dorje Buga Lhamo. She always strove after virtue, shied away from evil deeds, and felt great love toward less fortunate beings.

She was twelve when Jetsun Taranatha entered her womb. That night, she dreamt that from a golden vajra and a radiant sun, an incandescent shimmer permeated her and washed her completely. The light rays also pervaded the entire universe. All the beams of light, together with the stainless golden vajra, dissolved into the crown of her head and her bedroom glittered with a brilliance never seen before. Moreover, she found her body clothed in magnificent silks and her chair weighed down with precious gems. Young bejeweled maidens presented bowls of food, made prostrations and circumambulations, and showed her inconceivable honors. A black guardian, with a sash of golden cloth tied around his waist and a hooked knife in his hands, watched the door. In the sky, she saw young men and women who sprinkled water, made offerings, and sang praises. Their bodies were decorated with bone ornaments and great clusters of precious stones.

Such was the extraordinary omen that appeared in the dream of Dorje Buga Lhamo on the night Jetsun Taranatha entered her womb. When she described it to others, no one knew what to make of it. Some said it was just a dream and that she had better not get too carried away. Others advised her to do special long-life practices. Meanwhile, her father-in-law, the tantric master Tsultrim Gyamtso, was well versed in sutras, tantras, and other fields of study, and had worshipped many yidam deities and Dharma protectors. He saw the face of his yidam who spoke these words to him, "The lady Buga Lhamo had a most propitious dream and displays at present many auspicious signs. You should advise her to abandon impure foods. Do not talk about this to anybody."

Buga Lhamo was expected to give birth at dawn on the tenth day of the first month in the boar year.[230] The elder, Tsultrim Gyamtso, advised that wood, and not copper or iron instruments, should be used to dilate her. In the end, they used a wooden shuttle and comb-like reed. The baby was born white with a red hue, with special markings of drops of blood like an embroidery of vermilion thread. Both his hands and feet were embellished with wheel patterns. His lips were like an open lotus, exhuming a sweet fragrance of saffron, calendula, and marigold. His eyes, open as water-lilies, darted left and right, and three times he said the mantra, *Om Sumbhani Sumbha.* The umbilical cord did not even require cutting.

"Some time back," the elder said, "the Dharma lord Kunga Senge came from his monastery to bless the land and establish auspicious connections here. At the time, he said that a great being with mastery of all the classes of tantra would issue from our family. When this boy entered his mother's womb, all kinds of astounding dreams and omens took place. I myself had a dream in which a large being, ornamented with all the signs and marks of a Buddha, said he was the noble Manjushri. This dream being was carrying Dharma books. After I invited him to come into our shrine, he said, 'I am returning these to their rightful owner,' and goddesses handed over the books [he was carrying]. Such was my dream. Its meaning is that our newborn boy will be a scholar with complete understanding of the Buddha's words.

"This day of the boy's birth is an auspicious Padmasambhava day," the elder continued. However, I do see some minor obstacles. Therefore, so that he may overcome any such obstacles, we should name the boy Pedma Sichö Dorje, Diamond Lotus that Cuts through Obstacles. I am also told that his true name will be later given to him by a tenth-level bodhisattva." And the elder, Tsultrim Gyamtso, told many parables and meritorious stories.

Although it was fall, flowers bloomed in more than five hundred orchards that day. Roses revealed new buds, and peach and apricot trees bore fruit as if after a rain shower. Medicinal herbs, thistle, wildflowers, poppies, and the like shot up in no time at all. Even though the sky was bright and clear, for seven consecutive days flowers rained down, and the four heavenly rainbow mansions[231] could be seen. Everyone heard the sound of sparrows and was happy. Even the antelopes pranced about. Now, roses blossomed in the garden of the Lama's residence, their pigment, a deep red hue. Pomegranates grew to the size of a thumb, sour, bitter, and very spicy. Such were the events at the birth of Jetsun Taranatha. This first section briefly touches on Taranatha's entering the womb, and on his birth.

IT IS SAID that Taranatha was only ten days old when a blind man came from Eastern Tibet to see him, hoping to have his sight restored. He was accompanied by several other people from Lhasa and Samye, asking to be shown the bodhisattva who had been recently born. "Please, may we see your son?" they asked. But the parents were excessively protective of their baby and would not grant an audience. So the blind man and the others from Lhasa and Samye could do nothing but prostrate themselves before the residence, circumambulate, intone prayers, and then leave. When his parents and entourage approached him, Taranatha expressed his displeasure at their actions and scolded them [for not allowing the blind man and the others to meet with him].

The elder now said, "Ujön, a clairvoyant Lama, told me I would have a grandson with unmatched powers and abilities. At the time, I thought, 'But of course! We are, after all, the descendants of Ra Lotsawa. It's no wonder we have a great being in our family.' Lama Ujön read my thoughts and said, 'This boy will be far superior than anyone in your family!' 'How do you mean?' I was intrigued. And Lama Ujön elaborated, 'He will be a bilingual bodhisattva, intone vajra songs, and be a second Buddha in these degenerate times.'"

In a day, the supreme emanation matured as much as a normal baby would over a whole month. When he was eight months old, he was already walking. At twelve months, he spoke perfectly, meditated, and displayed other outstanding faculties. Without the slightest difficulty, he knew how to read and write the Buddha's teachings, visualize and intone the root mantras of yidam deities and Dharma protectors, celebrate tantric feasts etc. He seemed to have an innate understanding of all these things, although no one had actually taught him.

Now the household had several very old, dusty tankhas of six-faced black Yamantaka, Udaya Ayupati, Triloka Vijaya[232] and others, which the family ancestors had practiced over time. However, the tankhas were dirty and covered in such soot that neither the locals nor the parents could tell anymore which deity was on which tankha. The supreme emanation unrolled the old tankhas and immediately named

each individual deity. All the people experienced unswerving faith at
this wonder.

Although the family elder had named the boy Pedma Sichö Dorje—
Diamond Lotus That Cuts through Obstacles—the locals quickly came
up with the nickname Wönpo Sichö. But the boy appeared not to like
that, and he would say, "Why are you calling me Wönpo Sichö? I'm
the glorious Kunga Drolchok. Don't call me Wönpo Sichö!" And he
never answered when called by his nickname.

At that, the people became curious: "Kunga Drolchok? We've not
heard of any Lamas called Kunga Drolchok!" Taranatha casually explained the circumstances of his previous life [as Kunga Drolchok],
naming his previous patrons, schools, monasteries, chattels, empowerment objects, shrine objects, offerings and so forth.

Next, the boy went to Nakartse[233] with his attendant, Nyene Paljor,
where the governor, Tenzin, solicited a tantric feast on a grand scale.
Their return route took them through Karpung Pass, avoiding the
dark recesses of Rinpung. At the top of the pass, they ate part of the
offerings and left the rest in piles. They were descending the pass
when the supreme emanation saw his mother ahead, giving water to
some animals. He ran down to her and grabbing her skirts, he announced, "You know, my attendant Nyene Paljor once went to that
town over there." He pointed with his hand, and added, "Monks such
as Drunkun Chöpa, Chödrok Zhungwa, and Palwa also attended on
me. They lived in Chölung with their horses and mules, and I believe
they're still there, even now." And he went on to give detailed explanations of this.

Now it's a well-known fact that Taranatha's homeland was isolated.
Locals from the Drong foothills never ventured outside the small area
between the heights on one side and the valley at their doorsteps. In
contrast to the locals and their limited experience, the boy was talk-
ative, alert, and very healthy. To the locals he was like a god-child,
and they wanted to keep him indoors.[234]

Monks from Gangpa were performing a ceremony nearby when
one of them, Palne Chödze, fell seriously ill. It was decided that he
should go to Drong, accompanied by another monk, and seek treat-

ment. In Drong, the ailing monk and his companion came across the family elder, Tsultrim Gyamtso, in the company of the boy's uncle, who was a doctor. The elder and the uncle invited the two men inside. The sick monk was examined and given some medicine. Meanwhile, the supreme emanation, Taranatha, was teaching the Dharma to local men and women, expounding on the law of karma, the sufferings of samsara, and the rarity of having this precious human body endowed with leisures and opportunities. Seeing this astonishing boy, the two monks from Gangpa prostrated themselves and requested blessings, exclaiming, "This is a rebirth of our lord Lama Kunga Drolchok! He taught the Dharma in Central and Western Tibet. We've always had great faith in him. He gave many teachings to the monks from our monastery in Gangpa. Indeed, the two of us received precepts from him." They told stories of Jetsun Taranatha in his previous incarnation [as Lama Kunga Drolchok] to the parents and the locals, adding, "This boy is not like other Lamas! You people have great merit indeed!" The life of Kunga Drolchok was then told in great detail.

Namgyal Puntsok, one of the four husbands who shared the same wife, Buga Lhamo, was well acquainted with the visualizations of Yamantaka, the cycle of teachings of the Kagyu school, and the special instructions of Vajrapani, and could propitiate numerous protector deities, which he did over and over again, until his powers multiplied. He also felt a lot of affection for the boy, and thought, "This is my son, the apple of my eye. But I swear by the three jewels, whoever tries to train him as some kind of reincarnate Lama, I'll throw a torma at his backside! My boy must carry on the tradition of our family's golden lineage. He has to stay right here."

A few days passed. One evening, the boy and his family were gathered at mealtime. The dogs outside were quiet, the door did not creak or open. Yet a yogi magically appeared, claiming to be from Yarlung Valley. His skin was an azure blue, he was clad in cotton and a tiger skin, and brandished a freshly severed human head attached to a knife. The father and the others around were all terrified, but the supreme emanation looked delighted. The yogi prostrated before the boy and folded his hands in devotion, after which the two, yogi and boy, talked as if they had known each other in the past. They seemed to understand one another well, although none of the others present could grasp a word of what they were saying.

The yogi then performed a water purification over the supreme emanation, and gave him an iron dagger, explaining, "Padmasambhava gave this dagger, called Vajra-Thunder-Subduer-of-Mara, to Yeshe Tsogyal.[235] She hid it in Samye. Later, Lama Yungtönpa[236] found it after receiving prophecies from wisdom dakinis: on three occasions, he used it to subdue demons. Then he placed it back in the hands of the wisdom dakinis who kept it for a long time. Today I present it to you, so that you may have no trouble converting demons [to the Dharma]. Please keep it by your side."

The mother offered excellent beer, which the yogi accepted, saying, "This makes for a good connection." With the human head and tiger skin, he blessed the inner shrine and dispersed the offerings, which floated off as he intoned a prayer. Then, without going through the door, he disappeared, as if unseen by any human being. As instructed, the boy kept the knife by his side until he later gave it to the abbot Kenchen Lungrik Gyamtso, who placed it in a monastery, where it is now the central object on the offering shrine.

The supreme emanation, Taranatha, had great love for all beings, no matter what their shortcomings were, and established auspicious connections with many. This enabled him to tailor his teachings to the abilities of each individual. Immature beings received teachings commensurate with their aptitudes and old people were taught in a way appropriate for their condition. He also had compassion for animals, which he blessed and protected. This second section deals with those who brought up the supreme emanation, and the miracles he displayed from an early age.

*Namo Guru!* GREAT VAJRADHARA, all-pervasive nature of the Buddhas, lord of all the Buddha families, you are a guide to all who see, hear, remember, or come into contact with you!

At sunrise one day when the omniscient Jetsun Taranatha, protector of all beings, was three and a half years of age, two monks drew near and presented themselves as messengers of Chöje Tenzin. They said to the entourage of the supreme emanation, "We understand that you have here the rebirth of our great holy Lama. Chöje Tenzin Zangpo is on his way to see if it is indeed our Lama or not. Please stay here until he arrives. We came early to prepare you."

Chöje Tenzin arrived with his entourage and proceeded to the main residence of the family. He appropriated the larger throne for himself, while Taranatha was left to sit on a throne to his right. Chöje Tenzin did not prostrate, nor did he wait for the boy to drink first when tea was served. Instead, he shot out a stream of questions about the boy's place of origin and questioned whether the supreme emanation was his Lama.

Next, Chöje Tenzin pulled a red sandalwood *damaru* drum out of a little box and asked the boy, "Do you recognize this? What is it?" And the supreme emanation replied, "Of course I do! It used to be mine. One day, you asked for the empowerments of Chakrasamvara, Kalachakra, and Vajrabhairava. In order to establish blessings and a good connection with me, you needed one of the empowerment objects, so I gave you this *damaru* drum." This was enough to convince Chöje Tenzin that the boy was indeed the reincarnation of his Lama. He prostrated and offered a multi-colored silk scarf.

To the mother, he gave five sets of gifts with the words, "You have kept your boy clean, that's good. Please continue to do so. Make sure he doesn't hurt himself or fall off the stairs—he's our very special Lama." Chöje Tenzin continued, "I have previous engagements to attend to: I must spend a couple of days in Kharak for a consecration, and then move on to Mount Chuwori in Gongkar for the next several months. But after that, I'll be back to see our precious Lama." And Chöje Tenzin went on his way.

The boy's father was displeased by the situation. "My boy is like a god child!" he exclaimed. "This Chöje Tenzin Lama is obviously one of those opportunists who goes around saying the *mani* mantra to fill his purse and his belly!" So the father took a white silk scarf, some food, and a piece of silvery cotton. He ran after Chöje Tenzin to whom he presented the gifts. Then he said, "Our family has maintained the golden tradition of Ra Lotsawa unbroken, and my child will stay with us. He will become the next tantric master to combine wisdom and skillful means. What more, we have patrons to whom we are indebted. His mother and I are getting old and bent over like the horns of a goat and this boy is the apple of our eyes. You must understand, I will not grant your request to take him with you. He's just a little boy and should stay right here. Don't say he is some reincarnation of your Lama. Just take these offerings here and accept my decision."

Chöje Tenzin replied, "Please don't talk like that! Yes, your son must uphold the family tradition. But that's not all. I know with absolute certainty that he is the rebirth of a great, revered Lama. If that were not so, we would not insist. Now you and your wife are the parents of this great emanation. That is very special. So we shall offer you whatever is needed to make it up to you and to the local people in Drong. You know I have to go to Kharak for a few days, and then to Gongkar." He took a few of the father's offerings and went on his way.

Chöje Tenzin's return to invite the supreme emanation was delayed. After a time, he heard that another teacher, Kenchen Lungrik Gyamtso, had recognized and invited the supreme emanation to come with him. Chöje Tenzin was as disappointed as a monkey whose banana is taken from its hands! He felt so humiliated that from then on, he vehemently denied that the boy was in any way a reincarnation of his Lama. This completes the third section, which relates Chöje Tenzin's initial meeting with the supreme emanation.


*Namo Guru!* ON THE FIFTEENTH day of the eighth month in the tiger year, the great bodhisattva Kenchen Lungrik Gyamtso was performing a tantric feast. That night, he dreamt that he met the great Jetsun [Kunga Drolchok] who was happy and smiling and with whom he held a conversation as vivid as if Kunga Drolchok were there in person.

Toward dawn, throngs of women arrayed in dresses and gems drew near, cluttering the sky. They said together, "This reincarnation of Krsnacharya has come to benefit all beings. On the upper slopes of a popular gathering place for dakas and dakinis, known for its Indian and Tibetan scholars, stand Kharak and the Drong foothills, where the reincarnation [of Krsnacharya and Jetsun Kunga Drolchok] has gone. To you, genuine Lama Lungrik Gyamtso, we pay homage and advice that you quickly go there." Kenchen Lungrik Gyamtso immediately awakened. It was dawn. His body was saturated with a bliss quite unlike any previous one. His mind, too, was filled with an indescribable joy. He thought, "Now, I must find the reincarnation of my own Lama, no doubt about that." The extraordinary blissful feeling once again spread through his body.

The sun was rising and illuminating the land when his servant brought in tea, followed by an envoy from Nakartse. The envoy announced that in Drong, the reincarnation of Kunga Drolchok had been found and identified. Kenchen Lungrik Gyamtso sent out two messengers for further investigation. These two returned from Drong with confirmation of the news. At this, Kenchen Lungrik Gyamtso smiled in delight. He was filled with indescribable joy and his hair stood on end. He said, "I have dreamt of meeting my Lama. So these news make for a truly excellent connection. I've also got reports from the governor, Tenzin, confirming the prophecy that this is my Lama. I am so happy!"

That day, he deployed several students from his monastery as envoys, along with patrons and five or six horsemen laden with gifts. These were to convey Kenchen Lungrik Gyamtso's invitation to the supreme emanation. They had presents for the parents and for everyone in the area. The abbot from the monastery also went with eighty-five monks on horses. All these festivities and preparations were taking place on a most auspicious day in the ninth month. The caravan thus made for Drong to invite the great emanation.

Kenchen Lungrik Gyamtso and his people spent one night in Nakartse. To announce his coming, Kenchen dispatched two envoys with the order to quickly reach Drong and present the invitation.

That night, the attendants of the supreme emanation, Taranatha, looked out in the direction of Kenchen's camp and announced, "There are people coming, they'll probably be here at dawn. We'd better prepare ourselves."

This was not to the liking of the parents. When the two envoys sent ahead by Kenchen Lungrik Gyamtso arrived at the house of the supreme emanation, the parents warned, "We know very well that there are many more behind you. We know that you're trying to abduct our little boy. Why else would you have so many men and horses on the way? You two have come, you've seen for yourselves all you needed to see. You have no reason to stay, so leave now!"

And the father continued menacingly. "We won't let anyone take away our boy! If you people even think about abducting that child, you'll find yourselves our sworn-enemies. You may have all the teachers and abbots, but *we* are tantric practitioners, and anyone who's earned our hostility will be sorry, indeed. We have very powerful protectors under our spell and they respond to our commands faster than a dog going after wild animals! We won't let anyone insult us. But enough said! Now go!" The father threw the envoys outside where they found themselves face to face with locals who cried out in grief, "This special boy is born in our land and has brought us good fortune. Don't take him from us. If he's taken away, what will happen to us?"

His parents were upset, but the supreme emanation himself was elated. He declared that Kenchen Lungrik Gyamtso was a man of faith and ethics and should be welcome. Pointing to the two expelled envoys, he added, "These two should be given food and instructions. Listen, father, mother, don't be so upset. These are monks from my monastery. I must teach the profound Dharma for their benefit. I must labor day and night for the welfare of beings." Taranatha's exhortations mollified his parents. Through this and other means, he succeeded in comforting them. He proceeded to give a detailed reply to the two envoys and motioned for refreshments to be laid out for the arrival of Kenchen Lungrik Gyamtso.

The following day, Kenchen was heading the boy's way. In one of the towns, he asked for directions and people pointed toward the foothills of Drong, Taranatha's homeland. Presently, Kenchen Lungrik Gyamtso opened a letter of predictions his previous teacher given him, and found that it accorded with what he saw around him. "Those two mountains are similar to the drawing I have here," he concluded, and facing in that direction, he prostrated himself.

"Here is what my glorious holy Lama said about the mountains surrounding this main summit," Kenchen Lungrik Gyamtso explained, looking at the prophetic messages from his previous Lama. "He wrote that the mountain to the east resembled a mandala, the northern peak looked like a somber sky, and the snow-capped western mountain appeared as wide as a lotus blossom. The prophecy speaks of plants and roots growing by the brooks and streams gushing into the river basin with a sweet aroma. Birds and antelopes are prancing about in forests of bramble and buckthorn. I find that the surroundings concur with these auguries."

Kenchen Lungrik Gyamtso continued, "We are truly fortunate to meet with an omniscient master in this world! I remember that last year, a young boy was recognized as a reincarnation in Chushul, and was taken by someone else. The Chushul area looked pretty much like this and I thought that the boy was the emanation we'd been looking for. But one night, a black being riding a black horse stood out in space and said, 'I'm the protector of your Lama.' He whirled his bannered lance overhead and howled with laughter. The sky exploded in scarlet sheets of lightning and flame. 'Ha ha!' the protector bellowed, 'A supreme, genuine Lama has just been born. I'm going there to protect him!' Earth and sky shook violently. Knowing that I was to meet my Lama again made me very happy. And today, my greatest wish has come true. What a happy time for all!"

The party continued on their way in high spirits. When they were near, Kenchen dismounted from his horse, prostrated himself toward Taranatha's homeland, folded his hands in devotion, sank to his knees, said the seven-branch prayer, and then presented a full mandala offering. He proceeded the rest of the way with full body prostrations.

In this auspicious time of Kenchen's arrival in the Drong foothills, refreshing wine was brought out along with pitchers of beer and pots of tea. Kenchen said, "Everything, both external and internal, should make for auspicious connections." And he proceeded to prepare the 'golden line-up' ceremony usually performed to greet great beings: the monks were arranged in rows; two groups blew conch shells and one resounded a white conch; some played reed pipes and others beat drums; all created a resounding music. An incredible tent was erected in this great power place with large draperies inside and out. It mirrored the heavenly gods' realm, with stupendous banners, canopies, parasols, music, silken oriflammes hanging from the rooftops, and other objects beyond description. Jetsun Taranatha and the Dharma lord Kenchen Lungrik Gyamtso came together and held hands, conversing happily and each insisting that the other take the higher throne. Kenchen prostrated to the supreme emanation and offered twenty-five large handfuls of gold dust, silk robes, and more. At that moment, a rain of flowers descended from the sky and dazzling white rainbows appeared above Kenchen's tent.

After six days, Kenchen went to Gangkarda for a week and then returned to officially invite the supreme emanation, Taranatha, to his monastery. The arrangements were finalized over the next several days. During that time, Jetsun Taranatha came daily to Kenchen's camp. Each time he entered the tent, flowers rained from the sky as white rainbows shone and the sound of cymbals, conch shells, lutes, and hand drums could be heard.

On the fourth day of the tenth month, Kenchen and his party prepared to leave. Many locals went up to Trashita Rock to say goodbye to the supreme emanation. Trashita had been a plain old rock, but after Jetsun Taranatha touched it, letters appeared on the stone, the heart-syllables of Chakrasamvara.

Even birds and antelopes seemed sad at the departure of the supreme emanation. The locals, escorting Taranatha the last of the way, were all looking at him and telling him how much they cared for him. Some were making aspiration prayers, while others implored, "We're such unfortunate beings. Please don't forget us, please remember us in your compassion!" Some threw themselves on the ground as tears streamed down their faces, wondering what would happen to the region now. For the following ten years, the area saw outstanding harvests, more birds, and animals. The people there neither aged nor died, but lived to a ripe age. The place became very famous for this and even now, it is still being talked about!

Jetsun Taranatha left for Nakartse with Kenchen Lungrik Gyamtso and a large retinue. There, the supreme emanation gave the practices of Guru Yoga and the Avalokiteshvara textual transmission to the governor, Tenzin, and a great many teachers. His performance was astounding. "Such a little boy, yet such intellect and wisdom!" they all exclaimed with great faith.

On the fifteenth day, they reached Gyaltse Peak and were received by Lhawang Drakpa, Kunga Palzang, and other heart-disciples who had known the Lama in his previous life. They exchanged questions and answers just like old times.

Next, the supreme emanation was taught languages, mathematics, and rhetoric. He studied a vast number of sutras, tantras, and *shastras* with several teachers such as Je Draktöpa, Yeshe Wangpo, Kunga Trashi, Jampa Lhundrup, Lungrik Gyamtso, etc. His qualities and activity became greater and greater. But there is no need to speak of this, and we won't go into it here, as it is well known by both men on earth and gods above, and has been explained in detail in the complete life story of the omniscient Jetsun Taranatha.

This account of Taranatha's first four years is hopefully clear and free of mistakes. It was written by Tsitta who has no poetic ability or literary skill, but simply seeks to write without bias—be it flattery or ill will. May this benefit the precious teachings of the Buddha. May it benefit all sentient beings! May all be happy!

SARWA MANGALAM! EKATRI TSATSA!

# 23

# Nectar Rain of Realizations

*The Story and Cycle of Teachings on Mahakala, the
Glorious Six-Armed Wisdom Protector*

*Om Soti!* MAY THIS EXCELLENT explanation—an expanding, white, luminous cascade of the Buddha's compassion—open the mind's lotus-blossom to fortunate disciples, and, like the crown jewel of the wise, may it cure weariness.

With respect to the story and cycle of teachings on the swift wisdom protector—the three-fold visualization and recitation and so forth—we will present four sections: how the wisdom protector generated a compassionate aspiration; an account of Mahakala practices in India; an account of the transmission as it spread in Tibet, land of snow; an overview of the teachings as they are now known.

*How the wisdom protector generated a compassionate aspiration*

IN THE PAST, Avalokiteshvara, the Great Compassionate One, engendered bodhichitta. For countless eons, he gathered the two accumulations of merit and wisdom, attained the tenth level of a bodhisattva, and obtained the Great Light Rays Empowerment. He entered the ranks of the sons and daughters of the Buddha by sealing his aspiration with the vow, "I shall benefit beings in this samsaric world and throughout the ten directions. I shall remain in samsara to liberate all sentient beings from suffering, and until every one of them has attained supreme enlightenment, I myself shall not pass into nirvana. Only when all sentient beings have attained enlightenment, will it be all right for me to pass into nirvana. And if I ever break this vow, may by body be shattered into a thousand pieces!"

Avalokiteshvara stayed on Mount Potala. He performed emanations at every moment and brought to maturation and liberation countless beings, in ways far too vast to express. This he did for a great many eons, until one day he thought he should see what had developed, considering the many beings he had led on the path.

With his clairvoyance, he exerted his gaze on the world and saw that the realm of sentient beings was more confused than ever. Peoples' lives were getting shorter. Beings were mired in the five degenerations and it was difficult for them to avoid committing evil. Avalokiteshvara thought, "I haven't succeeded in liberating even a single sentient being!" This thought broke his vow. Consequently, his body split into a thousand pieces.

The spiritual guide who, as a result of the vow he originally made, always holds beings in his compassion, the noble protector of the world, the fully enlightened Buddha Amitabha, now appeared and said to Avalokiteshvara, "O noble son, you have broken your vow, that is not good! Now, you'd better renew your resolution, and in stronger terms this time!"

After he had finished speaking, Amitabha took the thousand pieces and formed eleven faces and a thousand arms for Avalokiteshvara. Then, he blessed him. At that point, Avalokiteshvara thought, "There is no possible way for me to renew my vow more strongly than before." So for the next seven days, he remained in a daze [of uncertainty].

When he came to, he perceived that by means of a wrathful form he could train sentient beings mired in the five degenerations. Seeing that even those who practiced Dharma were haunted by fears of the bardo, he recognized that in a wrathful form he could protect them from the frights of the bardo. Lastly, observing that beings in this degenerate age were poor and needy and experienced only suffering, he discerned that by means of a wrathful form he could provide them with an antidote to their suffering. Their needs and desires would be answered simply by expressing their wishes. Through this three-fold activity,[237] Avalokiteshvara was able to renew his vow in ways even more powerful than before and this was crystallized as the black-blue syllable HUNG at his heart, which transformed into the swift wisdom protector, Mahakala.

The earth shook in six ways in respect to Avalokiteshvara's compassionate aspiration. Buddha Amitabha, together with countless Buddhas, bodhisattvas of the ten levels, etc. exclaimed with one voice, "O noble son! This is a noble aspiration indeed! You shall have the powers of all the dakinis. You shall have the strength of Yamantaka.[238] And spirits, demons, harm-doers, and gods will perform activity [on your behalf]." Thus, the great wrathful emanation was granted the empowerments of the body, speech, mind, qualities, and activity of all the Buddhas of the three times. As of that time, the swift wisdom protector Mahakala guards the teachings in all the pure lands.

### An account of Mahakala practices in India

LONG AGO, WHEN Avalokiteshvara came to the town of Rajastan, a dancer aroused great devotion and offered songs, dances, and prayers. Six hundred years after the Buddha passed into nirvana, this devoted dancer was reborn as a human. His name was Shavaripa, Master of the Solitudes.

While staying in the charnel ground Shady Cool Grove,[239] the adept Shavaripa entered into a *samadhi* meditation devoid of elaboration.

One morning at dawn, he heard a *damaru* drum resounding in the sky. The wisdom protector actually appeared and made an offering of his heart mantra and all his practices to Shavaripa, whose life became like the sun and the moon. He performed the Joint Practice of the Four Blessings Deities, which included Avalokiteshvara, Vajrayogini, Tara, and the wisdom protector Mahakala.[240] Each of the deities also taught him their individual *sadhanas*.

One thousand years later, Maitri Gupta (Jampa Bepa in Tibetan, or known by his secret name of Nyime Dorje, Non-Dual Vajra)[241] was staying in Vikramashila monastery.[242] Although he was stable in the generation stage and had developed great powers, he did not have direct insight into the meaning of the natural state. So he prayed to the *adhideva*[243] deities and heard the prophecy, "Go to Mount Glory in the south. The protector will take care of you there."

Maitripa went to Mount Glory. There, he met the adept Shavaripa, Master of the Solitudes, under whom he studied Mahamudra precepts on the profound meaning. His insight into the natural state was as vast as the sky. Shavaripa commanded him to spread the teachings on the profound meaning and gave him the *sadhana* of the Joint Practice of the Four Blessings Deities. After practicing for twenty-one days, Maitripa had all the Dharma protectors at his service. He was presented with gifts from people five hundred miles away, and fulfilled the various wishes of beings. This is confirmed in other stories.

Some legends have it that Maitripa went three times to Mount Potala where he actually saw Avalokiteshvara as clearly as meeting someone face to face. He also went to the heavenly mansions of the gods, where he performed circumambulations and placed an offering at the foot of every pillar. At the entrance of the last colossal castle, he couldn't open the door, so he called out to the dakas and dakinis, "Please, open the door!"

They replied, "If we open the door, all the beings of the samsaric worlds—the nether-world, human realm, and heavenly sphere—will be angry and die." Hearing this, Maitripa directed a heartfelt prayer to Avalokiteshvara who manifested as a messenger and whose words opened the door without harm coming to any sentient being. Inside,

Maitripa saw the wisdom protector. He immediately said a prayer and asked for blessings, saying, "Please come to Jambudiva for the welfare of beings. Please protect the teachings of the Buddha!" The protector assented to his request, and from that day on, there has always been an emanation of the protector [Mahakala] in a recess of the Nyagrodha tree in the Shady Cool Grove charnel ground.

## An account of the transmission in Tibet, land of snow

GENERALLY SPEAKING, we know that many scholars translated the practice of the protector into Tibetan. In particular, Gyicho Daway Özer,[244] who studied with an attendant of Maitripa, worked on a translation of the short treatises of Shavaripa. His classification of the writings on the protector became known as the 'three-fold visualization and recitation.' Garö Tsultrim Jungne wrote a translation based on a text by the sage Shanta Akara. Then, the translator Garchözang studied with Atulyavajra and translated the *sadhanas* set down by Saraha and Shavaripa. Khyungpo's instructions were consistent with all these translations.

Some people claim that 'Ataya' is a misspelling, and that the yogi Advayavajra, or Atulyavajra, was in fact one and the same as Maitripa. It seems likely that spelling mistakes slipped in, such as a *da* instead of a *ta* or *ha*, or differences due to local dialects. But in the final analysis, these differences can be resolved: Atulyavajra [or Advayavajra, or Atayavajra], and Maitripa were all Lamas of the great scholar Khyungpo Naljor.

Although Khyungpo did study with these great masters, none of the teachings are extant except for the condensed version of the three-fold visualization and recitation, which has survived to this day only by a thread. Thus, the only complete, profound, and genuine cycle of teachings on the wisdom protector is that of the scholar Khyungpo

Naljor. It is an unparalleled blessings-stream of glorious, flourishing, all-pervasive activity.

Let us then briefly consider Khyungpo Naljor. He was born in Nyemo Ramang, to the Khyung family. He first became erudite in the Bön tradition and gathered more than seven hundred disciples. Next, he followed the Dzogchen teachings and soon gathered three hundred disciples. Finally, he went to the teacher Nirupa and studied Chakrasamvara, Yamantaka, and various Mahamudra teachings. At fifty-two years of age, he went to Nepal and spent the next fifty years wandering between India, Nepal, and Tibet. In India, he had a hundred and fifty teachers with whom he learnt sutras, tantras, grammar, logic, and oral precepts, all of which he fully accomplished. His common Lamas were the meritorious Dorjedenpa, Maitripa, Bebe Naljor, and Rahula. His two extraordinary Lamas were the wisdom dakinis Niguma and Sukhasiddhi. These six represent his principal Lamas.

Once, on his way back from a trip to India, he received the heart essence of countless sages, including the wisdom dakinis. He was almost all the way back to Tibet when he decided to give the lord Maitripa what little gold and provisions he still had left. Presenting himself to Maitripa, Khyungpo begged him, "Lama, my land—Tibet—is not a rich land. Please teach a practice for the quick accumulation of wealth."

Maitripa recounted the story of the wisdom protector, adding, "He is called the Great Compassionate Black One. He is also called the Protector of the Wish-Fulfilling Tree. As much as you rely on him, that much will your wishes and desires be answered. As much as you think [of him], that much will obstacles be removed, and enemies destroyed. Even if you don't do his practice, simply praying to him is enough to see his face and be protected from harm, illness, and impurities. Even if you gain only common achievements [of the protector's practice], extraordinary results will issue. I shall now teach you this Dharma protector known as the wish-fulfilling gem."

Having opened the door with a profound *samadhi* empowerment, Maitripa proceeded to give the complete precepts of the protector to

Khyungpo. When this was done, he said, "The general commitment is that one's vows to the protector never be violated. The particular commitment requires that torma offerings always include ground barley. Offer good incense and other natural substances. Practice without attachment. Do not throw rocks at black birds or black dogs. Most importantly, arouse faith and devotion and maintain your vows. If you follow this advice, you'll find that your life will be easy no matter what your circumstances—mountain solitudes or anything else. The protector will answer your every request. If you practice properly, you will definitely see the face of the protector with his retinue, in as little time as thirteen days."

This was Maitripa's prophecy to Khyungpo Naljor. Khyungpo returned to Tibet, and then went back to India to repay the kindness of all his Indian Lamas by performing a tantric feast in their honor. Since Maitripa was no longer staying in the area at that time, Khyungpo presented a beautiful golden mandala to the mighty woman yogini Gangadhara,[245] from whom he received Mahamudra precepts as well as very special omens about the protector practice. Following that, Khyungpo returned to Tibet where he worked extensively for the benefit of beings and had scholars study with him –such as Potawa and Langri Tangwa—out of the conviction that he was a genuine bodhisattva.

Once in a cave in Penyul, Khyungpo Naljor found himself alone and down to his last provisions. He recalled Lama Maitripa saying that the protectors would provide for his livelihood. He was in real need and felt like his life was about to end. So one night, he went to the door of his cave, shouting at the top of his voice, "Kshetrapala and you all! I was told by Maitripa that you'd help! Well, right now, I'm at the end of my rope and I can't finish my torma offerings!"

The following day, a big group of townspeople came to him with offerings of butter, tea, and clothes. Since many disciples had thus gathered, Khyungpo gave them a teaching. Within a month, the ranks of students swelled to the extent that they couldn't fit in his cave anymore. It was a decided that a monastery should be erected, and the monastery was named Cheka.

Khyungpo spent time in his Cheka monastery. He stayed in retreat at the beginning of each month, and during the waning moon, he taught the Dharma. Once at daybreak during the retreat part of the month, he heard a knock on the door. His attendant went to look and saw a yogi who asked to meet Lama Khyungpo. The yogi was pacing back and forth, but the attendant told him that the Lama was in retreat and would not see anybody. "Please," the yogi insisted, "I've come a long way to see him. I'm ill, let me just meet with him!" No sooner was he invited in than he cried out, "Quick, get me a doctor!"

Khyungpo examined him and declared, "You have a circulation problem. We need to let out blood." But the yogi replied, "Bleeding won't do! This is how a yogi deals with such disorders!" And he levitated about fifteen inches in space with a buzzing sound, while blood poured out from the blisters on his body.

Khyungpo took a special ointment and said, "Now I should massage you." But the yogi said, "Ha! Rubbing a salve won't do! Here is another way for a yogi to deal with such disorders!" And now he levitated in space just as before, with a buzzing sound. Semen poured out from the pores of his body and with a brisk sound was then withdrawn back in. His body glittered with a brilliant gloss. Khyungpo thought, "This man knows wonders indeed!" and asked the yogi where he was from.

The yogi replied, "I come from India. I left this morning before the sun was up, and crossed the Tibetan ravine at sunrise." Khyungpo asked him his name. The yogi replied, "I am Rahula Guptavajra.[246] I was told by Gunakara, Ratnakara, and Abhiyukta to go to Tibet where I would be of benefit to a yogi. So I came and now I've met you." And the yogi Rahula told Khyungpo his whole life story.

Rahula stayed in Cheka for seven months[247] and gave oral precepts and special instructions. In particular, Rahula transmitted to Khyungpo the extensive cycle of teachings on the wisdom protector, including instructions Khyungpo had not received from Maitripa. Rahula said he had sought suitable vessels for teachings on the protector but had found none except Khyungpo. Rahula then went into the sky and disappeared. It is not known where he went.

For the next twenty years, Khyungpo kept strict meditation in Penyul and Central Tibet. Finally, urged by repeated prophecies from the dakinis, he set out for Shang where he spent the next thirty years working extensively for the welfare of beings. He erected a hundred and eight monasteries but often left for extended stays in mountain caves.

Khyungpo once emanated a magical army in order to prevent war and thereby turned vast numbers of non-Buddhists to the Dharma. Many fantastic things occurred, which are quite beyond ordinary understanding. For example, he stayed for seven days inside a vase. Or again, during a stay at one of his monasteries, Khyungpo appeared in space on a hundred and eight thrones simultaneously, each emanation teaching the Five Treatises of Maitreya to vast assemblies.

Another time, his clairvoyant powers told him that a minor ailment he had was caused by defilements in the vows of some deluded monks from Eastern Tibet. Khyungpo received advice from the protector, "Prepare me torma offerings to dispel these negativities!" Teachers and students prepared tormas for the protector and performed the protector's *sadhana*. After thirteen days, the tormas began to display signs and when it was time to throw them out, the protector could be seen on top of the tormas, white in color, purifying obstacles. All the teachers and students saw this and Khyungpo's illness was immediately purified. Khyungpo recalled that this had been previously prophesized in a vision of Maitripa and his entourage.

Overall, many disciples received teachings on the protector from Khyungpo Naljor. One of them was the teacher Chökyi Sherab. Notes of the teachings were also found in the lineage of Zhutön Hralmo. However, until now, only four appear to have maintained an unbroken line for these precepts, namely the famous Kenchen Latöpa, Könchok Kar, Zhangom Chöseng, master of dakini union, and Mokchokpa Rinchen Tsöndrü, master of Dream Yoga and Illusory Body Yoga.

First, Kenchen Latöpa, a disciple of the great Sherab Barpa: Latöpa once found that he was followed by one of Khyungpo Naljor's tankhas of the protector, which was quickly nicknamed the Flying Tankha.

Latöpa thought he had better not take a hold of that tankha without the Lama's permission. So he retraced his steps back to Khyungpo and asked what to do with the Flying Tankha. Khyungpo said, "Do take it! Your merit will one day be even greater than that of your teacher Sherab Barpa." Later, Latöpa did indeed become powerful, and established monasteries in Chöding and the Nyang Valley. The transmission of the protector teachings that descended through Latöpa is known as the Early Protector System or the Upper Tibetan Tradition of the Protector.

As for Zhangom Chöseng: for a long time, he assisted the great scholar Khyungpo Naljor, and obtained many profound oral instructions from him. At the exhortation of his Lama, he spent seven years in meditation by the Monolith of Lake Tengri Nor.[248] He obtained a direct perception into the natural state and by opening up his central channel, received visions of numerous deities. For a number of years, he performed Mahakala practices. He lived like an ascetic but found that the protector looked after all the basic necessities. After many years of living in the mountains, he left for the Pure Land of the Dakini.

Next is the great Mokchokpa, whose achievements are as vast as the blazing sun. For twelve years, he stayed in a cave in Mokchok, practicing asceticism, and never once saw human food. As for the exalted states he reached, seven or eight years were spent on the Joint Practice of the Four Blessings Deities. One night, he looked to the wall of his cave and saw the protector with his retinue, amidst a blazing fire, rattling his *damaru* drum with a resounding sound. Mokchokpa was inspired to sing a paean and offer circumambulations, which greatly pleased the protector. From that time on, the protector acted as his servant without needing to communicate in human terms.

Mokchokpa, however, perceived all appearances to be like an illusion, and was fueled by intense love and non-referential compassion for the six kinds of beings. As a result, he never had recourse to the protector's powers for the subjugation of enemies.

Mokchokpa's enlightened activity spread, and alms began to pour in. One night, a large party of porters carrying offerings [for Mokchokpa] was overwhelmed by a group of villagers. Mokchokpa's monks formed themselves into an army, ready to fight [the villagers]. Meanwhile, the villagers had also stolen a yak that was, in fact, the protector's yak, and were trying to tie him but the yak rammed his horns every which way, trampled the ground with his hoofs, and emitted a loud sound as flames leaped from his horns with a crackling noise. The holy Mokchokpa sang the song that starts, "Asking your Lama for advice is the measure of your understanding of the path . . ."[249]

Then he told the assembled people, "My work consists only of Dharma. I want no army here, and no black magic either." Mokchokpa said a prayer, took a blanket, loaded his bag with his ritual objects, and left for the mountains. The monks gave up the notion of forming an army, the yak was returned, and Mokchokpa was graced with a vision of Tara[250] saying:

The flames of anger and attachment
Are quenched by the rivers of love and affection.
It is good, yogi, it is good!

Later, Kyergangpa presented himself to Mokchokpa, with whom he studied all the general precepts, and more particularly, the cycle of teachings of the protector who, it was prophesized, would wait on him like a servant.

After Kyergangpa established his monastic center, he labored extensively for the benefit of beings. During this time, he studied many profound teachings—including cycles of teachings on the protector which he had not studied with Mokchokpa—descending from such great masters as Zhangom Chöseng, the dakinis, Atulyavajra, and Maitripa. He thereby combined into one the oral instructions of Khyungpo's two heart-son disciples.[251]

Kyergangpa was a genuine master of bodhichitta. Once, he set out to build a monastery and erect walls around it.[252] However, the locals seemed bent on preventing this. They repeatedly broke the erected wall and fought among themselves until the protectors intervened by showing signs of impending death to two of the instigators.

The heart-son disciple of Kyergangpa was Rigongpa. One morning at dawn, Rigongpa approached Lama Kyergangpa and both did circumambulations when Kyergangpa suddenly said, "Look over there!" Rigongpa gazed in the distance. On the slope of Mount Takri was the protector, glaring in dazzling splendor. At his side, Kshetrapala was offering two human hearts, red and bloody. "What is this?" Rigongpa asked his Lama.

"Well," Kyergangpa explained, "these are the hearts of two men who yesterday caused havoc around the water mill." The day was breaking, and when Rigongpa approached to take a closer look, he saw that the water mill was destroyed and the two men were dead. This is how he saw his yidam deity without meditation.

Later when he was staying in Yöl, there was an explosion of thunder and Rigongpa was struck thirteen times by flashes of lightning. Yet he held the realization that the nature of reality is like an illusion. He sat in the center of a blazing fire and was unharmed by the lightning. He seized the thunderbolts in his hands, rolled them back and forth on the folds of his robes, and threw them against a nearby cliff. Since then, the rock has been marked by a reddish-brown trail. Rigongpa had the protector's help in this. He said that for him, there was no difference between friend and enemy. But further fights and retributions related to the protectors persisted with no end in sight until Palden Lhamo Remate shouted to Rigongpa, "Build a statue of the protector! It will help the situation!"

To which Rigongpa replied, "A man like me isn't up for that kind of task."

"What?" exclaimed Remate, "can't you even get a little mud from the water mill?"

Rigongpa seized the opportunity and bargained, "I will do it if you never kill any human beings again!"

A few days passed. Rigongpa was returning from the mill with a handful of clay, when he noticed a man in the doorframe leading to his room, holding yogic implements. Rigongpa showed him the clay and the man said, "I know all about clay. This is of excellent quality." Thinking that this was indeed an auspicious and special connection, Rigongpa invited the man inside. For the next few days, the two piled up their materials and, mixing together the different pigments of variegated colors, they began to fashion clay figurines.

When they were done, Rigongpa and the yogi lined up their confections. No sooner were they arranged than the statues took on the most perfect colors. The yogi declared, "The time has come to consecrate them." Knowing that the man was an emanation of the protector, Rigongpa replied, "You're the one who should perform the consecration." And the yogi dissolved into the statues, which became famed as the self-evolved protector and consequently carried tremendous blessings. Distinctive characteristics on the statues are still present to this day. Although the ever-increasing blessings of the protector are generally stronger when kept secret, these particular statues affect anyone who sees, hears, touches, or thinks about them. They are the activity of Avalokiteshvara. Even today, people worship the place where these statues came into existence.

The holder of the treasury of Rigongpa's secret body, speech, and mind was Sangye Tönpa, protector of beings, whose vast knowledge of the sciences was said to equal that of the greatest Lamas of the past. He turned his mind away from the eight worldly concerns. Perceiving samsara and nirvana to be like an illusion, he gained stable realization into the meaning of the natural state. With love and compassion vast as space, he beheld the faces of innumerable yidam deities and was served by dakinis and Dharma protectors. He counted thousands of disciples from Jalandhara and Uddiyana in the north to China in the east. Sangye Tönpa spontaneously brought benefit to others.

Once, in the residence of his disciple, Sangye Tönpa transmitted the essential precepts of the Shangpa practice lineage including the entire cycle of teachings on the protector, leaving nothing out. The disciple also received explanations on the instructions of the wisdom dakini, Niguma. This cycle of teachings on the protector became known as the Rigongpa Protector System, or the Lower Tibetan Tradition of the Protector.

There are, then, two distinct transmissions of the protector practice: on the one hand, the Rigongpa Protector System or Lower Tradition which spread from Rigongpa's monastic seat to many areas, and on the other hand, the Early Protector System or Upper Tradition. The adherents of the Upper Tradition concentrated chiefly on the three-fold visualization and recitation of the protector. Practitioners were versed in this tantric system and exhibited great powers, but many became conceited about their abilities. This Upper Tradition flourished early but has barely survived to this day, though it is not completely lost.

The Lower Tradition of Rigongpa was upheld by many great Shangpa Kagyu masters who not only practiced it properly, but also with certainty and faith, thereby loosening the knots in their mindstreams. The Shangpa Kagyu practitioners mastered self-arising Mahamudra, realized that appearances are like an illusion, and had genuine awareness, which kept them from [deviating] into exorcist recitations or mere harmful intentions. Within the relaxed mind, mental knots naturally loosened and the four types of enlightened activity manifested effortlessly.[253] In later generations, the Lower Tradition spread far and wide. It was taught to other schools by such masters as Jakchen Jampa Pal and the great Tsongkhapa.[254]

### An overview of the teachings as they are now known

THE DIFFERENT TEACHINGS on the protector can all be broadly grouped under two topics: the power practices on the fierce form, and the wealth practices on the peaceful form. Let us briefly look at the salient points differentiating these two practices.

In the power practices on the fierce form, the protector is black in color. He appears in various [mandala configurations]: as the sole

deity [of the mandala], with a consort, in a three-deity mandala surrounded by five haughty spirits, in a five-deity mandala with ornaments, in a thirteen-deity mandala as set out by Saraha, in a nine-
deity mandala, and so forth. His *sadhana* has such names as the Green
Wrathful Practice, the Yellow Wrathful Practice, the Retinue Individual Accomplishment, the Four Foundations, the Three Piths, and
so on—all, it is agreed, are genuine practices: the protector is a powerful medium for blessings.

In the wealth practices on the peaceful form, the protector is variously called the White Wish-Fulfilling-Jewel Protector, the Brilliant
Protector, the Eight-Faced Yellow Protector, the Yellow Wealth Protector, the Royal and Powerful Red Protector, the Long-Life Red Protector, the Green Protector Lord of Longevity, and so on.

Both power and wealth practices entail outer and inner oral instructions for the outer and inner clearing of obstacles, as well as
prayers to the inseparability of Lama and protector. Furthermore,
the Joint Practice of the Four Blessings Deities is a uniquely profound
method of connecting with the wisdom protector. I've written here
briefly about these practices. If you want to know more, a genuine
Lama will give you further teachings.

From his supreme, inexpressible wisdom and his ever-present, naturally skillful, unobstructed compassion, may swift-acting
Avalokiteshvara, who continually performs enlightened activity, grant
us excellent virtue. This was the brief story and cycle of teachings
concerning the Six-Armed Wisdom Protector Mahakala. Written by
Wangpo Kunga Rabten.

SARWA DAKALYA NIBHA WANTU! GEO! GEO! GEO!

# 24

# Conclusion

*Om Soti!* THE GLORIOUS SHANGPA Kagyu lineage—one of the Eight Great Chariots of the Practice Lineage in Tibet, land of snow—billows high like the tip of a victory banner. These have been the wondrous lives of this golden lineage, including an account on the Six-Armed Wisdom Protector.

By the noble intention of Karma Drupgyu and Kalu [Rinpoche] who set this down at the residence of Jamgon [Kongtrul], may all beings attain enlightenment and may the teachings of the Shangpa tradition flourish and last for a long, long time.

SARWA DA MANGALAM BHAWANTU!

# Appendices

# APPENDIX I: SHANGPA LINEAGE

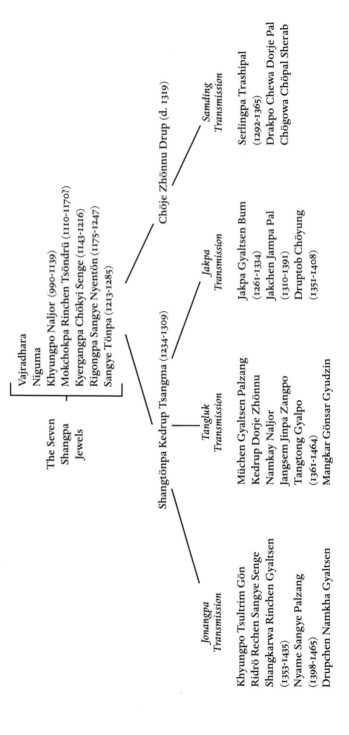

The Seven
Shangpa
Jewels

Vajradhara
Niguma
Khyungpo Naljor (990-1139)
Mokchokpa Rinchen Tsöndrü (1110-1170?)
Kyergangpa Chökyi Senge (1143-1216)
Rigongpa Sangye Nyentön (1175-1247)
Sangye Tönpa (1213-1285)

Chöje Zhönnu Drup (d. 1319)

Shangtönpa Kedrup Tsangma (1234-1309)

*Samding
Transmission*

Serlingpa Trashipal
(1292-1365)
Drakpo Chewa Dorje Pal
Chögowa Chöpal Sherab

*Jakpa
Transmission*

Jakpa Gyaltsen Bum
(1261-1334)
Jakchen Jampa Pal
(1310-1391)
Druptob Chöyung
(1351-1408)

*Tangluk
Transmission*

Müchen Gyaltsen Palzang
Kedrup Dorje Zhönnu
Namkay Naljor
Jangsem Jinpa Zangpo
Tangtong Gyalpo
(1361-1464)
Mangkar Gönsar Gyudzin

*Jonangpa
Transmission*

Khyungpo Tsultrim Gön
Ridrö Rechen Sangye Senge
Shangkarwa Rinchen Gyaltsen
(1353-1435)
Nyame Sangye Palzang
(1398-1465)
Drupchen Namkha Gyaltsen

Gyagom Legpa Gyaltsen
Kunga Drolchok
(ca. 1495-1566)
Chöku Lhawang Drakpa
Jetsun Taranatha
(1575-1634)
Jetsun Yeshe Gyamtso
Jampa Yönten Gönpo
Jalü Gönpo Paljor
Drupchok Gönpo Drakpa
Kyabdak Gönpo Namgyal
Katok Rikdzin Tsewang Norbu
Drupchen Kagyu Trinle
Mokchok Kunga Gelek Palwar
Kunga Lhundrup Gyamtso
Drupchok Kagyu Tendzin
Chokzik Karma Lhaktong
Karma Zhenpen Ozer

Kedrup Palden Darpo
Jetsun Sönam Tsemo
Kalzang Gyurme Dechen
(b. 1540)
Dzongpa Kenchen
Jamjang Sönam Gyaltsen
Ngawang Tenpa Dargye
Mangtö Sönam Chöpel
Kunga Legpa Jungne
Jamjang Sönam Palzang
Samdzong Chöde
Yeshe Gyalchok
Sakya Chödra Chenpo
Jamgon Dorje Rinchen
Jamjang Kyentse Wangpo

Jamgon Kongtrul Lodrö Taye (1813-1899)
Tashi Chöpel
Norbu Döndrup
Kyabje Kalu Rinpoche (1904-1989)
Bokar Tulku Rinpoche (1940-)
Yangsi Kalu Rinpoche (1990-)

# Appendix II

## Shangpa Tree of the Five Golden Teachings

THESE TEACHINGS WERE transmitted to Khyungpo Naljor from the dakini Niguma (who received them directly from Vajradhara) after he presented her with gold. The Five Golden Teachings are represented by a tree:

> The roots correspond to the Six Yogas of Niguma.
> The trunk is the Mahamudra Reliquary.
> The branches are the Three Ways of Integrating the Path.
> The flowers are the Red and White Forms of the Dakini.
> The fruit is Deathlessness and Non-Deviation.

### The roots: The Six Yogas of Niguma

NIGUMA'S YOGAS DERIVE from a direct inspiration she had of Vajradhara, the lord of all Buddhas. Similar to those of her brother or husband Naropa, but requiring an empowerment for each individual yoga unlike Naropa's, Niguma's yogas fall into six categories, thus six roots to the tree of the Shangpa teachings.

We start at the root, of course, but it should be noted that the teachings sketched by the tree take root after the ground has been worked. This means that preliminary practices—meditation and recitation of

the Five Tantric Deities mandala of Chakrasamvara as well as purification practices such as Empty Enclosure Resounding With A—should
precede introduction to these practices. The neophyte is enjoined to
receive the individual empowerment, blessing, authorization to practice, pointing-out instruction, and reading transmission for each of
the yogas. And before any tantric practice, she must connect with a
qualified, genuine Lama.

Since a version of the Six Yogas as brought forth by the Second
Dalai Lama already exists—admittedly a Geluk and not directly a
Kagyu interpretation—I will present only a short description here.[255]
The Six Yogas, when practiced with a genuine aspiration to benefit
others, lead the way for realization of Mahamudra.

## Inner Heat Yoga (gtum mo)

At times the term 'Path of Means' is used to refer to Inner Heat
Yoga. In a three-year retreat setting, this first yoga is practiced for
three months.[256] Inner Heat Yoga consists in practicing 'vase respiration' and exercises of the subtle body involving the seed essence (thig
le, Skt. bindu). Accomplishment in this practice produces heat and
bliss and leads to the Mahamudra realization of bliss-emptiness inseparable.

## Illusory Body Yoga (sgyu lus)

States of attachment and aversion disintegrate through this second
yoga, which is practiced for three weeks in a three-year retreat setting. The starting point for Illusory Body Yoga is an understanding
that phenomena are conceptual imputations. By mastering the seed
essence, the yogini produces an illusory body in the form of a tantric
deity, which appears to be real although it lacks substantial existence.

Practices cause the seed essence to enter the central channel and dissolve into clear light. Through familiarization, one comes to realize that the fundamental nature of all beings and all phenomena is void of inherent existence. Great compassion arises for beings who, not understanding the ultimate nature, create the causes of suffering.

## Clear Light Yoga (*'od gsal*)

THIS PRACTICE, THE focus for three weeks in a three-year retreat setting, essentially eliminates the darkness of ignorance, meaning that the yogini begins to experience the clear-light nature of mind.

## Dream Yoga (*rmi lam*)

PRACTICED DURING SLEEP (in a three-year retreat setting, three weeks are given for this yoga), Dream Yoga helps remove the subtle stains that obscure a direct understanding of reality. Dream yoga has several stages: first the yogini must realize, during the dream, that she is dreaming. Then various trainings can be applied—training, multiplication, emanation, and transformation—culminating in a realization of the nature of appearances.

## Transference of Consciousness Yoga (*'pho ba*)

IF THE YOGINI masters it, this yoga can be particularly helpful at the time of death. Khyungpo Naljor is an ideal exemplar for the Transference of Consciousness Yoga. At the moment of death, he advised all practitioners of this yoga to "'do like this'—and from the aperture at the crown of his head, he [Khyungpo] shot up in the sky. Transforming into sounds, iridescent lights and rainbows, he went off into space." In a three-year retreat setting, two weeks are given for this yoga.

## Bardo Yoga (bar do)

BUDDHISM SPEAKS OF intermediate states (bardos) within cyclic existence, of which life is only one. Through mastery of this last yoga, the realization dawns of the nature of the bardos or intermediate states of birth, dream, meditation, near-death, reality, and becoming. In a three-year retreat setting, two weeks are set aside for this yoga.

### The Trunk: The Mahamudra Reliquary

WHY 'RELIQUARY?' WHEN Khyungpo Naljor received these verses of teachings, he kept them on parchment paper that he rolled up and placed in a reliquary around his neck. Kalu Rinpoche also offers the explanation that Mahamudra "is thought of as a reliquary containing the nature of mind."[257]

The yogini first cultivates calm abiding (zhi gnas) and insight (lhag mthong) through a practice called Three-Fold Natural Flow (rang babs gsum) referring to naturalness of body, speech, and mind. Mahamudra is said to be "too close to be recognized, too profound to be grasped, too simple to be believed, and too marvelous to be understood conceptually."[258] The yogini seeks to overcome these four limitations by arousing primordial awareness, which is transmitted through a pointing-out instruction. When all doubts are resolved, Mahamudra manifests as the spontaneous presence of the bodies of enlightenment.

## The Branches: The Three Ways of Integrating the Path

THESE ARE THREE ways of maintaining Mahamudra experience at all times. Essentially, the yogini develops the understanding that appearances, sounds, and thoughts are meditated on as the Lama, the yidam, and the illusory nature of all things—with the last one corresponding to Illusory Body Yoga. In a three-year retreat setting, these are practiced for one week. Success in this practice is gauged by the yogini's realization of clear-light inseparable: bliss.

## The Flowers: Red and White Forms of the Dakini

WITH FOCUS ON both prayers and meditation, the yogini first practices the generation stage for the Red and White Forms of the Dakini and recites their mantras, ideally a hundred thousand times or more. Then she practices the completion stage, which involves Transference of Consciousness Yoga. Provided she keeps her vows, the yogini practicing these Red and White Forms of the Dakini can reach the Pure Land of the Dakini without leaving her physical body.

## The Fruit: Deathlessness and Non-Deviation

THIS IS THE ultimate realization—the true nature of mind is beyond birth or death, thus there can be no deviation into either cyclic existence (samsara) or perfect peace (nirvana).

In a three-year retreat setting, Deathlessness and Non-Deviation are practiced for one week, and they are very profound. They include Chakrasamvara visualizations. They also call for reflection on the absence of inherent existence in such notions as illness, death, enlightenment, and the samsaric experience. Sangye Tönpa advises to "meditate on the mind which is beyond death" and at the moment of enlightenment, it is precisely this realization that dawns: the mind's nature is beyond death, naturally liberated.

Body and mind do not deviate from samsara into enlightenment, or from enlightenment into samsara. Rather, they are seen in their clarity and emptiness, beyond birth or death. As confusion disappears, the yogini abides in an experience of reality free of extremes.

# Appendix III

### Song of Niguma

Whirling in the ocean of samsara
Are the myriad thoughts of love and hate.
Once you know they have no nature,
Then everywhere is the land of gold, my child.

If on all things, like an illusion,
One meditates, like an illusion,
True Buddhahood, like an illusion,
Will come to pass, due to devotion.

### Song of Sukhasiddhi

The sky is empty and non-conceptual.
Cut the root of this conceptual mind.
Cut the root and relax!

## Song of Niguma

འཁོར་བའི་རྒྱུ་མཚོར་བསྒྱུར་བ་ཨི།

ཆགས་སྡང་རྟོག་པ་སྣ་ཚོགས་འདི།

རང་བཞིན་མེད་པར་རྟོགས་ཚ་ན།

ཐམས་ཅད་གསེར་གྱིང་ཨིན་ནོ་བུ།


སྒྱུ་མ་ལྟ་བུའི་ཆོས་རྣམས་ལ།

སྒྱུ་མ་ལྟ་བུར་བསྒོམ་བྱས་ན།

སྒྱུ་མ་ལྟ་བུར་མངོན་སངས་རྒྱས།

ཆོས་གུས་སྟོབས་ལས་འབྱུང་བར་འགྱུར།


## Song of Sukhasiddhi

ནམ་མཁའ་རིག་མེད་སྟོང་པ་ལ།

རིག་བཅས་སེམས་ཀྱི་རྩ་བ་གཅུན།

རྩ་བ་གཅུན་ནས་ལྷུན་པར་ཞོག།

# Notes

1. Kalu Rinpoche, *Luminous Mind*, 22.
2. Dakini (*mkha' gro ma*), sometimes translated as 'sky-walker' or 'sky-dancer,' represents the primordial awareness of existence.
3. Conceptual thought (*rnam rtog*).
4. The Shangpa lineage is considered part of the Kagyu tradition, one of four major schools of Buddhism in Tibet. Its source of teachings is the Buddha Vajradhara, and a brief account of Vajradhara opens *Like an Illusion*.
5. See Appendix II: The Five Golden Teachings.
6. Readers may already be familiar with this master who, by his own account, was a rebirth of such great adepts as Krsnacharya and Kunga Drolchok. Taranatha is perhaps best known as a prodigious writer and historian. Many of the empowerments and *sadhanas* of the Shangpa lineage used even today were in fact composed by him.
7. The Empty-of-Other view on the ultimate nature uses mostly the terminology of Buddha nature, or *tathagatagarbha*. Jamgon Kongtrul posits the two truths according to the Empty-of-Other school as follows: "The imputed nature and the dependent nature are the relative truth; the ultimate truth is the perfectly present, self-aware primordial wisdom." (My translation from the Tibetan *kun brtags gzhan dbang kun rdzob don dam ni / yongs grub rang rig ye shes gzhan stong lugs*.) See Kongtrul, *Gaining Certainty*, 16. For a study of the Empty-of-Other position, see Stearns, *The Buddha from Dolpo*.
8. Nagarjuna's analysis, named Sparks of Vajra (*rdo rje gzegs ma*) is perhaps the most powerful of the various Middle Way (*dbu ma*, Skt. *madhyamika*) reasonings used to arrive at the view of emptiness by negation. Essentially, the argument refutes arising from any one of four extremes: the result (say, a flower) does not arise from itself (the flower), nor does it arise from something separate; it does not arise from both itself and something separate, nor does it arise causelessly. Since it does not arise, it does not abide or go out of existence. Therefore it does not inherently exist. See Hopkins, *Emptiness Yoga*, chapter 10.
9. Empowerment (*dbang*, Skt. *abhisekha*), a ceremony in which the Lama initiates the practitioner into a particular practice.
10. Here it is worth noticing that while the Life of Khyungpo was written as a first person account with some of the expected humility of an autobiographer, (he calls himself "an insignificant monk" (*ban chung*) for example), the

story was in fact compiled by four of his disciples and in many instances exhibits the praise of biography.

11. I am unable to felicitously translate the meaning of this famous verse by Sukhasiddhi. The Tibetan reads *nam mkha rig med stong pa la / rig bcas sems kyi rtsa ba gcun / rtsa ba gcun nas lhun par zhog* and is presented in Appendix III. The term *rig* is usually translated in its positive meaning as awareness: the Nyingma school speaks of 'Rigpa' as the natural wakeful state. In this context however, Bokar Rinpoche explained that *rig* refers to conceptual mind (information provided by Ngawang Zangpo in a discussion in Williams, Oregon, Fall 1999). The Tibetan verb *gcun* generally suggests subduing and pressing down, but in this context, it has the meaning of 'cutting,' which is the translation I chose.

12. Mahamudra (*phyag rgya chen po*).

13. Padampa Sangye (*pha dam pa sang rgyas*), an Indian yogi who brought the Great Pacifier (*zhi byed*) tantric tradition to Tibet. The teaching is called Great Pacifier because the power of its mantras pacifies all suffering.

14. We do not know the exact relationship between Niguma and the well-known Naropa because the Tibetan uses *lcam mo*, which can mean either 'sister' or 'wife,' to refer to Niguma. In Guenther's *Life and Teachings of Naropa*, she is cited as Naropa's wife and dismissed for her "countless faults." Kyabje Kalu Rinpoche, on the other hand, says that Niguma was Naropa's sister. See Guenther, *Naropa*, 18; Kalu Rinpoche, *Luminous Mind*, 213.

15. Other women in *Like an Illusion* include Sumatimaha, Gangadhara, Sumatikirti, Jena Teghanar, Ratnadevi, Drungdrup Chenmo, and others.

16. Bodhichitta (*byang chub gi sems*). See the discussion under the heading 'Compassion: Human All Too Human' in this introduction for an analysis of bodhichitta in its common meaning in *Like an Illusion*.

17. Afflictive emotions (*nyon mongs pa*, Skt. *klesha*), delusions that mediate the relationship between the poles of duality, starting with self and other. The self either likes what it perceives and wants more of it (attachment), doesn't like what it perceives and wants to avoid it (aversion), or regards it as irrelevant to its interests and ignores it (ignorance). Afflictive emotions drive the actions (karma) that bind us in samsara.

18. McLeod, *Morning Service*.

19. Vehicles (*theg pa*, Skt. *yana*), so-called because the practices transport the individual to the goal. The two 'lower' vehicles or hinayana (*theg pa chung*) aim at personal liberation. The 'higher' vehicle or mahayana (*theg pa chen po*) is the bodhisattva path endowed with the compassionate intention not to pass into nirvana until all beings are liberated. Within the mahayana is tantra, the adamantine vehicle (*rdo rje theg pa*, Skt. *vajrayana*), which includes powerful mantra recitations, visualizations and yogic practices that enable a practitioner to attain Buddhahood in a single lifetime. To keep the

text clear, I have used the word 'tantra' to refer to mantrayana, tantrayana, or vajrayana.

20. Kalu Rinpoche, *Luminous Mind*, 173.

21. From a quote of Nagarjuna in *Like an Illusion*.

22. Chang, *Milarepa*, 517.

23. Mani mantra, the mantra of Avalokiteshvara: om mani pedme hung. A detailed explanation of the mantra is found in Bokar Rinpoche, *Chenrezig*, 37-42.

24. This may be because Sukhasiddhi was a sixty-year-old ex-housewife when she attained realizations: she had not spent her life accumulating a stock of words to convey the experience she gained so rapidly.

25. More than sixty dreams are described in the text, not including brief references like "I then had many wonderful dreams."

26. Padmasambhava, the Lotus-Born (*padma 'byung gnas*), established Buddhism in Tibet in the 8th century. He is revered in Tibet as Guru Rinpoche, the Second Buddha.

27. Yidam deity (*yi dam*), meditation deity.

28. Dreams and visions feature in many other Buddhist life stories. The life of the famous poet-yogi Milarepa, for example, is full of them. See Chang, *Milarepa*. For the life stories of the Karmapas, another Tibetan Buddhist lineage also featuring many dreams, see Thinley, *Karmapas of Tibet*.

29. On the yogas of Niguma, see Appendix II.

30. Garuda (*khyung po*), in Indian lore, the mythical king of birds, half-human and half-bird.

31. Heaven of Thirty-Three, one the abodes of gods of the desire realm, believed to be located on top of Mount Meru. Indra is said to inhabit this heaven and it is common for its goddesses to appear to humans.

32. Yama, Lord of Death (*gshin rje*).

33. For further reading on the lives of great adepts, see Keith Dowman, *Masters of Mahamudra*.

34. Powers (*dngos grub*, Skt. *siddhi*), also translated as 'spiritual attainments.'

35. Vajra posture (*skyil krung*), the 'full lotus' or cross-legged meditation posture traditionally adopted by yogis.

36. Chakras (*gnas*), energy centers within the body, situated at the head; throat; heart (at the level of the heart, but in the middle of the chest); navel; sexual organs (this last often referred to as 'secret chakra').

37. Body of reality (*chos kyi sku*, Skt. *dharmakaya*).

38. Two truths (*bden gnyis*): the conventional truth (*kun rdzob*) is that all phenomena arise in dependence upon causes and conditions (*rten 'brel*). The ultimate truth (*don dam*) is emptiness (*stong pa nyid*) or the lack of inherent existence in phenomena.

39. According to the hinayana tradition, seven Buddhas have already appeared in this word. Kashyapa is the sixth and Shakyamuni, the seventh.

40. Saint (*dgra mchom pa*, Skt. *arhat*), a Buddhist practitioner who has attained the hinayana aim of personal liberation from suffering and therefore is worthy of respect. More challenging, however, is the mahayana aim to liberate not only oneself, but also all sentient beings.

41. *Nagas* (*klu*), serpent-like creatures that live in subterranean realms and have control over rain, ponds, rivers and soil.

42. Tanaduk (*blta na sdug*), literally Pleasing to Behold, the principal city of the god Indra on top of Mount Meru, according to ancient Indian cosmology. The whole city is made of gold and filled with special medicinal herbs.

43. According to Buddhist cosmology, Jambudiva (*'dzam bu gling*) is one of four great continents. It specifically represents ancient India, which included Kashmir at the time.

44. Sage (*mkhas pa*, Skt. *pandita*), a learned scholar-yogi.

45. The three pure states (*dag pa'i sa gsum*), the three highest levels on the path of a bodhisattva.

46. Four complete empowerments (*dbang bzhi yongs su rdzogs*), ritual steps performed by a qualified Lama initiating the neophyte to a practice: vase empowerment (*bum dbang*); secret empowerment (*gsang ba'i dbang*); prajna-jnana empowerment (*shes rab ye shes kyi dbang*); fourth empowerment (*bzhi ba'i dbang*), where the nature of mind is pointed out.

47. 'Tantric mahayana' is used to remind readers that the tantric vehicle is essentially part of the mahayana approach, as explained in note 19, since the aim for both is enlightenment for the sake of all beings.

48. Things as they are and things as they appear (*ji lta ba dang ji snyed pa*), the two truths. 'Things as they are' is the ultimate nature of phenomena—emptiness. 'Things as they appear' is the conventional nature—dependent arising. These two are not contradictory but are in fact inseparable.

49. Cloud of Dharma, the last of ten levels (*sa bcu*) on the bodhisattva path: levels of Very Joyful (*rab tu dg'a ba*); Stainless (*dri ma med pa*); Luminous (*'od byed pa*); Radiant (*'od 'phro ba*); Hard to conquer (*sbyang dk'a ba*); Manifest (*mngon du gyur pa*); Gone Afar (*ring du song ba*); Immovable (*mi gyo ba*); Good Intelligence (*legs pa'i blo gros*); Cloud of Dharma (*chos kyi sprin*).

50. Veil to the knowable (*shes bya'i sgrib*).

51. A realized being has three modes of being, or bodies of enlightenment (*sku*, Skt. *kaya*): the body of reality (*chos kyi sku*), the space-like nature of all phenomena; from the body of reality arises the enlightened enjoyment-body (*longs spyod rdzogs pa'i sku*, Skt. *sambogakaya*), perceived only by bodhisattvas; this in turn gives rise to the enlightened emanation-body (*sprul sku*, Skt. *nirmanakaya*), perceived by all beings. Taken together, the enlightened enjoyment-body and the enlightened emanation-body are the

form bodies (*gzugs sku*, Skt. *rupakaya*), forms that exist for the benefit of beings.

52. Abandonment and cultivation (*spang rtogs*), a synonym for enlightenment: abandonment of all delusions and obscurations; cultivation of all qualities.

53. Samadhi (*ting nge 'dzin*), a profound meditative state.

54. Three-fold purity ('*khor gsum*), a direct understanding of emptiness. 'Three-fold' refers to the perceiver, the perception, and the object of perception, all of which are to be understood as empty of inherent existence.

55. Starting with this line, the verse praises Niguma for her perfection (*pha rol tu phyin pa*, Skt. *paramita*) which is categorized in six, or as here, in ten aspects: generosity (*sbyin pa*, Skt. *dana*); ethics (*tshul khrims*, Skt. *shila*); patience (*bzod pa*, Skt. *ksanti*); perseverance (*brtson 'grus*, Skt. *virya*); meditative concentration (*bsam gtan*, Skt. *dhyana*); knowledge or wisdom (*shes rab*, Skt. *prajna*); skillful means (*thabs*, Skt. *upaya*); aspiration (*smon lam*, Skt. *pranidhana*); power (*stobs*, Skt. *bala*); primordial awareness (*ye shes*, Skt. *jnana*). Ordinary generosity is valuable, but it becomes a 'perfection' when it is accompanied by the wisdom that realizes emptiness, and likewise for the others.

56. Realm of reality (*chos kyi dbying*, Skt. *dharmadhatu*), the all-pervasive expanse wherein emptiness of inherent existence is realized as inseparable from dependent arising.

57. Great Light Rays Empowerment ('*od zer chen po dbang*), light rays emanating from the Buddhas and entering the bodhisattva. This is the final empowerment received by a tenth-level bodhisattva prior to attaining enlightenment.

58. Five paths (*lam lnga*), paths of accumulation; joining; seeing; meditation; no-more learning.

59. Ananda (*anan ta* or *kun dga bo*), the cousin and one of the ten close disciples of the Buddha, known for his superior knowledge of the scriptures. He recited the sutras by heart after Buddha Shakyamuni passed away.

60. Uddiyana (*O rgyan*).

61. Dakas (*dpa' bo*), heroic spiritual beings.

62. Virupa is one of the eighty-four great adepts. He was a great Vajrayogini practitioner. In a famous episode, Virupa went to a tavern and drank enormously. When it was time to settle his bill, he pledged the sun to the waitress, and simply held the sun up in the sky. After another two and a half days, the local king, frantic over the fact that the sun was no longer setting in his land, learnt in a dream of Virupa's doing. He went to the tavern and settled the bill for the yogi. For more details, see Keith Dowman, *Masters of Mahamudra*, 43-52.

63. Generation and completion stages, phases in tantric meditation: generation stage (*bskyed rim*, Skt. *utpattikrama*), transforming one's ordinary perceptions into a tantric experience whereby all sound is the mantra of the

deity being practiced; all form, the body of the deity; all thought, the wisdom of the deity. Completion stage (*rdzogs rim*, Skt. *sampannakrama*), dis-
solving the visualization and resting in the natural state.

64. Nairatmya (*bdag med ma*), literally She Who Has No Self, the personifica-
tion of liberation, and the consort of Hevajra.

65. Sacred outlook (*dag snang*), perceiving all phenomena free of dualism. Also
translated as 'pure appearances' depending on context.

66. Sadhana (*sgrub pa'i thabs*), meditation practice.

67. Referred to by its old name of Trulnang (*'phrul snang*) in the Tibetan text,
the Jokhang is the most revered temple in Tibet, founded by King Songtsen
Gampo in the 7th century to house images of the Buddha brought his
wives.

68. Three doors of emancipation (*rnam thar pa'i sgo gsum*), three types of
concentration leading to liberation: liberation through emptiness (*stong pa
nyid*); liberation through signlessness or unconditioned awareness (*mtshen
ma med pa*); liberation through wishlessness (*smon pa med pa*).

69. Here, body, speech, mind, navel, and secret organ also refer to the five
chakras: body (*lus*) refers both to the physical expression as well as the head
chakra. Speech (*gsung*) is both the verbal expression and the throat chakra.
Mind (*thuks*) is mental expression and the heart chakra. The last two chakras
are explicitly named.

70. Traditionally, Buddhism speaks of five Buddhas. Vajradhara is the source
of all the qualities expressed by the five Buddhas. In him, they are all
unified. Thus he is sometimes referred to as the sixth Buddha.

71. Bodhgaya (*rdo rje gdan*), literally Vajra Seat, is situated about five miles
south of the town of Gaya in India. It is said that every Buddha will attain
enlightenment in Bodhgaya.

72. Vinaya code of discipline, (*'dul*), a division of the Buddhist teachings.

73. The borderland of the red-faced demons (*srin po gdong dmar mtha' 'khob yul*),
a common expression to describe Tibet.

74. I have used 'becoming a monk' for the Tibetan *rab tu byung*, and 'full ordination' or 'taking the full vows of a monk' for the Tibetan *bsnyen rdzogs*.

75. Vairochana Rakshita was one of the disciples of Maitripa. Born in southern India in the late 11th century, he devoted himself early on to the study
of Buddhism, and was one of the first to transmit Mahamudra teachings
to Tibet. See Roerich, *Blue Annals*, 844-6.

76. Five Tantric Deities (*rgyud sde lha lnga*), principal deities of the Five Great
Tantras (*rgyud sde lnga*), the main tantras of anuttarayogatantra:
Chakrasamvara; Hevajra; Guhyasamaja; Mahamaya; Vajrabhairava.

77. Diamond-like bodhichitta (*rdo rje lta bu'i byang chub gi sems*), the unbreakable
vow to liberate all beings from suffering.

78. Two kinds of completion stages: with one's own body is the Path of Means, also called the Yoga of Inner Heat (*gtum mo*); with another's body is the practice of karma mudra (*las kyi phyag rgya*).

79. Eight great accomplishments (*dngos grub chen*), common attainments by realized beings: wielding the sword of awareness (*ral gri*); passing through matter (*sa 'og*); alchemical powers to transform substances (*bcud kyis len*); to dispense the nectar pill (*ril bu*); to dispense eye-salve (*mig sman*); swift-footedness (*rkang mgyogs*); ability to travel through space (*mkha la phur*); invisibility (*mi snang*).

80. See the discussion on *samaya* under the heading 'Renunciation and Commitment' in the introduction.

81. One of four mudras or tantric Mahamudra practices (*phyag rgya bzhi*): karma mudra (*las kyi phyag rgya*); samaya mudra (*dam tshig phyag rgya*); dharma mudra (*chos kyi phyag rgya*); shunyata mudra (*tsong pa'i phyag rgya*). Karma mudra can refer to union with a consort in tantric practice, but must not necessarily be interpreted literally since the higher tantras are written in ambiguous terms. In the lower tantras (Krya, Charya, Yoga), karma mudra is a ritual hand gesture.

82. The qualities of sensory objects (*'dod yon*) are to be elevated to the tantric path. In this particular context, sensual pleasure is the focus, but the point is that by directly recognizing things as they are, without clinging or rejecting, delusions no longer arise.

83. Kukkuripa the Dog Lover was one the eighty-four great adepts, as was the next lineage master, Luipa the Fish Eater. Short stories of both are found in Keith Dowman's *Masters of Mahamudra*.

84. Dombi Heruka, a disciple of the great adept Virupa, as was the dakini Sukhasiddhi.

85. There were several Indrabhutis renowned in Buddhist history. Indrabhuti the Young was one of the eighty-four mahasiddhas, and lived in the 9th century.

86. The four philosophical tenets (*grung mtha' gzhung chen bzhi*) at times refer to the great treatises of the four classical schools of philosophy—the Vaibhasika, the Sautrantika, the Cittamatra and the [Midle Way] Madhyamika. However, here Bokar Rinpoche lists them as: Vinaya; Abhidharma; Prajnaparamita; and Madhyamika (reference courtesy of Ngawang Zangpo, discussion in Williams, Oregon, Fall 1999). The vehicles are often separated as hinayana and mahayana, as defined in note 19. In this case, however, the vehicles are described as the causal vehicle of signs, which refers to the practices pointing to enlightenment, and the resultant vehicle of vajra in which the path itself is the end, as explained in the following lines of the text.

87. The three characteristics or three types of phenomena (*mtshan gsum* or *rang bzhin gsum*), imputed phenomena; dependent phenomena; and validly established phenomena. See Tsultrim Gyamtso, *Emptiness*, 47-9.

88. The thirty-seven limbs of (or auxiliaries to) enlightenment (*byang chub kyi chos gsum cu bdun*), four close contemplations; four perfect abandonments; four limbs of miracles; five powers; five forces; seven limbs of enlightenment; eightfold noble path.

89. Extreme views (*mtha' gnyis*): eternalism (*rtag pa*), which is a belief in inherent existence, and nihilism (*'chad pa*), which is a denial of cause and effect. Both delusions cause only suffering, but they can be countered by a clear understanding of emptiness and dependent arising.

90. Calm abiding (*zhi gnas*, Skt. *shamata*), a lucid meditative state free of conceptual thoughts. When the mind is calm, the meditator turns to insight (*lhag mthong*, Skt. *vipashyana*), an analytical meditation on the essential nature of mind. For detailed instructions on calm abiding and insight as practiced in the Kagyu tradition, see Bokar Rinpoche, *Door to Certainty*, 25-36.

91. Kshetavajra (*zhing gi rdo rje*), Atulyavajra (*mi mnyam rdo rje*), Ratnavajra (*rin chen rdo rje*).

92. The six times of day and night (*nyin mtshan dus drug*), the sessions traditionally recommended for meditation: morning; afternoon; twilight; late evening; midnight; early dawn.

93. Earth shakes in six ways (*sa rnam pa drug tu gyo*), an expression used to describe nature's homage to a Buddha or a bodhisattva: moving; shaking; rising; erupting; humming; shimmering.

94. This area of southern India is where Shakyamuni Buddha taught the Kalachakra.

95. *Damaru* drum (*da ma ru*), traditionally made of two human skulls, used in rituals to invoke deities.

96. Tormas (*gtor ma*), food offerings.

97. A metaphor for the long months that stretch as everyone goes hungry.

98. The fourteenth level of a bodhisattva (*bcu bzhi'i sa*), the final level on the path, which means full enlightenment. It is called the Ever-Luminous Vajra Ground (*kun tu 'od rdo rje'i sa*). Note that the path can also be graduated in ten levels with the tenth as the ultimate, as listed in note 49.

99. A ritual object in tantric practice. See Chapter 1: Vajradhara for the symbolism of the vajra.

100. Töling was at the time the capital of Gu-ge in far west Tibet and remained an active religious center until the cultural revolution, when many of its temples were destroyed. The Red Temple, one of the three main temples of Töling, was where Atisha and Rinchen Zangpo stayed. Batchelor, *Tibet Guide*, 373.

101. Little is known of Gayadhara, but the dating would accord with the possibility that this is the same individual whose name in Tibetan is sometimes

spelled *spring 'dzin,* and who had Naropa and Maitripa as Lamas. Gayadhara passed away in Kharak after years of expounding the Dharma. See Roerich, *Blue Annals,* 207.

102. Atisha Shrijnana, (*jo bo rje mar me mdzad,* 982-1054), an Indian master who came to Tibet in 1042, and received both the *Profound View* and the *Widespread Activity* lineages. We can date the episode in the text between 1042 and 1045, the first three years following Atisha's arrival in Tibet, which he spent at Töling.

103. Rinchen Zangpo, (*rin chen bzang po,* 958-1055), a translator whose works mark the beginning of the 'new schools' which include the Geluk, Sakya and Kagyu traditions. He brought the Dharma to Tibet, particularly Mahakala texts—as is explained in the last story in the compendium—and founded over fifteen monasteries. In this episode, Rinchen Zangpo was in his early eighties.

104. Reality itself (*chos nyid,* Skt. *dharmata*), the ultimate nature of mind and all phenomena, uncontrived, all-pervasive.

105. The imagery of the dream seems to imply that he would have many disciples and be a powerful teacher.

106. Vajrayogini; Avalokiteshvara; Green Tara; Mahakala.

107. Stupa (*mchod rten*), a shrine, literally 'receptacle for offerings.'

108. Empty Enclosure Resounding with A (*A'i stong ra*), one of the main purification practices in the Shangpa tradition.

109. The four guardian kings (*rgya chen bzhi*), part of the eight guardians of the world, each guarding a specific direction: King Dhritirashtra (*yul 'khor srung*) in the east; King Virudhaka (*'phags skyes po*) in the south; King Virupaksha, Lord of *Nagas* (*klu dbang mi bzang*) in the west; and King Vaisravana (*rnam thos sras*) in the north.

110. The three main lineage holders were Zhangom Chöseng, Meu Tönpa, and Mokchokpa.

111. Tara and Bhrukuti (a wrathful form of Tara).

112. Three chakras: head; throat; heart.

113. Six realms of samsara (*rigs drug*), the environment of sentient beings: gods (*lha*); demi-gods (*lha min*); humans (*mi*); animals (*dud 'gro*); hungry ghosts (*yi dvags*); hell-beings (*dmyal ba*).

114. Alakavati (*lcang lo can*), the abode of Vaisravana, guardian of the north and god of wealth.

115. Scent-eaters of the bardo (*dri za,* Skt. *gandharva*), spirits who subsist on odors.

116. The term 'wisdom being' (*ye shes sems dpa',* Skt. *jnanasattva*) specifically means the actual presence of the invoked deities (in this case, Khyungpo's Lamas), entering the visualization.

117. Three bodies (*lus gsum*), not to be confused with the three bodies of enlightenment. Here, the three bodies are the medium by which unreal-

ized beings experience existence: the fully ripened body (*rnam smin gyi lus*), of flesh and blood; the habitual body (*bag chags kyi lus*), which is projected in dreams as a result of the habitual imprints left upon the mind of the dreamer; the mental body (*yid kyi lus*), present during the bardo of becoming.

118. Note that Vajrabhairava is a wrathful form of Manjushri.

119. Non-humans (*mi ma yin*), spirits.

120. In this line in the Tibetan text, Khyungpo Naljor is referred to by the nickname Dubupa (*gdu bu pa* or *gdub bu pa*), literally The Man Wearing Bangles.

121. Tsampa (*rtsam pa*), parched barley-flour, a staple of the Tibetan diet.

122. Distorted conventional truth (*log pa'i kun rdzob*, Skt. *mithya samvrtti*), a misconception of cause and effect, such as the notion of a rabbit with horns. Pure conventional truth (*yang dag kun rdzob*, Skt. *samyak samvrtti*), a correct understanding of dependent arising. On the two truths, see note 38.

123. Nominal ultimate truth (*rnam grangs pa'i don dam*); actual ultimate truth (*rnam grangs ma.yin pa'i don dam*).

124. This rebuke is addressed to Mokchokpa several times, first by the practitioner Aseng in a section not included in this abridged version, and here again by the yogi Burgom Nakpo. Mokchokpa started as a disciple of Khyungpo but chose to travel in search of teachings from other masters (mere donkeys compared to Khyungpo) before returning to Khyungpo more than a decade later.

125. According to Buddhism, there are five major poisons (*dug lnga*) that have their roots in a false conception of self: attachment; aversion; ignorance; jealousy; pride.

126. In upper Shang, Western Tibet. Ferrari, *Central Tibet*, 159.

127. The Tibetan folio reads *rnam rtog* (conceptual thought) but the Chinese edition of the root text reads *mi rtog* (non-conceptual), which is more in keeping with the sense of Sukhasiddhi's teaching.

128. Kuklung Monastery (*lkuk lung*), set up in northern Shang. Later, Kyergangpa met Mokchokpa there for the first time, Gyaltsen Bum meditated there for three years, and Sangye Palzang, finding it in disrepair in the 15th century, strengthened the foundations and walls.

129. Draklha (*brag lha*), a township near Tanakpu north of Zhigatse. Gyurme Dorje, *Tibet Handbook*, 279.

130. Salt lakes and mountain ranges dot the windy and dry steppe plateau of northern Tibet and served as a stocking place for caravans heading south.

131. Stupidity, or ignorance (*ma rig pa*).

132. Fire *puja* (*sbyin sreg*), a ritual.

133. Four demons (*bdud bzhi*), challenges to overcome before attaining enlightenment: the demon of the aggregates (misconceiving the aggregates as

inherently existing); afflictive emotions (being confused by afflictive emotions); death (having one's practice interrupted by death); god-child (being
distracted by sensual pleasures).

134. There are four birth impulse (*skye gnas*) or types of birth taken by sentient
beings: birth from the womb (*mgal skyes*); birth from an egg (*sgong skyes*);
birth from heat and moisture (*drod gsher las skye ba*); miraculous birth (*rdzus
skyes*).

135. The four Tathagatas, or Buddhas: Jinaratnabahulya (*rgya ba rin chen mang*);
Jinasrupottama (*gzugs mdzes dam pa*); Jinarupaparyanta (*sku 'byams klas*);
Jinasarbodyvimuktasena ('*jigs pa thams cad dang bral ba*).

136. Mön (*mon*), present-day Tsona County, bordering Bhutan. Gyurme Dorje,
*Tibet Handbook*, 199; Wylie, *Geography of Tibet*, 119.

137. Note that Nairatmya is Hevajra's consort.

138. The Hell of Unceasing Torment, (*mnar med*, Skt. *avici*), the lowest of the
eight hot hells, and the one to which beings go who committed one of 'five
heinous crimes' (*mtshams med pa lnga*): killing one's mother; father; a saint;
causing a schism within the religious community; maliciously drawing blood
from a Buddha.

139. Pakmo Drupa Dorje Gyalpo (1110-70), one of Gampopa's disciples and the
founder of the Pakmo Kagyu tradition, one of the four major Kagyu schools.
For details on his life, see Roerich, *Blue Annals*, 552-69.

140. Three poisons (*dug gsum*), the fundamental delusions of attachment, aversion, and ignorance, from which all other afflictive emotions derive.

141. See the discussion on *samaya* under the heading 'Renunciation and Commitment' in the introduction.

142. Two accumulations (*tshogs gnyis*), accumulation of merit; accumulation of
wisdom.

143. Sutra of Advice to the Sovereign (*rgyal po la gdams pa'i mdo*).

144. The three whites (*dkar gsum*), milk; yogurt; butter. The three sweets (*mngar
gsum*), sugar; honey; molasses.

145. Ten virtues, (*dge ba bcu*), refraining from: killing; stealing; sexual miscon-
duct; lying; slandering; using harsh words; indulging in idle gossip; coveting;
hurting others; upholding wrong views.

146. The six consciousnesses: the five sense consciousnesses plus mind.

147. The Indian Middle Way philosopher Kamalashila (*ka ma la shai la*) was a
disciple of Chanti Rakshita. He visited Tibet in the 8th century at the request of the king Trisong Detsen and defeated the Chinese monk Hashang
Mahayana by proving the superiority of the gradual path as opposed to the
instantaneous path to enlightenment.

148. Ravigupta (*nyi ma sbas pa* or *nyi ma rtog ge pa*), well-known for his learning,
was once struck with leprosy. He isolated himself in a hut for three months,
and gained a vision of Tara. She asked what he wished for. "To be cured,"

he replied. Instantly, his body assumed its former appearance, except for a small sore on his forehead. See Roerich, *Blue Annals,* 1051.

149. Yöl (*yol*), south of Lhasa near Chushul in Central Tibet. Map reference courtesy of Keith Dowman.

150. Rigong (*ri gong*), in lower Yöl, west of the Kyichu River and north of the Brahmaputra River. Map reference courtesy of Keith Dowman.

151. The last chapter of *Like an Illusion* says that Rigongpa took the thunderbolt in his hand, played with it by rolling it back and forth on his robe and then threw it on a cliff nearby. It left an immense brown trail on the gray rock and this rock is now a place of pilgrimage.

152. Uddiyana (*O rgyan*), generally identified as Swat in Pakistan. Jalandhara (*dza len tra* or *'bar 'dzin*), present day Jalundur, a province in the Punjab. At the time of Sangye Tönpa, Jalandhara also comprised what we know as Kashmir.

153. A verse on the inseparability of our ordinary perceptions and enlightened awareness. See note 117 for the fully ripened body, habitual body, and mental body; see note 51 for the bodies of enlightenment.

154. Five heinous crimes (*mtshams med pa lnga*): killing one's mother; father; a saint; causing a schism within the religious community; maliciously drawing blood from a Buddha.

155. The three veils or three obscurations (*sgrib pa gsum,* Skt. *triny avaranani*), obscure the mind and prevent direct insight into reality as it is: the veil to the knowable (*shes bya'i sgrib*); the veil of afflictive emotions (*nyon sgrib*); the veil of habitual tendencies (*bag chags pa'i sgrib*).

156. Mount Chuwori (*chu bo ri*), sixty-five kilometers south of Lhasa, is said to have one hundred and eight hermitages, including one by Padmasambhava four centuries earlier, as well as one by the First Karmapa, etc.

157. The seven pure practices (*bdun rnam dag*), taking refuge; confession; rejoicing; generating the relative bodhichitta of aspiration; generating the relative bodhichitta of engagement; generating ultimate bodhichitta; dedication.

158. The five kinds of meat (*sha lnga*), traditionally presented as offerings, particularly to wrathful deities: elephant flesh; human flesh; horse flesh; dog flesh; cow flesh.

159. Vajra-word first transmitted, i.e. when Niguma first received the transmission from Vajradhara.

160. Increase of the five degenerations (*snyigs ma lnga bdo rtsod ldan*), lifespan is shorter; delusions are greater; persons are worse; the times are more degenerate; the view [of reality] is realized by fewer.

161. Awareness-holders (*rig 'dzin,* Skt. *vidyadhara*).

162. Vajra songs (*rdo rje glu,* Skt. *vajragitis*) set in verse after a spontaneous outburst of meditative experience, and combined with a melody. This dif-

ferentiates them from *doha* songs, which are generally sung in the moment of realization.

163. The old tradition (*snga 'gyur snying ma*), the Nyingma school. The Geluk, Sakya, and Kagyu schools are known as the new traditions.

164. The Tibetan lunar calendar accounts for thirty days in a month: the first of the month is the beginning of the waxing moon; the fifteenth is full moon; the thirtieth is no moon, or 'new moon.' Sangye Tönpa here is drawing a parallel between his waning self and the moon, with only one more day before it disappears.

165. These four constitute the 'four thoughts that turn the mind to Dharma.' Daily meditation on each of these helps the practitioner stay determined and diligent in her practice. Niguma wrote a brief text to be practiced in the morning, with verses on each of these four thoughts. See McLeod, *Morning Service*.

166. The Tibetan expression for 'cutting short distractions' is *blo sna thung*, a delicate expression to translate; it literally means 'short vision.' The term means giving up plans and activities, an attitude which arises as a direct result of meditating on the four thoughts that turn the mind to Dharma. The term is sometimes translated as 'mental simplicity.'

167. Eight worldly concerns (*chos brgyad*), reactions to mundane issues that a practitioner is advised to set aside: attachment to gain; fame; praise; pleasure; aversion to loss; infamy; blame; pain.

168. Three-fold inseparability (*lhun grub rnam gsum dbyer med*), the inseparability of a Buddha's enlightened bodies.

169. Eight leisures (*dal brgyad*) and ten opportunities (*byor bcu*) define a precious human life (*dal 'byor gyi rten*): leisure of not being born as barbarians; as extremists (see note 89 on extreme views); as imbeciles; in hell; among hungry ghosts; among animals; among long-living gods [who indulge in pleasure]; in a land where the teachings have not appeared. The opportunities include five with regard to one's own condition: born as a human; in a land where the Dharma is present; with good faculties; with faith; free of the five heinous crimes (see note 138). The second set of five opportunities concern the external conditions: being born when a Buddha has appeared; where a Buddha has taught the Dharma; where the Dharma has flourished; when there is a Sangha; when the individuals forming the Sangha have genuine compassion toward others.

170. Zhönnu Drup (*mkhas grub chos rje gzhon nu grub*), the other disciple of Sangye Tönpa to pass down a lineage, the Samding Transmission. See *Life of Zhönnu Drup*.

171. The three trainings (*bslab pa gsum*, Skt. *trisika*), ethical conduct (*thsul khrims*); mind or meditative concentration (*sems*); discriminating awareness (*shes rab*).

172. Sky (or space) as the body of reality, and the sun rays as the enlightened form bodies: a recurring metaphor in Tibetan Buddhism.

173. The two kinds of knowledge (*mkhyen gnyis*), knowledge of things as they are, in their simplicity (*ji lta ba mkhyen pa*), and knowledge of things as they appear, in their multiplicity (*ji snyed pa mkhyen pa*).

174. Three jewels: Buddha, Dharma, Sangha.

175. The three-fold duties of a scholar (*mkhas pa'i bya ba rnam gsum*), exposition (*'chad*); debate (*rtsod*); composition (*rtsom*).

176. The four elements (*byung ba bzhi*), earth; water; fire; wind.

177. The well-known adept Virupa, Sukhasiddhi's Lama.

178. The Tibetan expression *thod pa mgo la mi 'gel bar 'dug* literally translates as 'not having a skull on the head.' It means to not take rebirth as a human being, i.e. to be a Buddha in one's next life.

179. Six senses are the five senses plus mind. Mind is the sense faculty and thoughts are its objects.

180. Serious yogis and yoginis who practiced in intensive solitary retreat often abstained from any food prepared by humans and lived on berries or nuts. For example, Milarepa, the famous poet-yogi of Tibet, lived on nettles.

181. There are three main channels in Tibetan physiology: the central channel (*rtsa dbu ma*) through which the seed essence passes; and channels to the right (*ro ma*) and left (*rkyang ma*) of the central channel.

182. Four [channel] wheels are placed at the four chakras (the fifth chakra is mentioned at the end of the paragraph in the text): the wheel of great bliss at the head chakra; the wheel of enjoyment at the throat chakra; the wheel of phenomena at the heart chakra; the emanation-wheel at the navel chakra.

183. On the Six Yogas of Niguma, the Mahamudra Reliquary, Mind Deathlessness and Non-Deviation, and the Three Ways of Integrating the Path, see Appendix II.

184. State of no-returning (*phyir mi ldog pa*), a yogic realization.

185. Shangtönpa's full name is Ketsun Tsangma Shangtönpa (*gtsang ma shang ston pa*).

186. Exhaustion of all dharmas (*chos zad sar skyol*).

187. Probably referring to Kedrup Zhönnu Drup, the other main disciple of Sangye Tönpa and the founder of the Samding branch of the Shangpa Kagyu tradition.

188. Traditionally, a Lama's body is placed in a cremation shrine and a fire is ignited under it. When the cremation is finished, the shrine is opened and ashes, relics, and so forth are collected. These are used to make *tsatsas*—small shrines about eight inches in height.

189. Probably 1309 A.D., the female earth bird year.

190. Freedom from the two delusions (*dag pa gnyis ldan*), a synonym for full enlightenment, at which stage the two delusions—to liberation and omniscience—have been removed.

191. Nyang River Valley in Namam County, between Zhigatse and Gyantse. Gyurme Dorje, *Tibet Handbook*, 262. On the beneficial properties of the water in the area, see Ferrari, *Central Tibet*, 60.

192. Male side of the family, (*gdung rus*), literally the 'bone lineage,' while the maternal side of the family is called the 'flesh and blood lineage' (*sha khrag rus*).

193. Fifteen kilometers southwest of Zhigatse, the monastery of Narthang (*snar thang*) is best known for housing the woodblock compilation of the *Kangyur* and *Tangyur* texts. Narthang was destroyed during the Cultural Revolution. Some of the temples have been rebuilt in recent years. Gyurme Dorje, *Tibet Handbook*, 277.

194. Fighting against other Buddhist practitioners—other members of the Sangha—is a serious violation of the *samaya* vow. See the discussion on *samaya* under the heading 'Renunciation and Commitment' in the introduction.

195. Kunga Zangpo (*kun dga' bzang po*) held the regency from 1268 to 1280 during the Sakya school's rule over Tibet. The Blue Annals say that Kunga Zangpo was later killed by Mongol troops. See Roerich, *Blue Annals*, 216.

196. Zar (*zar*), in Tingkye County near Sikkhim.

197. Yuri (*gyu ri*), eastern part of Western Tibet.

198. Samding (*bsam sding*), five miles east of Nakartse, where Zhönnu Drup built his monastery in the late 13th century. Samding later became a center for the Bodongpa school. In 1716, the abbess of Samding is said to have transformed into a sow to escape Mongolian invaders. Batchelor, *Tibet Guide*, 273.

199. Dzogchen expanse or the Spatial Class of Dzogchen (*rdzogs chen klong*), a transmission of Atiyoga practice descended from Longde Dorje Zampa, Vairochana and others. Dudjom Rinpoche's authoritative book on the Dzogchen tradition describes its four aspects as: Black Space propounded as Absence of Causes (*klong nag po rgyud med du smra ba*); Variegated space propounded as Diversity (*klong khra bo sna tshogs su smra ba*); White Space propounded as Mind (*klong dkar po sems su smra*); Infinite Space in which cause and result are determined (*klong rab 'byams rgyud 'bras la bzla ba*). See Dudjom Rinpoche, *Nyingma School*.

200. Garab Dorje, (*dga' rab rdo rje*, Skt. *Surati Vajra*) received all the tantras, scriptures and oral instructions of Dzogchen from Vajrasattva and Vajrapani in person, making him the first human teacher of the Dzogchen lineage. He attained enlightenment through these Dzogchen practices and transmitted them to several disciples.

201. The Tsang River (*gtsang*), in the northern part of Western Tibet, not to be confused with the Tsangpo River which is also known as the Brahmaputra River.

202. Twin dimensions of enlightenment (*sku gnyis*), the body of reality and the form bodies.

203. Mount Sinpori sits in Chushul County, about forty miles southwest of Lhasa. Gyurme Dorje, *Tibet Handbook*,156.

204. Twenty-two kilometers south of Zhigatse, the monastic complex of Zhalu (*zhwa lu*) was founded in the 11th century. In the 14th century, it became the seat of the scholar Butön Rinpoche.

205. An obscure expression in the Tibetan, which literally translates as 'white storks with black tails' (*khrung khrung dkar la mjug ma nag pa*).

206. Gurgyi Gönpo (*gur gyi mgon po*), a protector deity of the Sakya school.

207. Kuklung (*lkuk lung*), a monastery in northern Shang founded by the Shangpa master Mokchokpa more than a century earlier.

208. One of the Six Yogas of Niguma. See Appendix II.

209. Tokar, perhaps Todo Karpo (*tho do dkar po*), to the northeast of the Ti-Se range. Wylie, *Geography of Tibet*, 122.

210. The Tibetan expression for 'learned, pure, and wise' (*mkhas btsun bzang gsum*) specifically means learned in the sense of vast intellectual knowledge; pure in all activities of body, speech and mind; and wise or good in the aspiration to benefit others.

211. The five precious objects: gold; silver; turquoise; pearl; coral.

212. Rangjung Dorje (*rang byung rdo rje* 1284-1339), the Third Karmapa.

213. Located in southern Tibet on the border with India, the Tsari region was considered a place of pilgrimage for many, particularly in the Kagyu tradition.

214. A detailed example of generation stage achievements. The next paragraph deals with the completion stage.

215. The Jonang monastic complex (*jo nang phun tshogs gling*), on the south bank of the Brahmaputra River in Lhartse County west of Zhigatse, originally founded by Tukje Tsöndrü and well known for its connection with Dolpopa Sherab Gyaltsen (1292-1361) who propounded the Empty-of-Other philosophical view (see note 7). For a brief look at the relationship between the Shangpa and Jonang schools, see the discussion under the heading 'Historical Background' in the introduction.

216. During ordination, the most senior ranking monk is the abbot (*mkhan po*) who blesses new articles for to the monk-to-be. The action teacher (*las lob*) recites all the necessary prayers. Vows are received. Then, the secret preceptor (*sang ston*) asks very personal questions of the recipient. A fourth monk states the exact date, month, day, time, and year, while a fifth monk assists.

217. Ngulchu Tokme (*dngul chu thog med*, 1295-1369), always called a bodhisattva for the great compassion he displayed. He also wrote the Thirty-Seven Practices of a Bodhisattva.

218. There are several places named Taktsang (*rtag tshang*), notably the hermitage in which Yeshe Tsogyal sought refuge after beings pursued by robbers, and the birthplace of the translator Taktsang Lotsawa. Here, it's most likely the area east of Chushul, by the Brahmaputra River, not too far from one of Mokchokpa's hermitages. Wylie, *Geography of Tibet*, 75.

219. Arjangchub Yeshe, (*Ar byang chub ye shes*) a famous exponent of the Prajnaparamita at Nalanda who literally died in the midst of an exposition on the text. Roerich, *Blue Annals*, 1081.

220. Lotsawa Jangchub Tsemo (*lo tswa ba byang chub rtse mo* 1243-1320), renowned as a great scholar, the abbot of Bodön monastery. Roerich, *Blue Annals*, 787-8.

221. Religious festivals (*dus mchod* or *dus chen bzhi*), celebrated on the four holy occasions of the Buddha Shakyamuni's life: from the first to the fifteenth of the first month, the period when Shakyamuni performed miracles; on the fifteenth of the fourth month, when Shakyamuni attained full enlightenment; on the fourth of the sixth month, when Shakyamuni turned the wheel of Dharma; on the twenty-second of the ninth month, when Shakyamuni descended from Tushita heaven. Accomplishment ceremonies (*bsgrub mchod*), great tantric ceremonies involving the creation of a mandala, offering of services and generation of self-deity.

222. Bodhichitta of aspiring (*smon pa'i sems bskyed*, Skt. *pranidhicittotpada*), the desire to attain enlightenment for the benefit of beings; bodhichitta of engaging (*jug pa'i sems bskyed*, Skt. *rasthanacittotpada*), the commitment to take the necessary steps to achieve such an aim.

223. Kuklung Monastery (*lkuk lung*), set up in northern Shang three centuries earlier by the master Mokchokpa, after his twelve years of solitary retreat. Also the site of Kyergangpa's first meeting with Mokchokpa, and Gyaltsen Bum's meditation place for three years.

224. Tangtong Gyalpo (*thang stong rgyal po*, 1361-1464), a great Shangpa adept who received teachings from Müchen and from Niguma in a direct vision. A superb scholar and a highly skilled musician, poet, and inventor, Tangtong Gyalpo also found a new method of iron-smelting and built several bridges in Tibet.

225. Sönam Tsemo (*bsod nams rtse mo*, 15th century), holder of the Shangpa Tangluk Transmission, which he passed on to Gyurme Dechen. His life story is not part of the compilation in *Like an Illusion*. See Appendix I for the lineage succession.

226. The four common sciences (*thun mong gi rig gnas bzhi*), the arts (*bzo*); linguistics (*sgra*); medicine (*gso ba*); and logic (*gtan tshig*).

227. Chökorling (*chos skor gding*), in Namling County, Western Tibet. Drong appears to be near Kharak in Rinpung, an adjoining county in Western Tibet. Wylie, *Geography of Tibet*, 75; Gyurme Dorje, *Tibet Handbook*, 248.

228. Twelve female Dharma guardians (*brtan ma bcu gnyis*), twelve women who have vowed to protect the Dharma in Tibet: Dorje Kundakma; Dorje Yamakyong; Dorje Kunzangma; Dorje Gegkyitso; Dorje Chenchikma; Dorje Palgyiyum; Dorje Drakmogyal; Dorje Lumokarmo; Dorje Bökamkyong; Dorje Menchikma; Dorje Yarmosel; and Dorje Yudrönma, under whose protection lay Jetsun Taranatha's homeland.

229. Ra Lotsawa (*rwa lo tsa ba*), a famed translator and practitioner of the Yamantaka cycle, as well as a master of Kalachakra. One of the two main branches of the Kalachakra in Tibet bears his name. Roerich, *Blue Annals*, 379.

230. Taranatha was born in 1575, in the wood boar year.

231. The four heavenly rainbow mansions ('*ja' od kyi gur khang*), to the north, south, east and west. Chandra Das describes them as 'imaginary pavilion[s] formed in the sky, canopied by rainbows, walled by rays of light supported by diamond posts and carpeted with variegated clouds, for the use of gods when they come to witness religious entertainments.' Das, *Tibetan-English Dictionary*, 222, under entry *gur khang*.

232. Six-faced black Yamantaka (*gshin rje dgra nag gdong drug*); Udaya Ayupati ('*char ka tshe bdag*); Triloka Vijaya (*khams gsum rnam rgyal*).

233. Nakartse (*sna dkar rtse*), southeast of Taranatha's homeland, in Southern Tibet. Gyurme Dorje, *Tibet Handbook*, 214.

234. It was common in Tibet to keep gifted children indoors, so that they would not be contaminated by the dirt and defilements of the outside.

235. Vajra-Thunder-Subduer-of-Mara, in Tibetan, *gnam lcags rdo rje bdud 'joms*. Yeshe Tsogyal was Padmasambhava's famous consort and attained enlightenment herself. Her life is recounted in Dowman's *Sky Dancer*.

236. Yungtönpa (*gyung ston pa*), an adept well-versed in the Kalachakra and a master of yogic practices (*krhul 'khor*) which made him famous for such feats as stopping water from leaking when his water bag was pierced, or not being burned when touching molten iron. Roerich, *Blue Annals*, 149-50.

237. That is, the three activities described in the preceding lines: subdue beings of these degenerate times; help beings in the bardo; bring prosperity.

238. Yamantaka (*gshin rje gshed*), a wrathful form of Manjushri who slays Yama, Lord of Death.

239. Shady Cool Grove (*bsil ba'i tshal*, Skt. *sitavana*), one of eight great charnel grounds of India. The practice of Mahakala involves visualizing him in the Shady Cool Grove.

240. Joint Practice of the Four Blessings Deities (*lha bzhi dril sgrub*) calls for self-visualization as Chakrasamvara. Above one's head is Vajradhara, sur-

rounded by the Four Blessings Deities: Vajrayogini to the right, Avalokiteshvara to the back, Green Tara to the left, and Mahakala in front. See Kongtrul, *Radiant Wisdom*. As with all tantric practices, it is necessary to receive permission and instructions from a qualified teacher before getting involved.

241. Different names for Maitripa.

242. Vikramashila (*bi kra ma sh'i la*), a monastery founded by King Dharmapala in Magadha, India, considered the best center of Buddhist scholarship after Nalanda. Atisha stayed there many years before going to Tibet. Vikramashila was destroyed in 1203 by Baktyar Ghiliji.

243. Adhideva deities (*lhag pa'i lha*), the highest of the gods.

244. Gyicho Daway Özer (*gyi co zla ba'i 'od zer*), 11th century scholar credited with the first Tibetan translation of the Kalachakra. Roerich, *Blue Annals*, 71, 755.

245. Gangadhara was Maitripa's consort. Roerich, *Blue Annals*, 731.

246. There are several well-known Rahulas in Buddhist history. Apart from Shakyamuni's son Rahula, and apart from a Rahula who was the last abbot of Nalanda (in the 13th century, too late to be a contemporary of Khyungpo Naljor) there was a Rahulabhadra said to be Saraha's teacher, and a student of Aryadeva. The dates suggest this was the Rahula encountered by Khyungpo Naljor. Rahula's story is recounted in Dowman, *Masters of Mahamudra*, 252-55.

247. A divergence from the Life of Khyungpo Naljor which states that Rahula stayed in the monastery of Cheka for eleven months.

248. Monolith of Lake Tengri Nor or Lake Namtso (*gnam mtsho rdo*), a site sacred to Bön practitioners. Dowman, *Central Tibet*, 131; Gyurme Dorje, *Tibet Handbook*, 139.

249. See the Life of Mokchokpa for the full song.

250. The Life of Mokchokpa states it was Avalokiteshvara, not Tara, who appeared and sang these lines. It should be noted that Tara is one of two retinues to appear at the side of Avalokiteshvara in the visions of the Shangpa Kagyu masters.

251. Mokchokpa and Zhangom Chöseng.

252. As readers of the Life of Kyergangpa will remember, he adamantly refused to take over the monastic seat left by his uncle Ba Thamche Khyenpa, and had to endure insults for it. However, after several years of solitary meditation, his own Lama ordered him to build a monastery and open the door of Dharma to other beings.

253. The four types of enlightened activity (*'phrin las bzhi*), pacifying; enriching; magnetizing; destroying.

254. Jampa Pal (*byams pa dpal*, 1310 -91), nephew of the Shangpa master Gyaltsen Bum whose story is recounted in *Like an Illusion*. See Appendix I for the lineage tree.

255. The existing version of the Six Yogas according to the Geluk tradition can be found in Mullin, *Dalai Lama II*, 92-151.

256. Jamgon Kongtrul, *Retreat Manual*. All references to the time span for the practice of the yogas are taken from this source.

257. Kalu Rinpoche, *Luminous Mind*, 222.

258. Kalu Rinpoche, *Luminous Mind*, 216.

# Bibliography

Batchelor, Stephen, 1987. *The Tibet Guide*. London: Wisdom Publications.

Bokar Rinpoche, 1996. *Opening the Door to Certainty*. Trans. from French by Christiane Buchet. San Francisco: Clear Point Press.

————, 1991. *Chenrezig, Lord of Love*. Trans. from French by Christiane Buchet. San Francisco: Clear Point Press.

Chang, Garma C.C., transl., 1989. *The Hundred Thousand Songs of Milarepa*. 2 vols. Repr. Boston: Shambhala.

Chen, C.M., 1982. *White Dakini Powa*. Trans. Matthew Kaptsein with assistance from Dezhung Rimpoche.Chenian Booklet Series No. 84. Berkeley, CA: Adi-Buddha Mandala.

————, 1982. *Shanpa Kargyu Golden Dharmas: Part I: Lineage & Outline*. Trans. Matthew Kaptsein with assistance from Dezhung Rimpoche. Chenian Booklet Series No. 125. Berkeley, CA: Adi-Buddha Mandala.

————, 1982. *Shanpa Kargyu Golden Dharmas: Part II: Non-Death Yoga*. Trans. Matthew Kapstein with assistance from Dezhung Rimpoche. Chenian Booklet Series No. 126. Berkeley, CA: Adi-Buddha Mandala.

Das, Chandra, 1996. *Tibetan-English Dictionary*. Repr. New Delhi: Gaurav Publishing House.

Dowman, Keith, 1985. *Masters of Mahamudra* . Albany: State University of New York Press.

————, 1984. *Sky Dancer: The Secret Life and Songs of the Lady Yeshe Tsogyal*. London: Routledge & Kegan Paul.

————, 1988. *The Power Places of Central Tibet: The Pilgrim's Guide*. London: Routledge & Kegan Paul.

Dudjom Rinpoche, 1991. *The Nyingma School of Tibetan Buddhism*. Trans. Gyurme Dorje and Mathew Kapstein. Boston: Wisdom Publications.

Ferrari, Alfonsa, 1958. *Mk'yen Brtse's Guide to the Holy Places of Central*

*Tibet*. Ed. Luciano Petech with collaboration of Hugh Richardson. Rome, Italy: Is. M.E.O.

Guenther, Herbert, 1986. *Life and Teachings of Naropa*. Boston: Shambhala.

Gyatso, Janet, 1998. *Apparitions of the Self: The Secret Autobiographies of a Tibetan Visionary*. Princeton: Princeton University Press.

Gyurme Dorje, 1999. *Tibet Handbook*. 2d ed. Bath, England: Footprint Handbooks; Chicago: NTC/Contemporary Publishing Group, Passport Books.

Hopkins, Jeffrey, 1987. *Emptiness Yoga*. Ithaca, N.Y.: Snow Lion.

Jamgon Kongtrul, 1996. *Creation and Completion*. Trans. Sarah Harding. Boston: Wisdom Publications.

———, 1997. *Gaining Certainty about the Provisional and Definitive Meanings in the Three Turnings of the Wheel of Dharma, the Two Truths, and Dependent Arising*. Trans. Anne Burchardi and Ari Goldfield. Kathmandu: Marpa Institute for Translation.

———, 1988. *Radiant Wisdom: A practice of the Glorious Shangpa Kagyu Lineage, in which the Four Deities are achieved in Conjunction*. 2d ed. San Francisco: KDK Publications.

———, 1994. *Retreat Manual*. Trans. Ngawang Zangpo. Ithaca, N.Y.: Snow Lion.

Jampal Zangpo, Ven. Tsering Lama, 1988. *A Garland of immortal Wish-fulfilling Trees: The Palyul Tradition of Nyingmapa*. Trans. Sangye Khandro. Ithaca, N.Y.: Snow Lion.

Kalu Rinpoche, 1997. *Luminous Mind: The Way of the Buddha*. Trans. from French by Maria Montenegro. Boston: Wisdom Publications.

———, 1995. *Secret Buddhism: Vajrayana Practices*. Trans. from French by Christine Buchet. San Francisco: Clear Point Press.

———, 1977. *The Invocation of Mahakala*. San Francisco: KDK Publications.

Kunga Rimpoche, Lama, and Brian Cutillo, trans., 1978. *Drinking the Mountain Stream*. Novato, CA: Lotsawa.

———, 1978. *Miraculous Journey: New Stories and Songs by Milarepa*. N.p.: Lotsawa.

Ling, Trevor, 1979. *Buddha, Marx, and God*. 2d ed. New York, N.Y.: St. Martin's Press.

Lopez, Donald Jr., ed., 1997. *Religions of Tibet in Practice*. Princeton: Princeton University Press.

McLeod, Ken, trans., 1975. *A Morning Service: The Total Flowering of Activity to Help Others*. Vancouver, B.C.: Kagyu Kunchab Chuling.

———, 1987. *The Great Path of Awakening: A commentary on the Mahayana Teaching of the Seven Points of Mind Training*. Boston: Shambhala.

Mullin, Glenn, trans., 1985. *Selected Works of the Dalai Lama II: The Tantric Yogas of Sister Niguma*. Ithaca, N.Y.: Snow Lion.

Orgyen Tobgyal, 1988. *The Life and Teaching of Chokgyur Lingpa*. Trans. Tulku Jigmey and Erik Pema Kunsang. 3d ed. Kathmandu: Rangjung Yeshe Publications.

Powers, Jon, 1995. *Introduction to Tibetan Buddhism*. Ithaca, N.Y.: Snow Lion.

Ricard, Matthieu, trans., 1994. *The Life of Shabkar: The Autobiography of a Tibetan Yogin*. Albany: State University of New York Press.

Rigzin, Tsepak, 1993. *Tibetan-English Dictionary of Buddhist Terminology*. Rev. 2d ed. Dharamsala: Library of Tibetan Works and Archives.

Roerich, George, 1976. *The Blue Annals*. 2d ed. Delhi: Motilal Banarsidass.

Snellgrove, David, 1987. *Indo-Tibetan Buddhism: Indian Buddhists and their Tibetan Successors*. 2 vols. Boston: Shambhala.

Stearns, Cyrus, 1989. *The Buddha from Dolpo*. Albany: State University of New York Press.

Stewart, Jampa Mackenzie, 1995. *The Life of Gampopa, The Incomparable Dharma Lord of Tibet*. Ithaca, N.Y.: Snow Lion.

Takpo Tashi Namgyal, 1986. *Mahamudra: The Quintessence of Mind and Meditation*. Trans. Lobsang Lhalungpa. Boston: Shambhala.

Tarthang Tulku, 1992. *Light of Liberation: A History of Buddhism in India*. Berkeley: Dharma Publishing.

Tharchin, Sermey Geshe Lobsang, 1984. *King Udrayana and the Wheel of Life*. Howell: The Mahayana and Sutra Press.

Thinley, Karma, 1980. *The History of the Sixteen Karmapas of Tibet*. Boulder, CO.: Prajna Press.

Tsultrim Gyamtso Rimpoche, Khenpo, 1986. *Progressive Stages of Meditation on Emptiness*. 2d ed. Trans. Shenpen Hookham. Oxford: Longchen Foundation.

Wylie, Turrel, 1962. *The Geography of Tibet According to the 'Dzam-Gling—Rgyas-Bshad*. Roma, Italy: Is. M.E.O.

# Index